The Descendants of
Rev. Joseph Rhea
of Ireland

Edward F. Foley

HERITAGE BOOKS
2007

HERITAGE BOOKS

AN IMPRINT OF HERITAGE BOOKS, INC.

Books, CDs, and more—Worldwide

For our listing of thousands of titles see our website
at
www.HeritageBooks.com

Published 2007 by
HERITAGE BOOKS, INC.
Publishing Division
65 East Main Street
Westminster, Maryland 21157-5026

Other books by the author:

The Descendants of Matthew "The Rebel" Rhea of Scotland and Ireland

The Prestons of Walnut Grove, Virginia

International Standard Book Number: 978-0-7884-0526-6

This book is dedicated to my father-in-law James Odell Bouton, whose stories about his family's history in Sullivan County, Tennessee got me interested in the subject of genealogical research. I will be forever grateful he shared these tales with me and his grandchildren so that this great story of the Rhea ancestry could unfold.

CONTENTS

FOREWORD

I have spent many years researching and corresponding with those who have come before me and recorded dates, stories and facts about the lives of the descendants of Rev. Joseph Rhea. In the course of this work I have to date identified over 2655 direct descendants and over 1114 of their marriages. In addition, I have been able to trace the ancestry of Joseph Rhea through Ireland to the Highlands of Scotland. If the family legends are true, the first identifiable ancestors include a number of great men of British history including William Marshall 1st Earl of Pembroke, Regent of England, Robert Bruce, 6th Lord of Annandale, father of Robert Bruce born 1274, King of Scotland and Gilbert 2nd Earl de Clare born 1180, Surety of the Magna Carta. Due to limitations of space in this first effort I have concentrated on only the descendants of Rev. Rhea who bear the Rhea name, as well as the first generation descendants from the families of Rhea women who married. This work thus includes 1652 of his direct descendants and their 799 spouses.

Great care has been taken to make this work as accurate as possible. However, there are most certainly facts which have been maimed or omitted since much of this information I received second- or third-hand, passed on from father and mother to son or daughter, or cousin to cousin. In addition, I know there are many descendants I lost track of as they moved west and more recently because our society has become so mobile I have not been able to locate them. I encourage the reader to help us update and/or correct any information about the family so the next edition can be that much more accurate. You can write the author at *Family Books Company*, 1111 Golf View Dr., North Myrtle Beach, South Carolina 29582.

Ed Foley
1996

ACKNOWLEDGMENTS

During the years of a research project such as this it is easy to lose track of the many persons who have rendered help on the project, and I can't hope to fairly acknowledge them all individually. This book is the result of an enormous effort of many members of the Rhea family who over the centuries have sought to record the heritage of this great family. Special thanks go to Frances Rhea Murphy in Memphis and Lula Faye Burton in San Diego, each of whom has turned over their years of compiled Rhea records to a new generation of researchers, for sharing not only information but contacts for the family history which have been invaluable. Thanks of course go to my wife Janet, a descendant of Rev. Rhea, who has shown great patience through these years of "genealogy widowhood."

1. Joseph RHEA born 1715, Loughborne Parish, Donegal
Co., Ireland, married 1752, in Ireland, Elizabeth MCILWAINE,
born 1732, "Tifannan" near Londonderry Ireland, (daughter of
John MCILWAINE and Margaret SCOTT) died 19-Dec-1793,
Bluff City, Sullivan Co. TN, buried: Weaver Cemetery., Weaver
Pike, Sullivan Co. TN. Joseph died 20-Sep-1777, Virginia, buried:
Piney Creek Church, Taneytown MD.

Born near Londonderry, County Donegal his home was of the
Parish Loughborne near also near St. Johnston which was on the
west bank of Lough Foyle between Londonderry and Lifford in Co.
Donegal. Joseph graduated from the University of Glasgow in
1742 at age 27 with honors, receiving his A.M. degree as a minister
of the Word of God. (Ministers signed themselves VDM which
signified Verbi Dei Minister) One reference to Joseph speaks of
him as "accounted one of the finest scholars in the North of
Ireland". While a student, Joseph wrote manuscripts comprising
translations from Latin poets, lectures, sermons and original essays
on philosophies and theology which bear witness to his intellect.
Some of these were preserved and some are part of the Rhea
Papers in the Archives in Nashville TN. In 1895 Rhea Anderson
owned one bearing Joseph's signature dated 3/1/1739 bearing dates
from 1739 to 1745. Also preserved are books which composed his
library including works of Tilloston and other divines of the 17th
century.

Rev. Rhea was ordained as a minister of the Presbyterian Church in
Letterkenny, County Donegal. He first preached at a little church
in Bun Cranaugh (now Buncrana) near the shores of Lough Foyle.
At the age of 27 he then became the regular pastor at the Fahan and
Inch Presbyterian Church in County Donegal at the parish of Fahan
(from 1742 - 1769). His salary was 24 pounds. Fahan is the small
fishing village community where Joseph's grandfather Matthew
Campbell Rhea, 'The Rebel', immigrated after his escape from
imprisonment on the Isle of Man. It was also became the home of
Joseph Rhea and his family. The village of Fahan can be

reached by taking the ferry across to the eastern side of Lough
Swilly from Rathmullan, a little resort port. The little church was
still standing in 1985.

In 1752, 10 years after becoming pastor in Fahan, Rev. Joseph
Rhea at the age of 37 married Elizabeth McIlwaine, born 1732,
daughter of John and Margaret Scott Anderson McIlwaine.
During the time that Joseph and Elizabeth lived in the parish of
Fahan, seven of their eight children were born. The older sons,
John and Matthew were educated at Trinity College in Dublin.
John, his eldest son prepared a manuscript about the Rhea
family in 1830 (a copy of which was in the possession of Rhea
Anderson, and is now a part of the Rhea papers housed in the
Tennessee State Library and Archives in Nashville). He stated
the following: He was the pastor of the Presbyterian church at
Fahan for over twenty years and then sent the following:

"As I have received the congregation of Fahan from the Presbytery
of Londonderry, I have labored in the work of the ministry above
twenty years in that place and as the congregation has fallen into
very long arrears and has been deficient in the original promise to
me which was 24 pounds yearly. I am unable to subsist any longer
among them and I do hereby demit my charge of them and deliver
them into the hand of them from whom I received them. Subscribed
this 16th Aug. 1769. Jos. Rhea"

"P.S. I have only this further request of the Presbytery that they will
see justice done me in that congregation in my absence."

The manuscript continues, "Having prepared for the same, he bid
farewell to his connection and friends, and with his wife and seven
children, the youngest about 2 years old, he embarked on board the
Brig 'George', Captain Richard Paul, Commander, bound for
America. They lay at anchor at Lough Foyle near Carmagniglaon
and on the 27th of September 1769 the brig hove up anchor and
sailed." Rev. Rhea kept a journal during the voyage. The journal
has been preserved and is part of the Rhea Papers at the State
Library and Archives in Nashville.

The Rhea family belonged to a period in Protestant Ireland when at least one of almost every family group pulled up roots and crossed the ocean for America. On the point of land not far from Fahan on the Northern coast of County Donegal are the Cliffs of Horn Head. Horn Head Castle was the name of the ancestral home of Elizabeth McIlwain's grandmother, Frances Stuart Scott. Ships from Belfast and Derry going to America could be watched from Horn Head as they passed by. A cairn, or pile of stones at the viewpoint is said to have been created by relatives who deposited a stone as a ship passed by carrying family members. Old Irish ballads still survive recounting these sad stories of long ago.

After a long passage across the Atlantic they arrived at their destination before the onslaught of the freezing winter. The brig sailed up the Delaware River and the passengers disembarked at Philadelphia. Arriving with the Rhea family was Fanny Dysart, Elizabeth's niece. For several weeks they lived in Philadelphia with a relative, Matthew Byers, but in the spring of 1770 they hired wagons and moved to Octorarah, Pennsylvania to the home of Joshua Anderson, Elizabeth's half brother. A wealthy man by the name of Joseph Miller (another Anderson relative) rented them with a house and small acreage with orchard and small field where they lived for about two years. The *Colonial Clergy of Maryland* notes Joseph settled in Cumberland, Adams Co., PA at Upper Marsh Creek Church, Gettysburg PA 1770-1771. In May 1771 the Presbyterian Synod met in Philadelphia, PA. Recorded in its minutes is a notation that the Presbytery of 'Donegal' had received as a member Rev. Joseph Rhea, lately from Ireland. In 1771, Joseph accepted a call to Piney Creek Church which is still in existence today. This church is west of Taneytown MD, a small city on the waters of Monocacy River. His salary was 112 pounds annually. Frances (Fanny) Dysart, who had come over with the Rheas married John McAllister, a storekeeper (and cousin) in Taneytown. Joseph Rhea and the McAllisters are buried next to each other at Piney Creek Church.

Frederick, Maryland deed records show that Joseph Rhea purchased a farm nearby on November 14, 1771 containing 201 acres of land called "the addition to Brooks discovery of the rich land". It was here on the Monocacy River they moved by 1772 and was here that their youngest child James was born on January 18, 1775.

The *History of Piney Creek Church* states "In June 1775 Rev. Rhea informed the Presbytery that he desired to visit some portions of Virginia and that his people had given him their consent to his absence." The Presbytery permitted him to carry out his purpose and furnished him with usual traveling credentials. The John Rhea manuscript states that Rev. Rhea in November 1775, at the age of 60, was in the Holston country (which later became eastern Tennessee), went with troops against the Cherokee Indians on the Little Tennessee; Micajah Adams, M. Depew and Joseph Beeler were with him; was out four weeks. He returned to Maryland immediately.

He was in the Holston Country again in 1776. His son John was with him. He bought land on Beaver Creek; Col. D Looney, George Maxwell and John Shelby and others entered into the Bond for payment.

His descendant Anne Rhea Bachman Hyde wrote in 1932 "There is a well founded tradition that he was in this country as early as 1771 he certainly preached in Sullivan County TN in 1775 under an old elm tree on the Bluff City road." This elm tree was located on the land which Rev. Rhea purchased and which is today known as the Philip Earhart farm on 11E just inside the Bristol Tennessee city limits. His descendant Rhea Anderson wrote, "It is believed he was here in 1775 and preached at Old Concord, now Weaver Church, also in the Forks (site of New Bethel) under the big Rhea Doak elm tree, at Taylors, and other places. He joined Rev. Charles Cummings, another Presbyterian minister from Wolf Hills (Abington VA) in service to the troops under Col. William Christian's campaign in 1776 as one of the chaplains in the Cherokee campaign and in this way became aquatinted with the

Holston country. An orderly's book, once the property of Joseph
Martin mentions the chaplains as follows:

"Six Mile camp. Oct. 5, 1776. Parole Wm. Burge, General
Orders: Mr. Ray will preach to the Augusta (County, VA) Line
at one o'clock and Mr. Cummins to the Fincastel (County VA)
Line. All others who chose to attend may do it."

Six mile camp was at Double Spring, near the headwaters of
Lick Creek at the foot of Chimney Top Mountain, six miles
southwest of Ft Patrick Henry. They had left the fort on
the long march to Cherokee country the first week Oct. 1776
and amounted to some eighteen hundred men. In their
capacity as ministers they were the first known to preach in
the territory that is now Tennessee. Progress was slow as
the men were mainly foot soldiers. The expedition crossed
the French Broad River and the Little Tennessee.

Fearing the advance of the white men, three thousand Indian
warriors fled. Col. Christian and his forces returned to the
settlements in November. Each soldier, upon his return home gave
a glowing account of the Tennessee country which was rich in
abundance of game, and carpeted with magnificent forests and deep
fertile soil for cultivation. Particular places were selected for future
settlement; Rev. Rhea's land purchase included about 2,000 acres.
He decided to locate there and to that end he secured land at the
mouth of Beaver creek.

After the Cherokee campaign, Joseph Rhea returned immediately to
Maryland. Several months later he wrote a letter in Latin to his son
John who was at that time in General Washington's army. (It was
very unusual for two individuals in the frontier to correspond in
Latin). "O son dear to me - I am well in body but anxious in mind.
The people on the Holston are afflicted again by the savages. I hear
that those below the hills (or on the other side of the hill) are for
the most part inactive within their fortifications. (probably referring
to people living beyond Eden's Ridge near Kingsport, where at that
time there was a Fort - R. Anderson). I think they are not going to

have a spring harvest. The fate concerning them will be, they in that section may not be able to live. I have sold my farm, and exactly on the fifth of June relinquish it. If the Holstonians do not send two wagons for my family about that time I will proceed, god willing, to Virginia and conduct them myself. One year with them; I now have no place in which to put my family. I do not despair, but I now think I sold over hastily. But nothing in this world is done in vain, nothing by chance fortune, but all things by the good omnipotent Ruler. I beg you write to me; counsel and take care of your brother Matthew. Mother and others at home are very well. I wrote you by Captain Thompson. This letter goes by Captain Boyer from Virginia and from the home of Chiliaribi McAllister and from the town of his name. Live both of you (John and Matthew) mindful of the future that is becoming that you behave yourselves. Flee women and wine, these you know have been the destruction of many. Live sober and secure the love of all, especially of the Captain. I hope God will surely guide me. I have done wrong in selling the farm so hastily but I trust the Governor of the whole world will return me to a good end. That God will be with you and will be to you a defense, prays a most loving father. Joseph Rhea 19 of April 1777.

P.S. Be kind to him who is an ...; he will give to Samuel Blair, he has been most friendly to me; he left family in Botetourt. (County, VA)"

The arduous Cherokee campaign and the strain of selling the farm and making his plans to move family to the wild frontier, as reflected in the above letter had been too much for the 62 year old man. Only five months after the letter was written, Joseph Rhea died of pneumonia. He is buried in the graveyard beside the Piney Creek Presbyterian Church on Harney Rd, 4 miles from the center of Taneytown Md. His resting place in marked by a simple, still legible (1993) 2x3' stone erected at the request and expense of a grandson of the deceased in 1839 by the Elders of Piney Creek Church where Joseph preached. The quiet cemetery is enclosed within a low brick wall and Joseph Rhea's marker is inscribed: "Sacred to the memory of Rev. Joseph Rhea who died in 1777 aged

62 years". Another monument to Joseph Rhea has been erected at Weaver Cemetery near Bristol, Tennessee at the place of his wife's grave and is inscribed: "Rev Joseph Rhea - Born 1715 - Died Sept. 20 1777".

After the death of Joseph, the family lived one year longer in Monocacy on the place of John Scott, and then in fall of 1778 the family set out for the Holston Country. They arrived in February 1779 at their new home on Beaver Creek - a little snow on the ground. Matthew Rhea was now in the army. Elizabeth, the wife of Joseph was a delicate woman and it was with great difficulty she reached her home which to her must have seemed a vast wilderness. Joseph Rhea had been so much impressed with the Holston Country that he influenced may of his Piney Creek Church members to follow him there - John and Finley Alison, the Gross', McKinleys, Hodges, Col. John Scott, Halls and others.

Children:

i   John Angus RHEA born 29-May-1753, Langborne Parish, Londonderry, Ireland, died 27-May-1832, Sullivan Co. TN. Licensed to plead law 1789; same year member of convention of NC that ratified constitution of US. Member of legislature. Member of Convention of 1790 that framed Constitution of TN. 1796-1797 member of Gen. Assembly of TN.

John was a man of high intellect and passion for public service. He was the author of many bills put before congress and of numerous opinions printed and now preserved with the Rhea Papers. He corresponded often with his family and his devotion to the Rhea clan is evident from these preserved letters. He was a handsome man. His portrait hangs in the Tennessee State Museum in Nashville which also displays his sword. Among his preserved works

is the brief genealogy he wrote of the Rhea family.
Although his dedication to family was great,
he never married nor had children of his own.

John Rhea was Representative from Tennessee
born in the parish of Langborne, County
Londonderry, Ireland in 1753. Emigrated to the
America in 1769 with his parents Joseph and
Elizabeth. They settled in Philadelphia PA,
moved to Piney Creek MD in 1771. Until 1779
Sullivan county was thought to be in Virginia.
The first grants in the area were actually
from that state. John came to Sullivan Co.
with his father in 1776 on an expedition
against the Cherokee Indians. Bought some land
in Beaver in 1776. With his widowed mother and
brothers he came back to Eastern TN in 1778, the
year after the death of his minister father.
He completed preparatory studies and graduated
from Princeton College in 1789. He was a member of
the patriot force in the Battle of King's Mountain
in October 1780. He became Clerk of the Sullivan County
court in proposed state of Franklin and
subsequently North Carolina 1785-1790. Member
of the House of Commons of the State of NC and
was Delegate to the State Convention that
ratified the Federal Constitution in 1789.
Delegate to the constitutional convention of TN
in 1796. Attorney General of Greene County TN
in 1796, member of the house of representatives
in 1796 and 1797. Elected as a Democrat to the
Eighth and to the five succeeding Congresses
(3/4/1803-3/3/1815). Appointed US commissioner
to treat with the Choctaw Nation in 1816.
Elected to the Fifteenth, Sixteenth and
Seventeenth Congresses (3/4/1817-3/3/1823)
Actively connected with higher education in TN.
During his time in Congress he served as Chairman

of the Committee of Post Offices and Post Roads,
Committee of Pensions and Claims.

After these many years of public service, John retired
from active pursuits and resided on the
Joseph Rhea Jr. plantation near Blountville, TN
where he died May 27, 1832. Interred in
Blountville Cemetery where a substantial
monument marks his resting place. His Epitaph:
"Sacred to the memory of John Rhea, who
departed this life March 27, 1832, aged 79 years".

2.	ii	Matthew RHEA IV born 14-Apr-1755.
3.	iii	Margaret RHEA born 27-Jun-1757.
4.	iv	William RHEA born 29-Jan-1760.
5.	v	Joseph RHEA Jr. born 24-Oct-1762.
6.	vi	Elizabeth 'Aunt Bettie' RHEA born 1767.
7.	vii	Samuel RHEA born 1769.
8.	viii	James RHEA born 18-Jan-1775.

Second Generation

2. Matthew RHEA IV. born 14-Apr-1755, Fahan Parish, Co.
Donegal, Ireland, married (1) 1-Nov-1778, in Virginia, Jannette
'Jane' PRESTON, born 1758, Walnut Grove, Washington Co. VA,
(daughter of John PRESTON and Eleanor FAIRMAN) died
1-Nov-1800, Sullivan Co. TN, buried: Weaver Cemetery, Weaver
Pike, Sullivan Co. TN, married (2) Martha MACKEY, born about
1760, Ireland?. Matthew died 18-Oct-1816 Sullivan Co. TN,
buried: Weaver Cemetery in an unmarked grave.

DAR Patriot Index - Matthew: b.1755 d.1816 m Jannette Preston
Lt. - Public Service. Served under General Greene at battles of
Camden SC and Guilford Courthouse. Rank of Major in the Fifth
Virginia Regiment of the Continentals.

Abstract of Rev. War Pension File R17386: Virginia - 1/2 pay & Bounty Land Warrant #2451-200 In March 1816 soldier was a resident of Sullivan Co. TN with a wife Martha and Children Joseph, Robert, Matthew, Margaret Rhea and grandchildren; Jennett and Amy Rhea. In December 1850 soldier's son Matthew Rhea was in Fayette Co TN and he received Bounty Land Warrant #22548-160-55.

Children:

9. i	Joseph McIlwaine RHEA born 14-May-1787.
10. ii	Robert Preston RHEA born 28-Jun-1791.
11. iii	Margaret RHEA born about 1793.
12. iv	Matthew RHEA V. born 23-Feb-1796.

3. Margaret RHEA born 27-Jun-1757, Co. Donegal, Ireland, married 28-Sep-1780, Robert 'Col.' PRESTON Sr., born 1750, Co Derry Ireland, (son of John PRESTON and Eleanor FAIRMAN) died 16-Dec-1833, Washington Co. VA, buried: Walnut Grove Cemetery Washington Co. VA. Margaret died 3-Jun-1822, Washington Co. VA, buried: Walnut Grove Cemetery, Washington Co. VA. W.L. Rhea in 1895 notes only child of Margaret and Robert was John.

Children:

13. i	Jane 'Jennie' PRESTON born 1781.
14. ii	John 'Col.' PRESTON born 8-Jul-1781.

4. William RHEA born 29-Jan-1760, Co Donegal Ireland, married 10-Jun-1795, in Abington, Washington Co. VA, Elizabeth BREDEN, born 5-Jun-1766, Ireland, (daughter of John BREDEN and Elizabeth DYSART) died 31-May-1835, Sullivan Co. TN, buried: Blountville, Sullivan Co. TN. William died 1836, Sullivan Co. TN, buried: Blountville, Sullivan Co. TN.

Lived on the old Joseph Rhea farm on Beaver Creek. William built a large imposing brick home known as "The Elms" in 1806. It still stands on the corner of 11E & Sperry Rd. in Bristol VA. It overlooks the great meadow which saw musters of Revolutionary

War militia and on the lawn formerly stood the Rhea-Doak Elm. Matthew fell from the top of a horse in January 1836 and died at 75 (his wife died the year before). The home was sold by James Dysart Rhea to John T. Earhart, husband of a cousin, and it has descended to the Philip Earhart family. (The old Earhart farm was adjacent).

Children:

15. i   Margaret Breden RHEA born 1798.
16. ii   Elizabeth RHEA born 1798.
17. iii   Joseph Campbell RHEA born 14-Feb-1800.
18. iv   James Dysart RHEA born 4-Jul-1802.
19. v   William Rockhold RHEA born 29-Aug-1804.
20. vi   Frances RHEA born 1-Feb-1808.
21. vii   John RHEA born 31-May-1810.

5. Joseph RHEA Jr. born 24-Oct-1762, Co Donegal Ireland, married 17-Mar-1789, in 'Brook Hall', Abington, Washington Co. VA, Frances BREDEN, born 17-Mar-1764, Ireland, (daughter of John BREDEN and Elizabeth DYSART) died 13-Apr-1850, Sullivan Co. TN, buried: Weaver Cemetery, Weaver Pike, Sullivan Co. TN. Joseph died 24-Feb-1825, Sullivan Co. TN, buried: Weaver Cemetery, Weaver Pike, Sullivan Co. TN.

Joseph owned the land on Back Creek, called 'Old Ireland' later the farm owned by Joseph Rhea, son of Robert P. Rhea (who owned it and raised his family there). The west end of the dwelling house, in which Joe lived, was built by the Grandfather of W.L. Rhea in 1800, the east end by Robert in 1826, three quarters of a mile from his father's Beaver Creek home. It was a mansion in those days, a log house of course, with rock chimneys, since then weatherboarded. The house had twelve rooms; the big old sitting room, with a huge fireplace; from this room you entered a hall running east and west; on either side of this hall there was a bedroom, then into the big hall running north south and across the back porch was the dining room and kitchen. Upstairs there were five bedrooms. The house was filled with handsome antique furniture made of cherry and walnut. Quite a bit of the furniture and many of the valuable heirlooms found in this old home were brought by the Rhea and Breden families when they came to this country and are treasured possessions of their descendants.

There was the Grandfather clock, the secretary, chest of drawers, all kinds of tables, handsome four poster beds, hand woven linens, the lovely old china and silver and everything in keeping with a real old southern home.

Many valuable documents were stored in this home including Joseph Rhea's commission as Lieutenant given over the signature of John Sevier, first Governor of Tennessee in 1796. Another is his commission as Captain of the militia of Sullivan Co TN in 1801. (These are now part of the Rhea Papers in the State Archives and Library in Nashville.)

Close to this house and home was built a log house and home for Grandmother Breden, Frances Breden Rhea's mother, wife of John Breden. Here she lived with her two sons Samuel and John until they were married. After that she lived with her daughter Frances until she died on Octber 1, 1825, being there 30 years and 91 years of age.

The nine children were taught the habits of industry and economy. They worked early and late, the boys on the machinery, agricultural implements or anything for lessening or lightening labor. All that was made or gained in that day was by hard licks and by the sweat of the brow. All material for the house and clothing was made on the farm. Sheep were raised for the wool, flax for linen, the wheels, reels and looms were kept busily playing in order to make jeans, linsey blankets, bed and table linens.

There were no colleges nor academies - nothing but a small log school house, so no opportunities for a higher education in that day. In the year 1783 though there was and Academy in Washington Co, East TN chartered as Martyn Academy. It stood near old Salem church. This academy was chartered as Washington College 1795. Then, it was for boys exclusively. Here his two sons, Samuel and Robert went for one year. Joseph, the father, died in 1825 from a wound which he received by using an adz, the tool slipping and cutting his leg, from which he never recovered.

'Old Ireland' was also the home of his brother John Rhea who remained unmarried, and died here in 1832.

As to the characteristics of Joseph, we know very little though from what we know and have seen in and from his sons and daughters - they were industrious and upright, and correct in all their principles and all led useful Christian lives.

In 1889 John Lynn Rhea bought from his cousin Joe a clock owned by Joseph and Frances. The old clock was bought in Philadelphia by Samuel for his parents paying $65. John Breden, Frances' brother made the casing of cherry wood. Still running in 1896.

Children:

22. i	Elizabeth RHEA born 28-Dec-1789.
23. ii	Margaret RHEA born 7-Aug-1791.
24. iii	Samuel RHEA born 3-May-1795.
25. iv	Eleanor 'Ellen' RHEA born 7-Apr-1797.
26. v	Frances 'Fannie' RHEA born 1-Mar-1799.
27. vi	Nancy RHEA born 25-Jun-1801.
28. vii	Robert Preston RHEA born 17-Sep-1802.
29. viii	Sarah RHEA born 1806.

6. Elizabeth 'Bettie' RHEA born 1767, in County Donegal, Ireland, married a cousin Robert 'Major' RHEA, born 1784, Kennecalley Farm, Fahan, Ireland, (son of William RHEA and Elizabeth LOCKHART) died 23-Aug-1841, Sullivan Co. TN, buried: Weavers Meeting House, Sullivan Co. TN. Elizabeth died 13-Mar-1821, Sullivan Co. TN, buried: Weavers Meeting House, Sullivan Co. TN. Came to America in 1769 with her parents and brothers.

Children:

30. i   Sarah 'Sallie' RHEA born about 1805.
31. ii   Joseph R. RHEA born 17-Nov-1805.
32. iii   Elizabeth M. RHEA born 1807.
33. iv   John RHEA born 1810.

7. Samuel RHEA born 1769, Maryland, married 24-Sep-1801, Nancy BREDEN, born 1776, Ireland, (daughter of John BREDEN and Elizabeth DYSART) died 7-Sep-1846, Sullivan Co. TN, buried: Blountville Cemetery Sullivan Co. TN. Samuel died 11-Dec-1848, Sullivan Co. TN, buried: Blountville Cemetery Sullivan Co. TN.

It was in Samuel Rhea's home that 20 persons signed a covenant that brought the Blountville Presbyterian Church into existence 9/20/1820. The first church was built in 1823 on Graveyard Hill. Samuel was one of the church elders. Born and died in America.

Lived on the farm on Muddy Creek 3 1/2 miles SW of Blountville. It is said he bought the farm and moved upon it in 1824. The house had been built by David Looney, one of the two magistrates of the "Watauga Association", within 50 yards of the Looney Fort. Samuel was a farmer and raised a large family. He and Nancy Breden Rhea were faithful members of the Presbyterian. Church and worshipped at Blountville Church.

He died in 1843 and Nancy died 13 years later in the winter of 1856 when there was a deep snow upon the ground. Nancy has lived to see all their children pretty well grown and settled in life except daughter Fanny who never married and lived to be 85 when she died in 1891.

Children:
34. i   Margaret P. RHEA born 1789.
35. ii   Samuel RHEA born 3-May-1795.
36. iii   Elizabeth 'Betsy' RHEA born 1803.
37. iv   John Nancy RHEA born 24-Apr-1805.
     v   Fannie B. RHEA born 1809, Sullivan Co. TN, died 1891, Sullivan Co. TN, buried:

Blountville, Sullivan Co. TN. 1850 census -
Fannie living with nephew John N. his family &
her mother Nancy. She never married. Lived in
part of the old homestead house as long as John
N. lived - with his family. Often she and the
colored girl Neasy would come to Blountville
for preaching. After her brother died she made
her home with brothers, sisters etc. She was
kind, patient and loving; had a mild sweet
gentle disposition.

38. vi   Ellen RHEA born about 1810.
39. vii   Joseph S. RHEA born 1812.
40. viii   Jane RHEA born 1813.

8. James RHEA born 18-Jan-1775, Taneytown, Frederick Co.
Maryland, married Elizabeth 'Betsy' SNAPP, born 1795, Sullivan
Co. TN, died 1882, Blountville, Sullivan Co. TN, buried: 1882,
Blountville Cemetery Sullivan Co. TN. James died 23-Mar-1855,
Sullivan Co. TN, buried: Blountville Cemetery Sullivan Co. TN.

Born in Maryland, he was but three or four when his mother's
family was brought to the Holston Valley by her oldest son John
then twenty years old, reaching their destination in 1779. He
owned land on Beaver Creek, five or six miles below where his
father first located. This land was probably deeded to him by his
father's estate as was his brothers'. After living on the farm for
some years, he left it, moved to Blou tville and engaged in the
mercantile business and never returned to his farm again as his
home.

He had a flouring mill upon it and the place took the name of
'Rhea's Mill'. In town he owned the property just east of the Court
House. His store house just in front of his dwelling house.
His great pleasure in life was his fondness for reading and especially
in reading Latin and Greek. He was studious, kept up on his Latin
and Greek as long as he lived. Would teach it and read it with his
children and grandchildren. He lived to be an old man, having his
own peculiarities, rode on horse back when he went to buy goods,

since in his day there were no railroads. If he was nearly out of a certain article of goods, he would not sell such articles to a customer but shake his head saying no, that would break my assortment and the customer would leave without it.

OBITUARY "Died in Blountville on Friday 4 am March 23rd in 1855. Mr. James Rhea in the 81st year of his age. The deceased was born in the State of Maryland, was the youngest of 6 brothers...received his education at Washington College TN under the late Rev. Sam Doak, and was considered one of the best Classical scholars of the day. In 1797 he settled in Blountville as a merchant and continued to sell goods for the greater portion of 58 years. As a tribute to the memory of the deceased, the writer must be permitted to say that, although he did not profess the Religion of Christ (which was lamented by his many friends), yet few were as moral. He was a man of sterling integrity, strictly honest, his virtues many, his faults few, and if he had an enemy he was not known" signed G.R.

Last Will and testament, recorded in Sullivan Co. TN: Microfilm Copy located in Tenn. Archives Nashville. Dated 18 Dec. 1854 Proved 2 Apr. 1855:

Be it remembered that I, James Rhea of the County of Sullivan and State of Tennessee being of sound mind and memory at the sealing of these .. do make this my last will and testament as respects my lands in Rhea County in the State of Tennessee. I give and bequeath to my son Theodore B. Rhea and to his heirs and should no heirs of his body to dispose of as he may see proper six hundred and forty acres in Rhea County on the north side of Tennessee River beginning at a stake on the bank of the Tenn. River...one hundred poles above the mouth of Piney River then down the Tenn. river crossing Piney to a stake a certain number of poles .. North eighty degrees west to my back line to include six hundred and forty acres of land with appurtenances thereof, know as the Hugh Rhea farm. I also give and bequeath to my son Theodore B. Rhea and his heirs as above all the upper part of thei sland above the line where said Theodore...fourth part commences with the appurtenances there of and this undivided fourth part and all the upper end of each said island with the appurtenances there of will be known as number one. I give and bequeath to Samuel Rhea and his heirs six hundred and forty acres in Rhea Co. on the north side of the TN with the appurtenances there of known as the John Biggle farm beginning at a stake on the bank of the Tenn. ... the lower corner of Theodore Rhea's land thence a certain number of poles down the Tennessee River to a stake thence north eighty degrees west a certain number of poles to my back line to include 640 acres of land. I also bequeath to my son Samuel Rhea and his heirs all above of the undivided fourth part of said Island in Tennessee River near said farm which is known as number 2. I also give to my son James Rhea and his heirs a certain tract of land in Rhea Co on the north side of the TN River beginning at a stake the lower corner of Samuel Rhea's land thence a certain number of poles down the River to a stake below Hornsby's ferry thence north eighty degrees west a certain number of poles to a bushy chestnut tree on the north side of the road near where the Pikeville Road intersects said road near southwest corner from the house where George Biggle formerly lived thence a straight line north eighty degrees west to my back line to a contain 640 acres of land more or less with apputurances thereof. I also give and bequeath to my son James 1/4 interest in island in Tennessee River near said farm known as number 3. I give and bequeath to my son John Rhea and his heirs 640 acres of land in Rhea Co. on the north side of Tennessee River with appurtenances. thereof. Beginning at a stake on the bank of said river below Hornsby's ferry, James Rhea's corner thence down the Tennessee river a certain number of poles to a stake on the bank of the river thence north 80 degrees west a certain number of poles to my back line to include 640 acres of land. I also bequeath 1/4 interest on an island in Tennessee River near said farm known as number 4. I give and bequeath to my daughter Margaret Snapp and to my daughter Frances Preston and to their heirs the remainder of my land lying between John Rhea's town line and my lower line with the appurtenances. I also give and bequeath to my daughter Margaret Snapp and to my daughter Frances Preston all my lots in the Town of Washington, Rhea Co. TN with all appurtenances. I do hereby constitute and appoint John Rhea, James Rhea, Samuel Rhea and Theodore Rhea my four sons Executors of this my will and testament as respects my lands in Rhea Co. TN and I do revoke all other wills by me respecting said land. Sealed this 18th day of Dec., 1854. Attest - John W. Cox, Wm. W. James, John C Rutledge. Proved the 2nd day of April 1855.

Children:

41. i	Margaret RHEA born 1815.	
42. ii	John Quintas RHEA born 1818.	
43. iii	James RHEA Jr. born 1820.	
iv	Elizabeth RHEA born about 1823, Sullivan Co. TN.	
44. v	Frances 'Fannie' RHEA born 1826.	
45. vi	Samuel RHEA born 1829.	
46. vii	Theodoric Bland RHEA born 21-Jun-1833.	

Third Generation

9. Joseph McIlwaine RHEA born 14-May-1787, Sullivan Co. TN, married 1806, Catherine 'Kitty' MYERS, born 28-Jul-1788, Rockingham Co. (?) VA, (daughter of Charles MYERS and Annie CASE) died 25-Feb-1860, Sullivan Co., Tennessee?, buried: Presbyterian Cemetery Sullivan Co. TN. Joseph died 14-Jun-1860, Sullivan Co. TN, buried: Presbyterian Cemetery Sullivan Co. TN.

Joseph Rhea at the age of 14 entered Washington College in TN. He graduated in 1805. In 1806 he married Catherine. Served in the War of 1812 as an Orderly Sergeant. Was in Canada as secretary to an officer. When he returned from the war they lived in Washington and Scott Counties in Virginia then came to the home place in TN called 'Soldiers Nest' where he lived till he died in 1860. Kitty died the same year. He was a farmer and school teacher, being highly educated and a great temperance lecturer. He, being a reformed man, knew the evils of this curse. He was often urged to accept public offices, but always declined. Helped build

the 'Pleasant Grove Church' of which he was an Elder to the time he
died. Had eleven children.

Children:

47. i Jennet 'Jane' Preston RHEA born 1808.
   ii Eliza Ann RHEA born 3-Jan-1810, Sullivan Co.
       TN, died 4-Jan-1811, Sullivan Co. TN.
48. iii Emma RHEA born 26-Feb-1811.
   iv Matthew RHEA born 12-Aug-1815, Sullivan Co. TN,
       died 1819, Sullivan Co. TN.
   v   Robert Charles RHEA born 13-Feb-1817, Sullivan
       Co. TN, died 1818, Sullivan Co. TN.
49. vi Margaret RHEA born 9-Dec-1818.
   vii Samuel Myers RHEA born 18-Oct-1821, Sullivan
       Co. TN, died 17-Oct-1840, Sullivan Co. TN,
       buried: Weaver Cemetery, Weaver Pike, Sullivan Co.
       TN.
50. viii Eleanor Fairman 'Ellen' RHEA born 14-Oct-1828.
51. ix Walter Preston RHEA born 12-Mar-1831.
   x   Edmund RHEA born 9-Feb-1834, Sullivan Co. TN,
       died Blythville, Arkansas. Married 3 times.
       Represented his county in the Ark. legislature
       for 2 terms. Went to Arkansas in 1860.

10. Robert Preston RHEA born 28-Jun-1791, Bluff City, Sullivan
Co. TN, married 1828, Nancy DAVIDSON, born 3-Mar-1801,
Kentucky, died 9-Oct-1875, Sullivan Co. TN, buried: Pleasant
Grove Cemetery. Robert died 31-Mar-1872, Sullivan Co. TN,
buried: Pleasant Grove Cemetery.

Educated at Princeton. Served in the War of 1812 under Gen.
Winfield Scott. Captured by the British, he was a prisoner of war
with brother. Kept for one year in Quebec, Canada, put in irons.

After living a while in Virginia. Moved to Sullivan Co. TN on the
land entered and located by his father lying on East TN and VA
Railroad two miles east of Bluff City TN (W.L. Rhea 1895). Was a

teacher, tutored Stonewall Jackson for West Point (recorded on his tombstone).

Will of Robert Rhea dated 4 February 1871 proven Sullivan Co., Tennessee 3 November 1873.

Wife Nancy. Our 3 children, Margaret Mary R. Matthew Rhea... "Hoping that they may all live together in the old mansion house..." 8 children (not named) an equal share in the old tract. 11 acres secured by an entry in two parcels adjacent to the old tract...Stock in East TN and VA Railroad. Exc. son, Robert C Rhea. Wit: N. Long, James D. Rhea. Signed Robert P. Rhea.

Children:

i		Jane RHEA born 1828, Sullivan Co. TN, married Mr. RIVERS, born about 1810.
52.	ii	John Preston RHEA Sr. born 20-Jul-1829.
	iii	Josiah Davidson RHEA born about 1830, Sullivan Co. TN.
	iv	Margaret RHEA born 1833, Sullivan Co. TN.
	v	Mary 'Mollie' R. RHEA born 1835, Sullivan Co. TN.
53.	vi	Robert Campbell RHEA born 19-Apr-1837.
	vii	Matthew RHEA born 1838, Sullivan Co. TN, married Sarah F. RHEA, born 1845, The Elms, Bristol, Sullivan Co. (daughter of James Dysart RHEA and Elizabeth Juliet CARTER) died 16-Nov-1893, Blountville, Sullivan Co., TN? Served in Company F 63rd Tennessee Infantry.
	viii	Sarah 'Sally' RHEA born 1840, Sullivan Co. TN, married Mr. JACKSON, born about 1820.

11. Margaret RHEA born about 1793, Sullivan Co. TN, married Abram FICKLE, born about 1790, Washington Co. VA?, buried: Greendale VA. Margaret and her young son left Washington Co. and resided in Sullivan Co.

A curious bequest appears in the will of Margaret's uncle Robert Preston Sr. of Washington Co. VA dated November 21, 1832. A comment on his relationship with Abram?

"I give to Edward Lathan of Washington, his Executors or Administrators in trust for the use and benefit of Margaret Fickle and her issue my negro woman named Ann, and her 3 female children and her future increase; $500 and bed and furniture such as have been common in my house, and a tract of land lying on Dudley's Branch in Lee Co. containing 278 acres, to be appropriated to the use of the said Margaret Fickle and her issue as her and their necessities or interests may require and I positively require that said Edward Lathan shall so manage the devise here made to him for the use and benefit of the said Margaret Fickle and her issue and that her husband, Abram shall at no time have any control over the same nor derive any use or benefit therefrom, and if the said Edward Lathan shall refuse to as trustee as aforesaid, I hereby authorize my Executor herein named to apply to the Court of the County of Washington to have a trustee appointed who shall perform the same duties.

I bequeath to Robert P. Fickle (her son age 10 at the time the will was made) a horse to be worth $50...to be furnished when the said Robert P. Fickle comes to be 18 years of age.

Children:

i   Robert Preston FICKLE born 1822, Washington Co. VA?, married 30-Oct-1850, Mary Elizabeth CHAMBERLAIN, born 27-Sep-1831, Washington Co. TN, died 1894, Sullivan Co., Tennessee? Robert died 23-Nov-1895, Sullivan Co. TN, buried: Blountville Cemetery Sullivan Co. TN. Man of good mind and retentive of general information on all topics of the day. Could tell what he knew and loved to tell it. A great historian of both ancient and modern history. Postmaster in Blountville (1895), Chairman of the Chancery Court for 6 years. Was Lt. in reserve corps for C.S.A.

12. Matthew RHEA V. born 23-Feb-1796, Sullivan Co. TN, married 13-Dec-1818, Mary 'Polly' LOONEY, born 10-Jun-1804, Sullivan Co. TN, died 11-Nov-1884, Sullivan Co. TN. Matthew died 7-Apr-1870, Sommerville, Fayette Co. TN?

Baptized under the old elm tree where his grandfather Rev Joseph Rhea preached, Matthew was baptized by Rev. Samuel Doak in 1798. Rev. Rhea and Rev. Doak used a large stone near the great tree for their pulpit. Matthew later attended Washington College where he boarded with old Dr. Samuel Doak. Matthew moved to West TN about 1836. As a surveyor, he surveyed the State of TN and made the first map of the state which was highly sought after by Union forces during the civil war. Was president of the Sommerville Female Institute.

Children:

54. i   Margaret Jane RHEA born 25-Jan-1820.
55. ii   Elizabeth Looney RHEA born 4-Mar-1822.
    iii   Ellen Preston RHEA born 15-Feb-1824, Sullivan
          Co. TN, died 21-Jun-1843. Died young. A
          sister born the year after her death was said
          to be named Ellen Preston as well (?)
56. iv   Sarah Lucinda RHEA born 28-Feb-1828.
57. v   John William RHEA born 1828.
58. vi   Abram Looney RHEA born 25-Feb-1830.
    vii   Matthew RHEA VI. born 8-Mar-1833, Sullivan Co.
          TN, married 15-Sep-1859, Harriet BEARD, born
          about 1833. Matthew died 7-Nov-1861,
          Belmont, Miss. Matthew Rhea was a 1st Lt. in
          Cavalry Co A, commanding the company. He
          carried his grandfathers sword. His father
          told him to remember how that sword came into
          our hands and bring no disgrace upon it. He
          replied to his father, 'Have no fears'.. He was
          a brave man and feared not death. ,Was in the
          battle fought at Belmont, Mississippi. The
          Confederates were compelled to fall back, a

young officer who was separated from his
command in the Federal Army came dashing upon
him and ordered him to surrender. His comrades
were too far off and scattered to give him
assistance. Matthew, waiving his sword in the
air uttered these words " I will never give up
my grandfather's sword!" and while that honored
blade glittered in the sunlight of heaven,
Matthew fell lifeless to the ground. That was
his first battle and his last. His sword it is
said was placed in the armory in Chicago. (W. L.
Rhea)

Had no children.

viii   Mary Annis RHEA born 2-Sep-1835, Sullivan Co.
TN, died 21-Oct-1844.

ix   Samuel Doak RHEA born 17-Nov-1837, Sullivan Co.
TN, died 21-Oct-1843.

x   Jennet Preston RHEA born 8-Feb-1840, Sullivan
Co. TN, died 20-Feb-1840.

59. xi   Walter Preston RHEA born 28-Jul-1841.

60. xii   Ellen Preston RHEA born 2-Sep-1844.

61. xiii   Mary Frances Bell 'Fanny' RHEA born 13-Jun-1848.

13. Jane 'Jennie' PRESTON born 1781, Washington Co. VA,
married 12-Apr-1798, in Washington Co. VA, Robert PRESTON
Jr., born 1772, Ireland, adopted son of Robert Preston Sr., died
9-Sep-1858, Washington Co. VA, buried: Walnut Grove Cemetery
Washington Co. VA. Jane died 24-Apr-1863, Washington Co. VA,
buried: Walnut Grove Cemetery Washington Co. VA.

John Preston in his will left 'to the two sons of Jenny Preston,
to-wit, Alexander R. Preston and John F. Preston all of my tract of
land lying on Opossum Creek in Scott Co to be equally divided
between them'. Robert Preston, her natural father, had large
holdings in Virginia and a number of tenants. It is said that he
conceived a child by the wife of one of his tenants. When the

husband died, the wife left the child of Robert on his doorstep. This daughter was Jennie. With and understanding heart, Margaret took the child in. Jennie's husband Robert was a relative brought over from Ireland and adopted by Jennie's father Robert Sr. as his own son.

Children:

i   James PRESTON born 17-Jan-1799, Washington Co. VA, married Jane COLVILLE, born about 1799, VA? James died 1828.

ii   Margaret PRESTON born about 1801, Washington Co. VA. Died young.

62. iii   Sarah Jane Gilliland PRESTON born 27-Jun-1803.

63. iv   Alexander R. PRESTON born 8-Dec-1805.

v   Fairman PRESTON born 28-Jun-1808, Washington Co. VA, died 1811. Died in an accident.

64. vi   John Fairman 'Capt.' PRESTON born 26-Apr-1811.

14. John 'Col.' PRESTON born 8-Jul-1781, Washington Co. VA, married 5-Oct-1802, in Smithfield, Washington Co. VA, Margaret Brown PRESTON, born 23-Feb-1784, Blacksburg, Montgomery Co VA, (daughter of William 'Col.' PRESTON and Susanna SMITH) died 4-May-1843, Washington Co. VA, buried: Walnut Grove Cemetery Washington Co. VA. John died 10-Oct-1864, Walnut Grove, Washington Co. VA, buried: Walnut Grove Cemetery, Washington Co. VA.

John inherited his parent's large estate and devoted life to farming. Named in the Preston Family Papers - Preston Davie Genealogical Collection, Filson Club, 118 W. Breckenridge St. Louisville KY 40203. John graduated in 1799 from Dickson College, Carlisle PA where he became a member of Union Philosophical Society in 1796. He studied law under St. George Tucker at the College of William and Mary in 1801-02 (Letter from Francis Preston 9 Nov. 1801, WMCP folder 126). Other sources indicate he was also a graduate of Princeton University.

On May 21, 1800 he was recommended by the Washington Co.

Court as an ensign in the 2nd Battalion of the 105th Regiment and the commission was issued July 28, 1800. Less than three months later he was commissioned a Captain of the company and on Sept. 22, 1802 he was commissioned Major of the 2nd Battalion. He became a Colonel of the 105th Regiment on January 19, 1805.

A lawyer by education, he never practiced his profession but was for more than a quarter of a century presiding judge of the county court of Washington Co. VA. He was appointed to the Court on 20 August 1803 and qualified January 17, 1804. He was presiding justice from 1820 until 1852.

John's father Robert built the original 'Walnut Grove' house for John who after his marriage to Margaret Brown Preston in 1802, began 'housekeeping' at the Grove. His large family of 14 children were born there. He was a farmer and from time to time had an interest in a number of mercantile firms in the county and in TN.

Near the present house (1937 - WPA notes) is an office building which belonged to the original home and it is in a very good state of preservation. Col. Preston being a very large slave holder, it was necessary to have such an office building.

In his will dated April 4, 1861 proved October 24, 1864 John Preston made liberal provision for each of his children. His youngest child was Henry Preston, and in his will he states: He gave to William R. Sheffey, Elizabeth Sheffey, and John P. Sheffey his great-grandchildren (descendants of his oldest daughter Susan) $1000 each to be paid by son Francis when the children came of age. He mentioned he had given land on Walker's Mountain to his son Francis. His great-grandchildren, the children of William C Edmonson and by his granddaughter Susan E. Rhea, were given about $900 each. He mentioned he had conveyed to his son Robert F. the plantation of which he lived and afterward had bought 300 acres of the same land for his own dwelling and that he had given to his son-in-law James L. White and daughter Margaret, both deceased, a

variety of property which he confirmed to their heirs. He
gave to his son William A. a tract in Lee County, the Wild
Cat Valley Place and the Dysart Tract in Wise County and the
property bought at a sale and loaned to him by deed in
Washington Co. including the Negroes in his possession. To
his daughter Ellen F. Sheffey he gave the money owned to him
by her husband James W. Sheffey. His sons John Preston of
Louisville and Walter E. Preston of Arkansas were to have
all the slaves they carried to Arkansas. He gave to his
daughter Elizabeth Madison Preston a tract on Beaver Creek
containing 765 acres and 100 acres he had lately bought of
Robert F. Preston, slaves, one half of the home stock of cattle,
horses, sheep, and hogs, and one half of the household and kitchen
furniture. To his son Francis he gave a small tract on the north side
of Island Road, and land west of Walker's Mountain. His daughter
Jane P. Craighead was given land in Sullivan Co. TN at the mouth
of Beaver Creek and forty shares of stock of the Exchange Bank of
Virginia (and he confirmed slaves already given to her). To his son
James T. he gave two tracts in Scott County on the north fork of
Clinch. To his son Thomas W. who already received land, Negroes
and money, he gave one slave. To his son Henry he gave his place
of residence and Henry's place of residence being all the land in his
grant of 4800 acres except 62 acres sold to Worley and 610 acres
conveyed to son Robert F. on the northwest side of the main road.
His grandson John, son of Francis, was given 200 acres on the
east end of the home place. His son Henry was to have the calves
and stock at his place. He stated he did not intend to devise the
Walnut Grove meeting house and the graveyard to his daughter
Elizabeth M. but gave it to his sons Robert F., William A., Francis ,
James and Henry as trustees for the use of the Old School Church.
He confirmed a Negro girl and her child to his daughter Ellen F.
Sheffey. The residue of his estate was given to his son James R.
and he named sons William A and James T. as executors.

By codicil dates April 4, 1861 he gave his son Robert F. 200 acres
opposite his residence, to his daughter Elizabeth M. 30 shares of
stock in Farmers Bank of Virginia and a bond for $1,300 and he
gave 15 shares in that bank equally to his granddaughters Mrs.

David Cummings, Mrs. Edward M. Campbell and Susan P. White. His library of books was given to his sons.

By codicil dated June 17, 1862 he revoked a gift of 100 acres to Elizabeth M. and gave that to Robert F. He also revoked a bequest of a slave to Henry and gave her to James T. Since his son William had died he named his son-in-law James W. Sheffey executor in his place.

A picture of Col. John Preston appears on page 476 Summers *History of Southwest Virginia.*

Children:

65. i   Susan Smith PRESTON born 17-Jul-1803.
66. ii   Robert Fairman PRESTON born 5-Dec-1804.
   iii   Margaret Rhea PRESTON born 26-Aug-1806, Washington Co. VA, married 27-Dec-1825, in Walnut Grove, Washington Co. VA, James Lowery WHITE, born 21-Dec-1804, Abington, Washington Co. VA, (son of James 'Col.' WHITE and Eliza WILSON) died 8-Dec-1838, Washington Co. VA. Margaret died 26-Mar-1860, Abington, Washington Co. VA, buried: White Family Cemetery Washington Co. VA. Born at 'Walnut Grove' and died at her home 'Fruit Hill'. Her will dates Feb. 17, 1860, proved April 16, 1860 in Washington Co. gave her estate equally to her children and the children of her deceased daughters Margaret and Jane and gave her silver plate to her daughter Susan White. Gave slave each to her son John P., to the children of Gordon Ogden and Jane his wife, and to the children of Wm. Y. C. Humes and Margaret his wife. Son James and son-in-law David Cummings were executors.
67. iv   William Alfred PRESTON born 21-May-1808.
68. v   John PRESTON Jr. born 10-Feb-1811.
69. vi   Eleanor Fairman PRESTON born 7-Nov-1812.
   vii   Elizabeth Madison PRESTON born 26-Aug-1814,

Washington Co. VA, died 5-Apr-1865, Washington Co. VA. Never married. Lived with her father at Walnut Grove.

viii   Thomas White PRESTON born 13-Aug-1806, Washington Co. VA, married (1) 19-Jun-1845, in Davidson Co. TN, Mary Jane CRAIGHEAD, born 1827, Nashville, Davidson Co. TN, (daughter of David CRAIGHEAD and Mary Hunt MACON) died 13-May-1849, Mississippi Co. ARK, married (2) Susan Booker MAGUIRE, born 12-Jul-1829, Columbia TN, (daughter of Patrick MAGUIRE and Martha KAVANAUGH) died 7-Aug-1906, Columbia, Maury Co. TN. Entered Georgetown U. October 22, 1834 and received BA in 1837. Received B.L. from U. of VA in 1840. Practiced law in St. Louis MO with P.C. Morehead and later moved in 1846 to Memphis. Thomas died 1-Apr-1862. During the Civil War he was on the staff of General Albert Sidney Johnston. Killed at the battle of Shiloh.

    ix   Walter Eugene PRESTON born 28-Jan-1818, Washington Co. VA, married Frances 'Fannie' HAYES, born about 1818, Jackson TN, (daughter of Samuel Jackson HAYES and Frances MIDDLETON) died 1891. Walter died 23-Apr-1866, Phillips Co. ARK? He studied law at the University of Virginia 1835-37. Moved to Phillips Ark. where he was a planter and a member of the House of Representatives 1848-49 and 1850-51. Had no children.

x   Jane PRESTON born 26-Jun-1822, Washington Co. VA, married (1) 27-Dec-1846, James B. CRAIGHEAD, born about 1822, VA?, married (2) Mr. MARSHALL, born about 1822, VA? Jane died in Alabama. Father John left her "a tract of land lying and being in Sullivan Co TN at the mouth of Beaver Creek. I likewise give her 40 shares of bank stock in the Exchange Bank of VA,

unless I dispose of them or the proceeds of
them during my lifetime. I likewise give to her
any money or slaves (including Lizzy) that I
may have given her heretofore."

70. xi   Francis PRESTON born 26-Mar-1822.

71. xii   James Tecumseh 'Col.' PRESTON born 1-Apr-1824.

xiii   Joseph PRESTON born 1-May-1826, Washington Co.
VA, died 11-May-1847. Never married.

xiv   Henry PRESTON born 20-Nov-1828, Washington Co.
VA, married 8-Sep-1952, in Albermarle Co VA,
Anne Cary CARTER, born 19-Apr-1833, Redlands,
Albermarle Co VA, (daughter of John Coles CARTER
and Ellen Monroe BANKHEAD) died 12-Jan-1895,
Walnut Grove, Washington Co. VA, buried: Walnut
Grove Cemetery Washington Co. VA. Henry died
17-Jul-1899, Washington Co. VA, buried: Walnut
Grove Cemetery Washington Co. VA. Henry's father
made generous provisions for this his youngest
son. He was devised 4800 acres of Virginia
land, "families of slaves: Isaac and Lucy and
their family of children; Aggy and sons Ned and
George; Mary and her children; Jane and her
children; Andy and Hirshey and their family;
Betsy and Clary and her children and Bill. I
likewise devise to my said son Henry all of the
stock of every kind on my place at my death
after fulfilling the foregoing devise. I give
to my son Henry the remaining half of my
household and kitchen furniture"

He lived after his marriage on Preston land on
Sinking Creek until the death of his father at
which time he inherited the Homeplace.

Henry was a big farmer and slave holder and
contributed largely to the support and care of
the widows and orphans of the Confederate
soldiers and to the needy in the County.

During the war he and a brother furnished the
Confederate Government with a large number of
slaves to aid in ditch and trench building

A newspaper clipping tells of Henry Preston:
"Death of Henry Preston Sr...One of Washington
County VA's most prominent citizens: Henry Preston
Sr. died Monday night at 10 o'clock at his
handsome farm home 6 miles east of Bristol.
Mr. Preston had been an invalid for 4 years of
rheumatism. He is survived by 10 children, 8
daughters and 2 sons, his wife having preceded
him a few years."

Henry was the last surviving son of Col. John
Preston of Walnut Grove. Henry made his will
Sept. 4, 1895 "..I give to my son Henry the
portrait of my father, to son Percy I give the
portrait of my brother Thomas, and to my
daughter Cary, I give my silver spoons and cup.

I further direct that the interests of my 6
unmarried daughters in my lands..."

15. Margaret Breden RHEA born 1798, Sullivan Co. TN, married
1828, in Sullivan Co. TN?, Samuel Wood NETHERLAND, born
18-Nov-1796, Powhattan VA, died 1832, Sullivan Co. TN.
Margaret died 1864.

Children:
i   Elizabeth Rhea NETHERLAND born 1830,
Sullivan Co. TN, married 18-Dec-1850, William
Philip BREWER, born about 1830, Bristol, Sullivan
Co. TN. Elizabeth died 9-Sep-1896.

ii   Harriet S. Woods NETHERLAND born about 1832,
Sullivan Co. TN, married John KING, born about
1827, Sullivan Co. TN, (son of Rev. James KING).

16. Elizabeth RHEA born 1798, Sullivan Co. TN, married
Reyburn BUCHANAN, born about 1798, died Bristol, Sullivan
Co. TN. Elizabeth died 1856.

Children:
i   William BUCHANAN born about 1827, Sullivan Co.
       TN, married Addie HILL, born about 1827,
       died Morristown TN. William died Morristown
       TN. Served in the 63rd TN Infantry for the
       C.S.A. under Col. Abe Fulkerson.
ii   Elizabeth 'Lizzie' BUCHANAN born 1828,
       Sullivan Co. TN, married James KING Jr., born
       about 1825, Sullivan Co. TN, (son of Rev. James KING).
       Elizabeth died 1900, Sullivan Co. TN.
iii   John BUCHANAN born about 1829, Sullivan Co. TN,
       married Martha 'Mattie' CROSS, born about 1829,
       Sullivan Co. TN. Served the C.S.A. in its
       Western Army.

17. Joseph Campbell RHEA born 14-Feb-1800, Sullivan Co. TN,
married (1) 2 1824, in Washington Co. VA, Susan Smith
PRESTON, born 17-Jul-1803, Washington Co. VA, (daughter of
John 'Col.' PRESTON and Margaret Brown PRESTON) died
2-Nov-1828, Blountville, Sullivan Co. TN, buried: Blountville
Cemetery Sullivan Co. TN, married (2) 1831, in Pulaski, Giles Co.
TN, Margaret FIELD, born about 1800, Pulaski TN?, died 1832,
Pulaski TN?, married (3) 31-Mar-1836, in Giles Co TN, Catherine
C. REYNOLDS, born 25-Apr-1815, died 4-Aug-1857, Pulaski,
Giles Co. TN. Joseph died 15-Jul-1853, Pulaski, Giles Co. TN.

Moved to Pulaski TN in 1831 after death of Susan. He was a
member of the Blountville Presbyterian. Church. Did much to
persuade his fellow men to lead better lives with his uncle Robert P.
Rhea. Often stumped the county making temperance speeches.
(W.L. Rhea-1895)

Assisted his cousin Matthew Rhea in making the first map of
Tennessee. He was a colonel in the Tennessee Militia. Merchant
with John McNabb until 1827.

Children:

72. i   Margaret RHEA born 1823.

  ii   William RHEA born 1825, Sullivan Co. TN,
died 7-Jan-1847, Monterey, Mexico, buried:
Mexico. Graduated from West Point. Was First
Lieutenant in United States Army during the
Mexican War. Died of measles in Mexico while in
the service and was buried there. Cadet from
1841 to 1845. Commissioned 2nd Lt. in 6th Inf.
Served on frontier duty at Fort Gibson, Indiana
Territory (Oklahoma) in 1845-6 and was
transferred 3rd Inf. September 21,1846 where he
was in service till he death.

73. iii   Susan E. RHEA born 3-Aug-1828.

  iv   John RHEA born 1836, Pulaski, Giles Co.
TN, died 1-Mar-1836, Pulaski, Giles Co. TN.

74. v   James David RHEA born 7-Feb-1838.

75. vi   Mary Amanda RHEA born 1840.

  vii   Anna V. RHEA born 1842, Pulaski, Giles
Co. TN, died 1845, Pulaski, Giles Co. TN.

76. viii   Ellen Catherine 'Kate' RHEA born 17-Dec-1846.

77. ix   William Samuel RHEA born 16-Aug-1849.

18. James Dysart RHEA born 4-Jul-1802, Sullivan Co. TN,
married (1) 15-Dec-1831, Elizabeth Juliet CARTER, born
10-Feb-1814, Carter Co. TN, died 22-Apr-1857, Sullivan Co. TN,
buried: Blountville Cemetery Sullivan Co. TN, married (2)
Margaret Jane RHEA, born 25-Jan-1820, Sullivan Co. TN,
(daughter of Matthew RHEA V. and Mary 'Polly' LOONEY) died
17-May-1880, Sullivan Co. TN, buried: Pleasant Grove Cemetery
Sullivan Co. TN. James died 29-Nov-1886, Bluff City, Sullivan
Co. TN, buried: Pleasant Grove Cemetery.

Born on his father William.'s farm, now owned by the Earharts. Lived to be an old man. Chose profession of law and spent his last years farming. Was an elder in Presbyterian Church. After selling the farm to John Earhart he moved to Bluff city. He lived in the Stone House on the north side of the river with one of his married daughters. His wife was the sister of General Sam Carter. 1850 census shows him with property worth $10,000.

Children:

i   Frances E. RHEA born 11-Dec-1833, Sullivan Co. TN, died 4-Nov-1870, Sullivan Co. TN, buried: Blountville Cemetery Sullivan Co. TN.

ii   Matilda Wendel RHEA born 1834, The Elms, Bristol, Sullivan Co. married William George RUTLEDGE, born about 1835 (son of George Washington RUTLEDGE and Sarah Casell COBB). Died soon after marriage leaving no children.

iii   William RHEA born 1835, The Elms, Bristol, Sullivan Co Never married.

78. iv   Elizabeth 'Bettie' RHEA born 22-Oct-1836.

v   Alfred Carter RHEA born 11-Oct-1838, Sullivan Co. TN, died 16-May-1869, Sullivan Co. TN, buried: Blountville Cemetery Sullivan Co. TN. Never married.

79. vi   Margaret RHEA born 1841.

vii   John H. RHEA born 1843, The Elms, Bristol, Sullivan Co died 1863, at Chicamagua TN. Never married. First Corporal in Company G, 19th Tennessee Infantry, C.S.A. Wounded at Chickamauga in 1863 and died from his wounds.

viii   Sarah F. RHEA born 1845, The Elms, Bristol, Sullivan Co married Matthew RHEA, born 1838, Sullivan Co. TN, (son of Robert Preston RHEA and Nancy DAVIDSON). Sarah died 16-Nov-1893, Blountville, Sullivan Co, TN?

80. ix   James Taylor RHEA born 17-Jun-1847.

81. x   Mary Ellen RHEA born 1849.

xi   Susan Elizabeth RHEA born 1853 died 1905.

xii   Matthew Belmont RHEA born 22-Feb-1833, Sullivan Co. TN, died 27-May-1863 buried: Pleasant Grove Cemetery.

19. William Rockhold RHEA born 29-Aug-1804, Sullivan Co. TN, married 1-Oct-1833, Mary Ann Mosely ROCKHOLD, born 1816, Sullivan Co. TN, (daughter of William R. ROCKHOLD and Harriet NETHERLAND) died 1-Dec-1887, Sullivan Co. TN, buried: Bethel Church, Sullivan Co. William died 5-Dec-1861, Sullivan Co. TN, buried: Presbyterian Cemetery, Kingsport TN.

Elder in Presbyterian Church. Born on the farm of William Sr. on Beaver Creek. Obituary in Christian Observer & Presbyterian Witness, Richmond. VA 1862.

Children:

82. i   Harriet Netherland 'Hattie' RHEA born 10-Aug-1834.

ii   Elizabeth Breden 'Lizzie' RHEA born 21-Feb-1837, Sullivan Co. TN, died 7-Jan-1925, Sullivan Co. TN. Lived in Mexico Texas with her brothers but died in Sullivan Co., Tennessee. Never married.

83. iii   Frances R. 'Fanny' RHEA born 1838.

84. iv   William Rockhold RHEA Jr. born 20-Oct-1840.

v   George Duffield RHEA born 12-Mar-1843, Sullivan Co. TN, married Charlotte Jane 'Lottie' ROSS, born about 1855. Married Lottie Jane Rhea (nee Ross) the widow of his brother James. No children.

85. vi   John Adolphus RHEA born 1848.

86. vii   Charles Wells RHEA born 23-Jun-1853.

87. viii   James Campbell RHEA born 2-Sep-1855.

20. Frances RHEA born 1-Feb-1808, Sullivan Co. TN, married Montgomery IRVIN, born 14-Mar-1802, died 14-Apr-1857. Frances died 23-Jun-1854, buried: 25-Jun-1854.

Children:

i   Elizabeth IRVIN born 6-Jun-1840, died
30-Jun-1841. Born on a Monday evening and died
12 months and 24 days later.

ii   William Rhea IRVIN born 25-Mar-1842, married
1-Jul-1868, in Rhea Co TN, Josephine EARLEY,
born about 1832, died 1880, Dayton,
Rhea Co TN. William died 27-Sep-1875,
Cofferville, Miss. Served through Civil War. Was
in Gen. Joe Johnston's command at the surrender
at Bentonville NC.

iii   Margaret Jane 'Maggie' IRVIN born 27-Jun-1844,
TN?, married 24-Aug-1864, in Sullivan Co. TN,
George W. 'Capt.' ALLEN, born 14-Dec-1840,
Jackson Co. AL, died 1931, Texas.
Margaret died 29-Jul-1879.

88. iv   Mary 'Mollie' Rhea IRVIN born 6-Jan-1846.

89. v   Sarah 'Sallie' Harriet IRVIN born 26-Jan-1848.

21. John RHEA born 31-May-1810, Sullivan Co. TN, married
22-Dec-1840, in Jonesboro, Washington Co., Elizabeth Looney
RHEA, born 4-Mar-1822, Sullivan Co. TN, (daughter of Matthew
RHEA V and Mary 'Polly' LOONEY) died 8-Jun-1892,
Sommerville TN. John died 24-Aug-1862, Jonesboro, Washington
Co Died in the War age 50 (another source notes he died March
24, 1862).

Children:

i   Mary Elizabeth RHEA born about 1840, Sullivan Co.
TN. Never married.

90. ii   William Abram RHEA born 30-May-1844.

91. iii   Matthew Robert RHEA born 5-Jul-1846.

92. iv   James Samuel RHEA born 11-Feb-1849.

93. v   Sarah Frances 'Fanny' RHEA born 6-Sep-1853.

94. vi   John Rufus Wells RHEA Jr. born 1855.

vii   Walter RHEA born 1858, Sullivan Co. TN,
died 11-Sep-1876.

viii   Lucinda Harriet RHEA born 1858, Sullivan
Co. TN, died 1884.

22. Elizabeth RHEA born 28-Dec-1789, Back Creek, Sullivan Co
TN, married (1) 12-Jan-1812, in Sullivan Co. TN, Audley
ANDERSON, born about 1790, The Block House, Sullivan Co
(son of John ANDERSON and Rebecca MAXWELL) died
5-Apr-1818, Blountville, Sullivan Co. TN, married (2) Nicholas
FAIN, born about 1790, Sullivan Co., Tennessee?, died
Rodgersville TN. Elizabeth died 9-Apr-1853, Blountville, Sullivan
Co. TN, buried: Blountville Cemetery Sullivan Co. TN.

Lived in Rodgersville with her second husband until his death, then
with her daughter Rebecca till she died. (W.L. Rhea-1895).

Children:

i   Fanny Rhea ANDERSON born 1813,
Blountville, Sullivan Co. TN, married about 1830,
William K. MCALISTER, born about 1810, Nashville,
died 1892, Nashville, buried: Nashville.
Fanny died 1856, Nashville buried: Nashville.

ii   Rebecca ANDERSON born 8-Sep-1814, Blountville,
Sullivan Co. TN, married William B. GAMMON,
born 1807, Blountville, Sullivan Co. TN,
died after 1866, Blountville, Sullivan Co. TN,
buried: Blountville, Sullivan Co. TN. Rebecca
died 21-Mar-1863, Blountville, Sullivan Co. TN,
buried: Blountville, Sullivan Co. TN. Born, as
her sisters were, in the counting room of the
Stone House. Attended School in Knoxville under
Easterbrook. Sister Nancy married Rebecca's
husband's brother Abraham.

iii   Eliza ANDERSON born 1-Aug-1816, Blountville,
Sullivan Co. TN, married Richard Gammon
'General Dick' FAIN, born about 1815, Sullivan
Co. TN, (son of Nicholas FAIN and wife of
Nicholas FAIN) died before 1890, Rodgersville TN.
Eliza died 18-Jan-1892, Rodgersville TN. She

with her sister Nancy attended school in
Knoxville. Was fond of letter writing. After
death of Dick, made her home at Mossy Creek
with Sallie. Died at the home of her daughter
Fanny. (W.L. Rhea-1895).

95. iv   Nancy ANDERSON born 1818.

  v   Elizabeth 'Lizzie' FAIN born about 1836,
Rodgersville TN, married Rutledge POWELL, born
about 1838.

23. Margaret RHEA born 7-Aug-1791, Back Creek, Sullivan Co
TN, married 16-May-1816, Isaac 'Col.' Campbell ANDERSON,
born 3-May-1789, Block House, Carters Valley, Sullivan County
TN, (son of John ANDERSON and Rebecca MAXWELL) died
7-Feb-1872, Sullivan Co. TN, buried: Morrison's Chapel, Scott Co
VA. Margaret died 24-Apr-1873, Scott Co VA, buried: Morrison's
Chapel, Carters Valley VA.

Obituary "Departed this life April 24, 1873, Mrs. Margaret Rhea
Anderson was 81y 3m 17 days. She survived her husband about 15
months. She had borne testimony for 50 years to the religion of
Jesus Christ, and in her death she was not forsaken by him. She was
blessed with uninterrupted health until 5 weeks before her death,
although her last sufferings were severe... (W.L. Rhea-1895)
She died after an illness of 6 weeks.

Children:

  i   Rebecca Maxwell ANDERSON born 12-Jun-1818,
Scott Co VA, married 26-Nov-1835, Joseph
NEWLAND, born 13-Nov-1809, Blountville,
Sullivan Co. TN, died 28-Oct-1867, Blountville,
Sullivan Co. TN. Rebecca died 23-Jul-1893,
Sullivan Co. TN. Rebecca died at the home of
her daughter Martha. (W.L. Rhea-1895). She was
born at the Anderson home, the 'Blockhouse'.

  ii   John Rhea ANDERSON born 25-Oct-1819, Bristol,
Sullivan Co. TN. Born at the Blockhouse and
raised there until his 14th year.

96. iii   Joseph Rhea ANDERSON born 25-Oct-1819.
97. iv   Audley ANDERSON born 28-Jan-1821.
v   Frances 'Fanny' ANDERSON born 6-Oct-1824, Scott
Co VA, married 1859, James I. HUGHES,
born 2-Sep-1806, Sullivan Co. TN, (son of Abner
HUGHES and Rebecca WOODWARD) died 21-Jun-1890,
Sullivan Co. TN. Frances died 1874.
vi   Eliza F. ANDERSON born 7-Mar-1826, Scott Co VA,
married 15-Jun-1845, David J. CARR, born about
1825, Washington Co. VA, died 1889, Carrville,
Washington Co. Eliza died 13-Sep-1890,
Bristol, Sullivan Co. TN. Died at
the home of her son Aaron in Bristol.
vii   Sarah Ann ANDERSON born 1827, Scott Co
VA, married Henry KANE, born about 1830,
Estilville VA, died 13-Jun-1876. Sarah died
1906, Virginia Springs VA.
viii   John ANDERSON born about 1828, Scott Co VA.
ix   Mary 'Mollie' S. ANDERSON born 30-Jul-1830,
Scott Co VA, married Jessie R. EARNEST, born
about 1830, Fullen's Depot, Green Co TN, died
Earnestville. Mary died 18-Feb-1897,
Earnestville. Obituary...in 1775 her parents
entered the Blockhouse in Scott Co. VA. In this
historic place she was born July 30, 1830. On the
banks of the Chucky River they buried her...
x   Samuel Rhea ANDERSON born about 1832, Scott Co
VA. In Mexican War Samuel was a Lieutenant in
Shaver's Co, Col. McCLellan commanding. Was in
2 battles.
xi   Isaac Campbell ANDERSON Jr. born 1832,
Scott Co VA, married Nannie STEWART, born about
1832, VA? Isaac died 16-Feb-1876.
98. xii   Jane ANDERSON born 1833.
xiii   Caroline ANDERSON born about 1836, Scott Co VA.

24. Samuel RHEA born 3-May-1795, Back Creek, Sullivan Co TN,
married (1) 1-Feb-1826, Ann M. RUTLEDGE, born 27-Dec-1804,

(daughter of George 'Gen.' RUTLEDGE and Annis ARMSTRONG) died 22-Feb-1827, Blountville, Sullivan Co. TN, married (2) 3-Jan-1832, in Sullivan Co. TN, Martha LYNN, born 22-Dec-1810, Kingsport ,Walnut Hill, Sullivan Co (daughter of John LYNN and Martha FLEMING) died 4-Nov-1878, Knoxville, Knox Co. TN, buried: Blountville Cemetery, Sullivan Co. TN. Samuel died 7-May-1863, Blountville, ullivan Co. TN, buried: Blountville Cemetery Sullivan Co. TN.

Attended Washington College in 1813. In 1814 he clerked in Blountville with uncle Audley Anderson. Partner and owner of the business on Audley's death. Bought goods in Baltimore and Philadelphia twice a year. Took cousin Joe Anderson as partner. First wife died four weeks after the birth of their first son in 1927. Aunt Betsy Rhea cared for young Samuel Audley Rhea till he was five. Widower for five years. Samuel then married Martha at Walnut Hill. 1853 moved to Bristol. Died at his residence after a lingering illness.

Children:

99. i   Samuel Audley RHEA born 23-Jan-1827.

   ii   John Lynn RHEA born 28-Oct-1832, Sullivan Co. TN, died 1910, Knoxville, Knox Co. TN. He and his brother William Rhea owned a prosperous mercantile business in Knoxville. Had a home with their sister Ellen in Knoxville where they were active members of the Presbyterian Church. Never married. John always loved languages and mathematics in school. He also progressed in sciences. But before he could finish his education, father needed his assistance in the store. Showing to an inclination in that direction he put in at the store at 17. Mother and teacher were opposed to this. Having the good and systematic training of his father, he soon learned to sell goods and had a good memory and remembered what he read and could tell it. Soon he began gathering in

choice books of history, poets and other
celebrated writers for his library. He clerked
under the firm of Samuel and J. R. Anderson. In
1854 Joseph, and R A withdrew from the Business
and moved his family to Bristol. John became
partner with his father. After fathers death
he carried on the business by himself. During
this partnership the war came on in 1861. He
at once volunteered. In May 1863 his father
died John felt it his duty to get a discharge
from the army and come home. He with his
cousin Joseph Anderson were his father's
executors. He hired a substitute and stayed
home during the rest of the war. Only went out
with the 'Home Guards'. He acted as Register
of Sullivan Co. at that time.

On Sunday September 20, 1863 the Federals were
skirmishing round, woke up John from his
morning nap and demanded all his fire-arms.
They claimed him as their prisoner, took him
off to Zollicoffer. Mr. Fain went with him, did
what he could to have him released in which he
succeeded and they returned to their homes in
Blountville. The two armies continued
skirmishing. The fight commenced, the
Confederates still retreating and stopped in
Blountville. All were ready to go into thecellars but
then they saw Col. Carter planting his cannon in the
middle of the Main Street in front of the Rhea
house! So they went out through meadow north
of town to Miss Betsy Shrights. The next day
they returned to nothing but smoldering ashes,
destruction and discouragement everywhere.
Soon as they could make ready, they and the
girls kept house in the Ensor House until the
war closed.

After that the house was built and lived in
until moving to Knoxville in 1869. Soon as he
could he rebuilt the store on the old stand,
moved all his effects to it and continued
merchandising. In 1868 he bought a store in
Knoxville on Gay Street one door South of Baptist
Church; also bought a lot on Church St. on which
he built his home in 1874. In 1869 he moved
his stock of goods to Knoxville. His brother
Brainard was also there and they formed a
partnership which continued till 1872.

100. iii   Fannie 'Fannie' Anderson RHEA born 6-Mar-1834.
101. iv   Mary Martha RHEA born 14-Aug-1836.
102. v   Joseph Brainard RHEA born 8-Apr-1838.
    vi   James Alexander RHEA born 5-Dec-1840,
Blountville, Sullivan Co. TN, married
17-Jun-1868, in Montgomery, AL, Sarah 'Sallie'
WHITING, born about 1840, Montgomery, AL, died
5-Jul-1896, Birmingham, Jefferson Co. AL.
James died 31-Dec-1871, Montgomery, AL. Buried
in Mr. Whiting's vault in Montgomery. Student at
Amherst College. Was 1st Lt. in Company G 19th
Infantry; later the 16th Regiment. Later
elected Major and afterward Lt. Col. He had
been wounded in the eye. Again was wounded an
captured by Federals and recaptured by his own
men. Fought at battle of Shiloh April 6,7,
1862. Wounded in the hip on the 7th. Wounded
at the battle of Piedmont VA June 5, 1864.
Fleeing Union retribution he moved to
Montgomery after the war, his health shattered.
103. vii   Robert Morrison RHEA born 14-Oct-1842.
    viii   Eliza Eleanor RHEA born 22-Aug-1844,
Blountville, Sullivan Co. TN, died 1914.
Never married.
    ix   William Lynn RHEA born 6-Jun-1847, Blountville,
Sullivan Co. TN, died Knoxville, Knox Co. TN.

Never married. Owned mercantile business with
brother John. He was the author of the manusript W.L.
Rhea-Genealogy of Rhea Family - 1895.

104. x   Margaret Elizabeth RHEA born 24-Jul-1849.
   xi   Charles Stoddard RHEA born 23-Dec-1851,
      Blountville, Sullivan Co. TN, died 1856,
      Blountville, Sullivan Co. TN. Died of scarlet
      fever.

25. Eleanor 'Ellen' RHEA born 7-Apr-1797, Back Creek,
Sullivan Co TN, married 8-Nov-1818, Edward B. ANDERSON,
born 1795, Rockbridge Co VA, died 8-Oct-1862, Blountville,
Sullivan Co. TN, buried: Blountville Cemetery Sullivan Co.
TN. Eleanor died 5-Jul-1865, Blountville, Sullivan Co. TN,
buried: Blountville Cemetery Sullivan Co. TN.

In an agreement with the other heirs of Joseph Rhea, her
grandfather, she and her husband Edward received about 265 acres
from the homestead of Joseph. They built a large two story home 2
1/2 miles from Blountville where they raised their family. At one
time Edward bought the historic Anderson Townhouse on Main
Street, Blountvile from brother-in-law Robert Rhea.

Children:

i   William Rhea ANDERSON born 1821, Sullivan
      Co. TN, married Louise SMITH, born 1827,
      TN, died 2-Jan-1890, Blountville, Sullivan Co.
      TN, buried: Blountville, Sullivan Co. TN.
      William died after 1895, Blountville, Sullivan
      Co. TN. Born in the house 2 1/2 miles from
      Blountville, Sullivan Co. Grew up on the
      farm. Loved to read and talk. When a young man
      traveled through the far west. Held places of
      trust in Sullivan Co. Was an enrolling
      officer and belonged to the reserves during the
      civil war.

ii   Joseph Rhea ANDERSON born 24-Feb-1825, Sullivan
      Co. TN, died about 1851, Big Pine, Imayo Co,

42

California. Lost in the California Gold Rush.
Left home in 1850 to find gold. Was sick in
Kern Co, Died at Big Pine, Imayo Co,
California.

105. iii   Audley 'Doc' ANDERSON born 1826.
106. iv   Fannie ANDERSON born about 1830.
107. v   Margaret E. ANDERSON born 1832.
   vi   Robert R. ANDERSON born 1834, Sullivan
        Co. TN. Was in Company G. 16th Tennessee
        Cavalry in service to the C.S.A.
108. vii   Samuel R. ANDERSON born 1834.

26. Frances 'Fannie' RHEA born 1-Mar-1799, Sullivan Co. TN,
married 1-Mar-1825, in Sullivan Co. TN, Jonathan BACHMAN,
born 1801, Sullivan Co. TN, died 1844, Sullivan Co. TN. Frances
died 3-Jun-1850, Sullivan Co. TN, buried: Old Kingsport
Presbyterian Cemetery, Kingsport TN.

Children:

   i   Joseph Rhea BACHMAN born 1827, Sullivan
        Co. TN, died 1850. Was enroute to
        California to the Gold Rush when he heard of
        his mother's death. He wrote he was returning
        but he was never heard from again. He was
        supposedly shipwrecked.
109. ii   Ann Peoples BACHMAN born 9-Mar-1827.
   iii   Frances BACHMAN born about 1829, Sullivan Co. TN.
   iv   Elizabeth 'Betty' BACHMAN born about 1830,
        Sullivan Co. TN, died 22-Aug-1883, Fullen's
        Depot, Green Co TN, buried: Kingsport, Sullivan
        Co TN. Never married. Was a great sufferer
        the greater part of her life. When about grown a
        'white swelling' began developing in her left
        limb. For years this gave her much trouble and
        suffering. Was in Jonesboro at different times
        under treatment with Dr. Cunningham. She seemed
        to grow and recover but the limb was shorter
        than the other. Always walked lame. During her

last years was afflicted with asthma, terrible spells.
Finally died from one of these spells at B.F.Earnest's.
Took care of the home and children after oldest
sister left, so long as she was able.

v   Nathan BACHMAN born 1832, Sullivan Co.
TN, married Sarah Jane CUNNINGHAM, born about
1830, Jonesboro, Washington Co. Nathan
died 1914. A Presbyterian minister, he was born
at the home on Horse Creek, grew up on the
farm. Ambitious about an education. Older
brother went to college but he had to care for
widowed mother and other 8 younger children,
going to school and teaching in Jonesboro.
Made a profession of religion early in life.
Graduated Emory and Henry College VA just
before the war came on. He and his brother
Jonathan went on to Union Theological Seminary
in NY to study. Not there too long before the
war came on. Jonathan came back to his home
in the south and enlisted, made chaplain, while
Nathan, not feeling to be right to take up arms
against the Union, remained in the north and
completed his courses, taking also a year at
Princeton. He returned and was ordained and
preached at various churches in Kingsport and
Arcadia. Some time in 1866 he took the 2nd
Presbyterian Church in Knoxville as pastor for 10
years. In 1878 he took the Evangelical work,
holding a series of meetings in the south and
west, wherever called. (W.L. Rhea, 1895).

vi   Samuel Rhea BACHMAN born about 1833, Sullivan
Co.
TN, died about 1863. Enlisted in a Hawkins
Co TN Company for the C.S.A. Died of fever at
Cumberland Gap in the early part of the war.

vii   Mary Jane BACHMAN born about 1835, Sullivan Co.
TN.

110. viii   Jonathan Waverly BACHMAN DD. LDD. born 9-Oct-1837.

111. ix   John Lynn BACHMAN born 23-Jan-1841.

     x   Robert Lucky BACHMAN born 1844, Horse Creek, Sullivan Co married Mary ROSE, born about 1850, Grand Rapids, MI, died 2-Mar-1890, Utica NY. Robert died Sullivan Co. TN. Robert was born on Horse Creek, spent his first years and grew to manhood at home, attending school and working some on the farm. Before he was fully grown the war was over our country, he went into the army belonging to his brother Col. J W BACHMAN, was in the Vicksburg siege. Served in the 16th Tennessee Cavalry, Co. G.

When the war closed he with his brother Lynn and cousin C. E. Lucky entered Hamilton College, where he graduated. While in college he carried off two medals, one for oratory the other for the best composition in his class. He came out and taught five months in the school Lookout, then returned to Hamilton and complete the course. After this he began preparing for his life work, went through the Theological Seminary course in NY of 3 years. He preached a while in Syracuse NY, pretty soon had a call to the largest church in Utica NY which call he accepted and was pastor. Robert BACHMAN married Mary Rose soon after he took charge of the Church in Utica NY. He was pastor for 16 years. Wife died leaving him and 3 children in March 1890. In summer of 1896 the 2nd Presbyterian Church of Knoxville gave him a call to be their pastor. After much prayer and deliberation, he accepted, giving his resignation to his Presbytery. He preached his first sermon there on September 27, 1896. (W.L. Rhea, 1895)

27. Nancy RHEA born 25-Jun-1801, Sullivan Co. TN, married
25-Nov-1825, in Kingsport, Sullivan Co TN, John LYNN Jr.,
born 13-Apr-1798, Boltsagh Ireland, (son of John LYNN and
Martha FLEMING) died 1-Apr-1883, Sullivan Co. TN. Nancy
died 7-Oct-1839, Kingsport, Sullivan Co TN.

Born at fathershome on Back Creek. She, like her sisters, had
limited education as in those days very poor opportunities for
education. She married John Lynn of Kingsport and moved there.
All her children born there. She died there a triumphant death. She
had a long lingering illness but was patient and uncomplaining.
(W.L. Rhea-1895).

Children:

112. i   Martha Fleming LYNN born 23-Feb-1827.
    ii   Frances Rhea LYNN born 7-Feb-1829, Sullivan Co.
         TN.
    iii   Ellen A. LYNN born 27-Jun-1830, Back Creek,
         Kingsport, Sullivan Co died 3-Aug-1861,
         Kingsport, Sullivan Co TN. Never married.
    iv   Joseph Rhea LYNN born 15-Aug-1833, Sullivan Co.
         TN, died 3-Jan-1857, Kingsport TN?
    v   Mary Ann LYNN born 24-Nov-1835, Kingsport,
         Sullivan Co TN, married 30-Oct-1855, Joseph
         Rodgers WALKER, born 24-Aug-1831, Rodgersville
         TN, died 18-Sep-1931, Rodgersville TN. Mary
         died 15-Dec-1871, Rodgersville TN. Died leaving
         her youngest an infant, his aunt Ella Walker
         took him as her special case.
113. vi   James LYNN born 9-Sep-1837.
114. vii   Samuel Alexander LYNN born 9-Jul-1839.

28. Robert Preston RHEA born 17-Sep-1802, Back Creek,
Sullivan Co TN, married 17-Oct-1826, in Abington, Washington
Co. VA, Sarah Jane Gilliland PRESTON, born 27-Jun-1803,
Abington, Washington Co. VA, (daughter of Robert PRESTON Jr.

and Jane 'Jennie' PRESTON) died 20-Jul-1874, Sullivan Co. TN, buried: Blountville Cemetery Sullivan Co. TN. Robert died 26-Mar-1881, Sullivan Co. TN, buried: Blountville Cemetery Sullivan Co. TN.

Robert P. Rhea was always a citizen of Sullivan Co lived and owned the home of his father, there all his children born and reared. In 1896 it was owned by his oldest son Joseph, living there with his family. This was a very dear spot to all the nieces and nephews who loved to visit his home. He was always lively and cheerful. They would enter heartily and enter into sports and plays, get a crowd together and they would play "Blind Man's Bluff" he being the Blind man. His school days were spent in the log school house near his father's home. He also went to Washington College TN, to old Dr. Sam Doak 1819 & 1820. Came out of school and carried on farming extensively on his land, owned many slaves, forty or fifty, big and little, male and female. They did all kinds of work, belonging to the farm, had a sugar camp where maple sugar and syrup was made. He was kind and good to these slaves, never cruel and they loved and respected him.

His wife was a very managing and industrious and energetic woman, up early and late planning her work. She had spinning and weaving carried on, long as they owned these slave in the house. While granny Breden lived there (1828) they spun, wove and made cloth from wool, flax and cotton all raised on the farm (except the cotton) and made up into clothes, blankets, sheets, table linen for the house. It was laborious work to raise the bread meat and grain for so many mouths. That day is all past (1896).

Robert was a high toned honorable citizen, had the esteem and respect of all who knew him. Held co. offices and places of trust though' he never sought them. He made a profession of religion and united with the Presbyterian Church in Blountville TN. In that Church his place was never vacant. It was his joy and pleasure to be found in the Sanctuary and to do the work of the Sanctuary. He was and elder in the church for many years until he died. He was a great Temperance lecturer, gave much of his time and attention to this cause, going through' his country holding temperance meetings and making speeches. He could always draw a crowd. Along this line he did much good in the way of reforming the drunkard and lifting him up our of the mire.

He was also much interested in public affairs, helping to build the East Tennessee and Ga. Railroad. Was one of the Board of Directors and also one of the thirty, who saved the Charter of the Road. He was a pure, true man, honest and upright. When he passed away he was greatly missed by all who knew him. He had a large circle of relatives and friend. When the last summons came, he was ready. Had fought and the fight finished his course and was laid away amid the regrets of a large number of people. From manuscript *Genealogy of the Rhea Family* by W.L. Rhea (1895), son of Samuel.

1850 Sullivan Co. TN census he was a farmer with property valued at $8000.

1870 after the war, he is enumerated as head of household with wife Sarah G. and son Joseph and his wife Elizabeth, daughter Jane P. Vance, living there following the death of Belfor Vance, Delia Wadkins (keeping house at age 16) and infant Robert Rhea born July 1870. Real estate value $4000 property $2102.

Col. John Anderson Townhouse on Lot 26 is one of Blountville's original dwellings were legend and deed disagree as to its beginnings. The lot was originally bought by Dr. Elkanah Dulaney probably as an investment property and the log house there today was probably built by him for rental purposes. In 1811 he sold lot 26 and 27 to Joshua Miller for 500 dollars. Miller sold lot 26 "including the house at present occupied by Joshua Russel's family to Robert Rhea for $300. Robert kept the property for 2 years then sold it to his brother in law Edward B. Anderson for $600. He may have made improvements and it was probably he who built the frame rear section which was at first connected to the log house by a "dog trot".

Children:

i   Jane Preston RHEA born 1829, Sullivan Co.
TN, married (1) Belfour VANCE, born about 1800,
Abington, Washington Co. VA, married (2) Audley
'Doc' ANDERSON, born 2 1826, Sullivan Co.
TN, (son of Edward B. ANDERSON and Eleanor
'Ellen' RHEA) died 1-Feb-1864, Sullivan Co. TN,
buried: Blountville Cemetery Sullivan Co. TN.
Jane died aft 1896. Was lively, kind, pleasant
and very industrious. A great comfort to her
parents in their declining years. Her married
life with Mr. Vance was short and spent in VA.
She came back to her father's house to spend
her widowhood. Later she married Audley. They
lived a while in Bristol, where he was selling
goods in cousin Joe's store. His health began
failing and they moved to the 'Blockhouse',
the old homestead, then called 'Lucille'. They
were both members of the Presbyterian Church.

115. ii   Joseph RHEA III born 12-Dec-1830.

116. iii   Frances "Frank" Elizabeth RHEA born 31-Dec-1832.

117. iv   Margaret 'Peggy' Preston RHEA born 22-Jun-1835.

v   Robert James RHEA born 18-Dec-1837, Sullivan
Co. TN, died 17-Sep-1864, Forsyth GA. Youngest
Son of Robert and Sallie, born on Back Creek,
educated at home in Blountville TN. Rode out
every day a distance of four miles to Jefferson
Academy. For a while was a student at Emory &
Henry College, VA. After that to Maryville
College for year or two. War came up, he
enlisted in C.S.A. was engaged in several battles:
Fishing Creek, Shiloh. Was sick, came home with a
spell of fever for a year. In 1864 he returned
to his Regiment. In battle near Atlanta July 22,
1864 received a wound and never recovered.

vi   Sara Sells RHEA born 1841, Bristol,
Sullivan Co. TN, died 1934, Sullivan Co.

TN, buried: Blountville Cemetery Sullivan Co.
TN.

29. Sarah RHEA born 1806, Sullivan Co. TN, married
6-Dec-1831, in Sullivan Co. TN, Seth J. W. LUCKY, born 1799,
died 14-Apr-1869, Jonesboro, Washington Co buried: Jonesboro E.
TN Cemetery. Sarah died 9-Sep-1862, Sullivan Co., Tennessee?

Bright and intellectual. In her day, colleges for women were
unheard of but she was fond of reading - history, biography, poetry.
Memorized hymns and scripture while spinning flax on the little
wheel. Read Burns poems and Humes history of England when at
her knitting. (W.L. Rhea-1895) Died after and an illness of 2
weeks leaving 6 children.

Children:

i		Frances A. LUCKY born about 1832, Jonesboro, Washington Co buried: Jonesboro, Washington Co TN.
118.	ii	Sarah Jane LUCKY born 6-Feb-1834.
119.	iii	Ellen LUCKY born 18-Feb-1836.
	iv	Sophia LUCKY born about 1836.
	v	Joseph LUCKY born about 1838.
	vi	Cornelius Eugenia LUCKY born 1841, Jonesboro, Washington Co married Julia SIMMS, born about 1845, Dalton GA. Fought at Vicksburg 1863. Served in Co. K, 16th Tenn. Infantry. In the year 1858 he entered Henry and Emory College, VA. While there the war began. He came home and went into the Southern army in 1862 though his father was a strong Union man. He was in several battles and at the surrender of Vicksburg July 4, 1863. When the strife was quiet he pursued his studies in Hamilton College NY. When he graduated he was offered a position in Roberts College. He considered this offer but declined, having chosen law as his profession and life work. He moved to Knoxville and read law with Judge S.T. Logan

then with Honorable John Goe (who died in
1896). He and Edward Stanford were partners.
His church was the 4th Presbyterian.
(W.L. Rhea-1895).

vii   Martha McAlister 'Pet' LUCKY born 13-Feb-1843,
Jonesboro, Washington Co married about 1860,
John E. WILLIAMS, born about 1840, Carter Co. TN,
died 26-Dec-1886, Knoxville, Knox Co. TN.
Married young.

viii   Agnes Mitchell LUCKY born 13-Jul-1845,
Jonesboro TN?, married Joseph R. WALKER, born
about 1845, Rodgersville TN. Agnes died
1903. Her mother died when she was 17.
Made her home with her stepmother until they
moved to Knoxville, then she lived with her
sisters until she married.

ix   Elizabeth Dysart "Bettie" LUCKY born
9-Feb-1847, Jonesboro, Washington Co
married George W. HAMILTON, born about 1845,
Dalton GA. Elizabeth died Dalton GA. Lived
with her stepmother until the father moved to
Knoxville. She then lived with her sisters till
she married and moved to Dalton GA. Very smart
and sarcastic. (W.L. Rhea-1895).

30. Sarah 'Sallie' RHEA born about 1805, Sullivan Co. TN,
married 22-Jun-1826, George Woodson GAINES, born about
1800. Sarah died 27-Jan-1849.

Children:

120. i   John Rhea GAINES born 1827.
121. ii   Robert J. GAINES born 1829.
iii   August Pendleton GAINES born 1831
married Dorcas HENDERSON, born about 1830
died Sweetwater TN? August died 1902,
Sweetwater TN? Augustus had 3 children.
(W.L. Rhea-1895) Lived on their farm near
Sweetwater TN and were noted for their

hospitality.
iv   William J. GAINES born 1834, died
1854.
v   Elizabeth McCuin GAINES born 1837,
married (1) John Franklin BOGART, born about
1835, married (2) John BOGART, born about 1840.
Elizabeth died 1873.
vi   Sarah GAINES born 1849, Sullivan Co. TN,
married John W. JOHNSTON, born about 1849
died Sweetwater TN. Sarah died 1901,
Sweetwater TN.

31. Joseph R. RHEA born 17-Nov-1805, Sullivan Co. TN,
married 1830, Emaline M. ALEXANDER, born 11-Nov-1805,
Hawkins Co., Tennessee, died 10-Dec-1891, near McKinley,
Texas. Joseph died after 1895, near McKinley, Texas.

Livedin Loudon Co TN then TX in 1855, bought lands and raised
family there. Owned a flouring mill in McKinney, Collin Co. TX.
The town became known as Rhea Mills.

Children:

i   Robert P. RHEA born 7-Nov-1831, Loudon Co TN,
died 7-Apr-1915.
122. ii   William Alexander RHEA born 23-Feb-1833.
123. iii   John W. RHEA born 1835.
124. iv   James Calvin RHEA born 11-Apr-1837.
125. v   Mary Elizabeth RHEA born 2-May-1840.

32. Elizabeth M. RHEA born 1807, Sullivan Co. TN,
married Joseph ANDERSON, born about 1800, Sullivan Co. TN,
died Loudon TN. Elizabeth died 1853, Loudon TN.

Children:

i   Robert ANDERSON born 1832, Sullivan Co.
TN, married Emily HUFF, born about 1832. Robert
died 1-Jun-1895, Loudon TN.
ii   Sarah G. ANDERSON born about 1834, Sullivan Co.

TN.
iii   Isabelle J. ANDERSON born about 1836, Sullivan
Co. TN.
iv   Adeline ANDERSON born about 1836, Sullivan Co.
TN.
126. v   Elizabeth M. ANDERSON born 1840.
vi   John A. ANDERSON born 1842, Sullivan Co.
TN, married Isabella HOTCHKISS, born about 1842,
Sullivan Co. TN? John died 1868. Died
of exposure while serving in the First
Tennessee Infantry for the Union Army.
vii   Samuel ANDERSON born 1845, Sullivan Co.
TN, married Margaret HUFF, born about 1845,
Sullivan Co. TN? Samuel died 1900.
viii   Rachel A. ANDERSON born 1848, Sullivan
Co. TN, married Ebb J. CROWDER, born about 1848,
Sullivan Co. TN? Rachel died 1911.
ix   Amanda ANDERSON born 1851, Sullivan Co.
TN, married John Taylor LOWERY, born about 1835.
Amanda died 1907.

33. John RHEA born 1810, Sullivan Co. TN, married
1838, Elizabeth Adeline DODSON, born about 1810, Sullivan Co.
TN, (daughter of Alexander DODSON and Elizabeth ROBERTS)
died Loudon Co TN. John died 1863, Loudon Co TN.

Moved to Roane Co where he owned large tracts of land also a
large tract at Loudon Co. Raised his children on this farm. He left
the tract to Alexander.

Children:
127. i   Alexander Dodson RHEA born 16-Jun-1841.
128. ii   Sarah Elizabeth 'Bettie' RHEA born 1843.

34. Margaret P. RHEA born 1789, Sullivan Co. TN, married
Wendell STURM, born about 1800. Margaret died 7-Sep-1846,
Sullivan Co. TN, buried: Blountville Cemetery Sullivan Co. TN.

Children:

i   Nancy STURM born about 1830, married Fulton
HALL, born 1837 (son of Jane (Stephens?) HALL).

ii   Frances 'Fanny' STURM born about 1832,
married 23-Oct-1867, Richard Shipley CARTRIGHT,
born 1-May-1834, Sullivan Co. TN, (son of
William CARTRIGHT Jr. and Elizabeth SHIPLEY)
died 1-Jul-1920, Sullivan Co. TN, buried:
Gunnings Cemetery, Sullivan Co. TN.

iii   Catherine 'Kate' STURM born about 1834,
married Samuel HALL, born 1839 (son of
Jane (Stephens?) HALL).

35. Samuel RHEA born 3-May-1795, Sullivan Co. TN, married
(1) Martha wife of Samuel RHEA, born 22-Dec-1810, Sullivan
Co., Tennessee?, died 4-Nov-1878, Sullivan Co. TN, buried:
Blountville Cemetery Sullivan Co. TN, married (2)
3-Jan-1832, Ann WASELL?, born 26-Dec-1804, Sullivan Co.,
Tennessee?, died 22-Feb-1827, Sullivan Co. TN, buried:
Blountville Cemetery Sullivan Co. TN. Samuel died 7-May-1863,
Sullivan Co. TN, buried: Blountville Cemetery Sullivan Co. TN.

Children:

i   Samuel A. RHEA born 1827, Sullivan Co. TN, died
2-Sep-1865, Ali-Shad Persia, buried: Persia.

36. Elizabeth 'Betsy' RHEA born 1803, Sullivan Co. TN,
married Thomas CRAWFORD, born 1795, Sullivan Co. TN,
died 12-Mar-1874, Blountville, Sullivan Co. TN. Elizabeth
died 22-Apr-1876, Blountville, Sullivan Co. TN, buried:
Blountville, Sullivan Co. TN.

Children:

129. i   John R. CRAWFORD born 1831.

130. ii   Seraphine 'Sarah' CRAWFORD born 1833.

131. iii   Samuel H. CRAWFORD born 1835.

iv   Joseph R. CRAWFORD born 1837, Sullivan
Co. TN, married Cornelia ROGAN, born about 1840,

Knoxville, Knox Co. TN, buried: 1891,
Blountville, Sullivan Co. TN. Joseph died
Blountville, Sullivan Co. TN. On the farm with
his father until 1859 when he came to
Blountville TN and was clerk in Samuel Rhea's
store for several years. He was 3rd Sergeant
Co. G, 16th Infantry and later Captain of Co. G
16th Cavalry.

   v   Nancy 'Nannie' CRAWFORD born 1840,
       Sullivan Co. TN.

37. John Nancy RHEA born 24-Apr-1805, Sullivan Co. TN,
married 17-Jan-1837, Ruth M. ROCKHOLD, born 20-Mar-1821,
Sullivan Co. TN, (daughter of William R. ROCKHOLD and
Harriet NETHERLAND) died 30-Sep-1892, Blountville, Sullivan
Co. TN, buried: Blountville Cemetery Sullivan Co. TN. John
died 2-May-1876, Blountville, Sullivan Co. TN, buried: Blountville,
Sullivan Co. TN.

Born on the farm of his father. Lived, farmed, raised his family and
died there. He was a regular attendant at the Presbyterian Church in
Blountville.

Children:
   i   William R. RHEA born 22-Dec-1837, Sullivan Co.
        TN, died 22-Dec-1837, Sullivan Co. TN.
132. ii   Elizabeth Crawford 'Lizzie' RHEA born 23-May-1839.
133. iii   Samuel Wood RHEA born 12-Jun-1841.
134. iv   John M. RHEA born 9-May-1848.
135. v   Harriet Nancy RHEA born 15-Jul-1851.
136. vi   Mary A. 'Mollie' RHEA born 1854.
137. vii Joseph S. RHEA born 25-Nov-1861.
138. viii Margaret R. 'Maggie' RHEA born 15-May-1865.

38. Ellen RHEA born about 1810, married Washington
MONTGOMERY, born about 1800.

Children:

i   Nannie MONTGOMERY born about 1830 married
Mr. JONES, born about 1830.

39. Joseph S. RHEA born 1812, Muddy Creek, Sullivan Co
TN, married 17-Aug-1837, in Carter Co. TN, Sarophina L.
WILLIAMS, born about 1800, Carter Co. TN, (daughter of
Archibald WILLIAMS and wife of Archibald WILLIAMS) died
Knoxville, Knox Co. TN, buried: Grays Cemetery Knoxville TN.
Joseph died 26-Oct-1886, Ringold, GA, buried: Grays Cemetery
Knoxville TN.

When he was a young man he sold goods in Blountville for Sam
Rhea (W.L. Rhea's father). Chose dentistry as a profession and
prepared himself for it. After marrying lived in Blountville for a
while then bought a farm on Watauga River. Lived there several
years. Bought property in Jonesboro and moved family there until
1871 when they moved to Knoxville and he practiced there. Upon
death of wife he and Nannie moved to GA and lived with his
daughter Rhoda until his death.

Children:

139. i   Rhoda RHEA born 1833.
140. ii   Archibald W. 'Archie' RHEA born 1838.
    iii   Nannie A. RHEA born about 1840, Blountville,
          Sullivan Co. TN.
141. iv   Samuel RHEA born 1850.

40. Jane RHEA born 1813, Blountville, Sullivan Co. TN,
married John Fairman 'Capt.' PRESTON, born 26-Apr-1811,
Washington Co. VA, (son of Robert PRESTON Jr. and Jane
'Jennie' PRESTON) died 16-Jan-1875, Abington, Washington Co.
VA. Jane died 4-May-1876, Abington, Washington Co. VA.

Children:

i   Nannie Montgomery PRESTON born 4-May-1838,
      Washington Co. VA, married 1866, John
      'Col.' C. SUMMERS, born 1-Feb-1839, Union VA,
      died 19-Jun-1907. Nannie died 13-Jun-1906.

ii   Robert James PRESTON born 25-Jan-1841, Washington Co. VA, married 19-Oct-1875, in Smythe Co. VA, Martha E. SHEFFEY, born 15-Mar-1849, Marion, Smythe Co. VA, (daughter of James White S. SHEFFEY and Eleanor Fairman PRESTON) died 4-Nov-1898, Baltimore Co. MD. Robert died 20-Aug-1906, Lewiston NY. Born at "Locust Glen" near Abington. Successful and noted physician in Marion. Superintendent of the Southwestern State Hospital in 1888. He had attended Abington Academy and Emory and Henry College 1859-61. Joined Capt. James Campbell's Co. C.S.A. and was elected 1st Lt. but when ordered to Richmond resigned. 25 May 1861 enlisted as private in Co. K 37th VA Inf. until September 9, 1862. Re-enlisted 15 June 1863 in Co. C. 21st VA Cavalry. and was elected 1st Lt. Practiced medicine in NY, Abington VA and Marion VA.

iii   Sarah Ellen PRESTON born 21-Oct-1843, Washington Co. VA, married 29-Feb-1872, David 'Col.' Flourney BAILEY, born 23-Jan-1845, VA, died 30-Oct-1922, Bristol, Sullivan Co. TN. Sarah died 22-Jun-1927, Bristol, Sullivan Co. TN.

142. iv   James Brainard PRESTON born 3-Dec-1845.

v   Samuel Rhea PRESTON born about 1848, Washington Co. VA, married in Columbia SC, Ida SUTPHEN, born about 1850, Columbia SC, died Bristol, Sullivan Co. TN. Samuel died TN? Minister in Columbia SC. Then in Bristol and Johnson City TN Churches.

vi   Jennie Fairman PRESTON born about 1850, Washington Co. VA, married Thomas James NEWMAN, born about 1850, VA?

41. Margaret RHEA born 1815, Sullivan Co. TN, married 1832, John Pemberton SNAPP, born 1808, Green Co. TN, (son of Samuel SNAPP and Hannah 'Dianah' PEMBERTON)

died aft 1860, Green Co. TN, buried: Mt. Zion Church Cemetery. Margaret died 23-Oct-1897, Green Co. TN, buried: Mt. Zion Church, Green Co. TN.

Children:

i   Elizabeth Rhea SNAPP born 1833, Green Co TN?, married 1815, Alexander Adams BLAIR, born about 1839. Elizabeth died 1857. Had no children.

ii   Florence Diane SNAPP born 1835, Greene Co TN, married 10-May-1865, Paul Michaux WILLIAMS, born about 1845, Knoxville, Knox Co. TN. Florence died 1908.

iii Vivoline M. SNAPP born 1839, Green Co. TN, married (1) Alexander Adams BLAIR, born about 1839, married (2) John BRAZELTON, born about 1845 died before 1895. Married Alexander after the death of his first wife, her sister Elizabeth. After his death (they had no children) she married James Brazelton. One girl.

143. iv Cynthia Lodoville SNAPP born 1844.

v   John Raymond SNAPP born about 1844, Green Co. TN.

vi   Tulen Velosso SNAPP born 1847, Green Co. TN, married Isaac EARNEST, born about 1856, Earnestville Tulen died before 1895.

vii Cicero DeForest SNAPP born about 1848, Green Co. TN.

42. John Quintas RHEA born 1818, Blountville, Sullivan Co. TN, married (1) 1843, in Sullivan Co. TN?, Nancy LYNN, born circa 1810, married (2) Cynthia WILLIAMS, born about 1800, (daughter of Mr. WILLIAMS and Nancy COPELAND) married (3) Cornelia C. WILLIAMS, born about 1806, Sullivan Co., Tennessee?, (daughter of Mr. WILLIAMS and NancyCOPELAND). John died 1883.

After wife Cynthia died, Mary Lucita, her sister came and kept house and took care of the children. Sometime afterward John married another sister Cornelia C. Williams and had one girl.

Children:
i   Joseph RHEA born 15-Aug-1833, Sullivan Co. TN, died 3-Oct-1857, Sullivan Co. TN, buried: Old Methodist Cemetery Kingsport TN. Died of fever.
ii   Margaret Frances RHEA born about 1834, Sullivan Co. TN.
iii William Fort RHEA born about 1836, Sullivan Co. TN.
iv   James E. RHEA born about 1838, Sullivan Co. TN.
v   John RHEA born about 1840, Sullivan Co. TN.
vi   Elizabeth RHEA born about 1842, Sullivan Co. TN.
144. vii Anna Cornelia RHEA born about 1850.

43. James RHEA Jr. born 1820, Sullivan Co. TN, married 1847, Louise SMITH, born 1827 died 2-Jan-1890, Blountville, Sullivan Co. TN, buried: Blountville, Sullivan Co. TN. James died 1891.

Children:
145. i   Wright Smith RHEA born 1848.
146. ii   James RHEA III. born 1850.
iii Alexander Smith RHEA born 1852, Sullivan Co., Tennessee?, married Sarah 'Sallie' Virginia HARRIS, born about 1852.
147. iv   Bryant Whitefield RHEA born 1854.
v   Priscilla Ada RHEA born 1856, Sullivan Co. TN, married J. G. IVEY, born about 1856.
148. vi   Florence RHEA born 1859.
149. vii David M. RHEA born about 1862.
viii Robert Lee RHEA born 1872, Sullivan Co. TN, died 1909.
150. ix   Thomas B. RHEA born 1873.

44. Frances 'Fannie' RHEA born 1826, Sullivan Co. TN,

married 1-Aug-1850, James Tecumseh 'Col.' PRESTON, born
1-Apr-1824, Washington Co. VA, (son of John 'Col.' PRESTON
and Margaret Brown PRESTON) died 9-Dec-1883, Washington
Co. VA?, buried: Walnut Grove Cemetery Washington Co. VA.
Frances died 1888, Sullivan Co. TN, buried: Walnut Grove
Cemetery, Washington Co. VA.

A refined, educated and handsome lady. Read and studied Latin
and Greek with her father. Sabbath school teacher. (W.L.
Rhea-1895).

Children:

151. i   John PRESTON born 21-Jul-1851.

ii   James Rhea PRESTON born 22-Jan-1853, Washington
Co. VA, married 18-Dec-1902, in Natchez, Miss.,
Elizabeth Alice VAUGHAN, born 1-May-1875,
Clinton LA, died 2-Jun-1972, Jackson, Miss.
James died 3-Apr-1922, Jackson, Miss. Born at
"Walnut Grove". Superintendent of schools in
Mississippi. He was a student at Geo. Washington
U. and later at Emory and Henry College 1871-73
and there received A.M. degree. Moved to Miss.
in 1874 as a teacher. While Superintendent of Water
Valley Schools he was chosen by the legislature
to be State Superintendent - an office he held from
1886-96. 1896 he was a graduate student at U.
of Edinburgh. 1898 he founded Stanton College
at Natchez Miss. and Belhave College which
burned in 1910. Composed state motto "Virtue et
Armis".

iii   Walter Eugene PRESTON born about 1856,
Washington Co. VA, died Texas. He was a student at
Emory and Henry College 1871-73 and received B.A. He
died unmarried.

iv   Robert Fairman PRESTON born 1-Apr-1857,
Washington Co. VA, married 12-Feb-1896, in
Washington Co. VA, Elizabeth McDonald PRESTON,
born 1870, VA?, died 1934,

Washington Co. VA, buried: Walnut Grove Cemetery
Washington Co. VA. Robert died 1929, buried: Walnut
Grove Cemetery Washington Co. VA. Lawyer
living in VA (W.L. Rhea-1895).

v   Frances 'Fanny' Rhea PRESTON born 1859,
Washington Co. VA, died 1881, Washington
Co. VA, buried: Walnut Grove Cemetery Washington
Co. VA. Died as a child.

vi   Frances 'Frank' McIlwaine PRESTON born
1864, Washington Co. VA, died 1907,
Washington Co. VA, buried: Walnut Grove Cemetery
Washington Co. VA.

45. Samuel RHEA born 1829, Sullivan Co. TN, married
1857, Lucy J. WILLIAMS, born 22-Apr-1836, Sullivan Co.,
Tennessee?, (daughter of Mr. WILLIAMS and Nancy
COPELAND) died 17-Mar-1916, Sullivan Co. TN. Samuel died
1902.

Family lived in Grainger City for some time, then in Rhea County.
Moved to Sullivan Co lived at Rhea's Mill awhile, then moved to
Bristol where they lived in 1895. Has met some misfortunes in life.
Lost his oldest son in a railroad wreck. Lost his property.

Children:

152. i   James Copeland RHEA born 1862.
153. ii   Samuel Williams RHEA born 1864.
154. iii   Thomas Humes RHEA born 1866.
155. iv   Mary Lucy RHEA born 1868.
    v   Anna Elizabeth RHEA born 1870, Sullivan
Co., Tennessee?, married William T. ENSER, born
about 1870.
156. vi   Kate RHEA born 1873.
    vii   Hal Henry RHEA born 1877.
    viii   Fanny McIlwaine RHEA born 1879.

46. Theodoric Bland RHEA born 21-Jun-1833, Sullivan Co. TN,
married 1856, Frances "Frank" Elizabeth RHEA, born

31-Dec-1832, Sullivan Co. TN, (daughter of Robert Preston
RHEA and Sarah Jane Gilliland PRESTON) died 4-Nov-1870,
Blountville, Sullivan Co. TN, buried: Blountville Cemetery
Sullivan Co. TN. Theodoric died 15-Nov-1868, Sullivan Co.
TN, buried: Blountville Cemetery Sullivan Co. TN.

Died two years before wife. When she died in 1870 the children
were sent to live with Frances' younger sister Margaret and
husband John T. Earhart, until they were old enough to follow the
oldest boy Robert to Texas. The oldest child was only 14 when her
mother died.

Children:

157. i	Elizabeth 'Bettie' Dysart RHEA born	1856.
ii	Elizabeth B. RHEA born 1857, Sullivan Co. TN.	
158. iii	Robert Preston RHEA born 6-Mar-1859.	
159. iv	James Theodoric RHEA born 1860.	
160. v	Sarah 'Sally' Gilliland RHEA born 1862.	

Fourth Generation

47. Jennet 'Jane' Preston RHEA born 1808, Sullivan Co.
TN, married 15-Sep-1831, in Sullivan Co. TN, Elkanah
WOLFORD, born 29-Aug-1806, Sullivan Co. TN, (son of George
WOLFORD and Catherine SMITH) died 18-Dec-1842, Sullivan
Co. TN, buried: Old Wolford Cemetery Blountville TN. Jennet
died 28-May-1884, Texas Co. Missouri.

In 1860 Jennet sold the farm and with four of her children moved
by covered wagon to Texas Co. Missouri. There she bought land
from Samuel Hughes. When she died she left 4 children and 10
grandchildren and 1 great-grand child.

Children:
161. i   Joseph Rhea WOLFORD born 18-Apr-1834.

ii   Catherine 'Kitty' WOLFORD born 13-Mar-1837, Sullivan Co. TN, died 21-Aug-1867, Texas Co. Missouri. Twin of Margaret.

iii   Margaret Jane WOLFORD born 13-Mar-1837, Sullivan Co. TN, died 29-Nov-1915, Marion Ill. Twin of Catherine. Margaret kept a diary of the trip from Sullivan Co. TN to Texas marking their progress as far as Richland Co. Illinois. Died unmarried. Margaret kept a diary of the trip from Sullivan Co. TN to Texas marking their progress as far as Richland Co. Illinois.

She was 23 when the family moved west.

From Margaret Jane's diary:

Sullivan Co. TN. Left the old native home the 12th day of Sept. '60 destine for Mo. To cairnes camp ground and camped the night. 19th thence across the north fork River to old Mr. Cleak's and there eat dinner. Thence through Estilville west of there some miles to an old still house and there camped with solum thoughts of the night before impressed upon our minds. 20th thence to Col. Neal's and eat dinner. Thence to Patinsville. Here struck Towel's Mountain. Across it camped at the foot of it at Stickleyville, a beautiful place, Lea Co. 21 from there we struck Walling's ridge, thence to Jonesville and on to the widow Ewings and there camped in a beautiful grove of oaks. 22nd thence to Mrs. Daughety's and eat dinner in the Towel's Valley thence to Mr. Hoskins. Here encamped for Sabbath and 23rd in the bend of the creek in full view of Cumberlin (sic) Mountain. Thence past Ealy's Store in Knox Co. KY and to Cumberlin Gap. Here eat dinner at Dickenson's Thence to the log mountains. Camped

at them in a store. 25th thence to Cumberlin
River 3 miles from it and eat dinner. Thence
through Mersburg (Now Middlesboro) 6 mile west
there camped in a beautiful water scarce. 26th
Thence through Barbrasville west 8 miles and
eat dinner in desert place well calculated make
people homesick. Thence to Lorrel Co KY to and
old horse mile an there camped. 27th thence 3
miles through London 3 miles west and eat
dinner at a smith shop and store. Thence west.
Heard some rain that night. Nothing hurt.
28th thence 5 miles to big rock castle River in
Rock Castle Co. KY to Mrs. Hackney's and eat
dinner. Thence through Mt. Vernon on mile and a
half est and camped in a swamp where we had to
lay down fence rails to put beds on. Traveled
until 8 o'clock to get any place to get water.
29th thence 11 miles to the crab orchard and
eat dinner. Here we struck the turnpike to
Lincoln Co Ky. Thence through the walnut flat
west some 5 mile and here camped over Sabbath
in one mile of Stanford in a nice green lot. A
wet day the 30th Sabbath. October 1 1860
thence through Stanford 12 miles through
Danville, a beautiful town in Boilan Co. KY
thence 5 miles and eat dinner. Thence into
mercer Co KY 5 miles to Haredsburg. Thence 4
miles and camped upon the narrow bank of the
pike. Buggies running all night thick by the
side of clever folks. 2nd thence Edwards
thence Salvicy. Here the annual fare going on.
Thence 5 miles to Anderson KY Ripleyville. 3
miles to Laranceburg. One mile and eat dinner.
Thence rough and ready thence 7 mile into
Franklin Co. and camped near an old brickyard.
3rd thence through Andersonville. Thence
Shelby Co. Clayvillage. Thence Shelbyville 3
mile and eat dinner at a toll gate. Thence

Simosnville. Thence Boston Jefferson Co and
camped at Mr. Nelson's. 4th Thence Middleton
thence through Louisville across the Ohio into
New Albina (New Albany). Floid Co Indiana
thence Moreesburg and camped. 5th thence
Soleno, thence Greenville. Thence Harrison Co.
to a beautiful swamp grove and eat dinner.
Thence Palming thence Fredricksburg, thence
Blue River Washington Co, 2 mile and camped.
6th thence Hartinsburg, thence Orange Co.
thence Chambersburg thence 2 mile and eat
dinner. Thence 5 miles and camped over
Sabbath. 7th beautiful place. 8th thence Lost
River down it mile and eat dinner. Thence Maron
Co. 8 miles and camped (tonight our dog was
stoled (sic) 9th thence East fork of White River
foryed (Forded?) thence Mt. Pleasant thence
Davis Co. 3 mile and eat dinner near an old
pond. Thence Knox Co Washington. Thence west
fork of White River forged. 8 mile and eat
dinner. Thence Vinvannes and cross the Wabash
River into Ill. and camped near the bank near
the river. 11th thence Lawrence Co. Ill.
thence Laranceville some mile and eat dinner,
thence through Prairiation west some miles and
camped in a prairie and bought firewood
tonight. 12 thence Richland Co. through Olney
west of it and eat dinner. Thence Nobel west 4
miles and camped at old Mr. Barkers.

Signed Margaret J. Wolford.

Lived in the same house as her mother in Texas
Co. until Martha died. Then moved to the home
of her niece Jennie Wolford Hughes, Marion Ill
and died there. She never married.

162. iv   William Owen WOLFORD born 17-Dec-1838.

v   Martha E. WOLFORD born 22-May-1841, Sullivan Co. TN, died 8-Jun-1909, Texas Co. Missouri.

48. Emma RHEA born 26-Feb-1811, Sullivan Co. TN, married Pharoh RILEY, born about 1810. Emma died 11-Jun-1887, Sullivan Co., Tennessee?

Children:

i   Ann Myers RILEY born 1-Jul-1837, Sullivan Co., Tennessee?, married James DAVIS, born about 1830, TN? Ann died 1879, Sullivan Co., Tennessee? Left 5 children when she died.

49. Margaret RHEA born 9-Dec-1818, Sullivan Co. TN, married Joseph HODGE, born about 1820. Margaret died 1-Mar-1895, Sullivan Co. TN.

Children:

i   Robert Bruce HODGE born about 1850, Sullivan Co. TN, died Pulaski TN? Preaching at Brick Church, Pulaski TN - 1895 (W.L. Rhea).
ii   J. Frank HODGE born about 1852, Sullivan Co. TN.
iii   Anderson HODGE born about 1854, Sullivan Co. TN.
iv   Rhea HODGE born about 1856, Sullivan Co. TN.
v   Ellen HODGE born about 1858, Sullivan Co. TN.
vi   Laura HODGE born about 1860, Sullivan Co. TN, married C. W. BELL, born about 1860.

50. Eleanor Fairman 'Ellen' RHEA born 14-Oct-1828, Sullivan Co. TN, married 20-Nov-1851, in Sullivan Co. TN, John MILLARD, born about 1820, Sullivan Co. TN.

Children:

i   Marshall Wallace MILLARD born 20-Jan-1853, Sullivan Co. TN, married 1879, in Prince Edward Co. VA, Ellen C. NORTON, born about 1855, VA?. Had 7 children. Graduated from King College, Bristol TN in 1877, from Union

Theological Seminary 1880. Spent four years in
Texas preaching, 10 years in Tennessee. Lived
in Bethsada, Williamson Co. TN (1895).
(W.L. Rhea-1895).
163. ii   Joseph Rhea MILLARD born 24-Jan-1856.
   iii   Jennet Rhea MILLARD born 27-Jun-1862, Sullivan
Co. TN, married 1880, in Sullivan Co.,
Tennessee?, George L. F. FLEENOR, born about
1860, Sullivan Co. TN.
   iv   Nancy Margaret MILLARD born 26-Jul-1866,
Sullivan Co. TN.
   v   James Abia MILLARD born 5-May-1871, Sullivan
Co. TN.

51. Walter Preston RHEA born 12-Mar-1831, Sullivan Co. TN,
married 1858, Sarah Jane PYLE, born about 1830, Sullivan
Co. TN. Walter died 1897, Washington Co AR?

Lula Burton 1994 had 2 post cards from Joseph Rhea Wolford
calling him Jannet Rhea Wolford's brother. Also had a etter from
WP Rhea to Margaret and Martha Wolford after Joseph Rhea's
death in 1896. He was in Washington Co AR each time. In 1867
removed to Salem Ark. Had 8 children, 6 boys 2 girls. Served the
C.S.A. under Col. Fulkerson as 1st Lt. in Co. F, 63rd Tennessee
Infantry.

Children:
164. i   Laura Ella RHEA born 1856.
   ii   David Charles RHEA born 1858,
married Miss RIPTOE, born about 1858.
165. iii   Joseph Matthew RHEA born 1862.
166. iv   Margaret Lillian RHEA born 1862.
   v   Edmond George RHEA born about 1866. Did not
marry.
   vi   Elizabeth Eleanor RHEA born 1868, married
E. N. KEIGER, born about 1868.
167. vii   Oscar Lee RHEA born 1876.
   viii   Kitty RHEA born about 1877. Died young.

168. ix   Holmes Gans RHEA born 1878.

52. John Preston RHEA Sr. born 20-Jul-1829, Clarke Co. WV,
married 10-Aug-1857, Matilda Ann LONGACRE, born
19-Feb-1834, Sullivan Co. TN, (daughter of Joseph Addison
LONGACRE and Mary EDWARDS) died 5-Mar-1922, Sullivan
Co. TN, buried: Pleasant Grove Cemetery. John died
13-Mar-1896, Sullivan Co. TN buried: Pleasant Grove Cemetery.

A country doctor. Sergeant in Reserve Corps during the War.
Was the First Master of the Masonic Lodge at Zollicoffer (Bluff
City). 1870 census shows his property valued at $2100 - no real
estate.

Children:

   i   J. Edward RHEA born about 1857.
   ii   Mary RHEA born 10-May-1858, Sullivan Co. TN,
      married E. J. BURKEY, born about 1860, Sullivan
      Co., Tennessee? Mary died 1-Mar-1902,
      Sullivan Co. TN, buried: Pleasant Grove Cemetery.
   iii   Kalla Warren RHEA born about 1858.
   iv   Matthew B. RHEA born 20-Jan-1862, Sullivan Co.
      TN, died 17-May-1896, Sullivan Co. TN?, buried:
      Pleasant Grove Cemetery Sullivan Co. TN.
169. v   Robert Orestes RHEA born 3-May-1864.
   vi   Nancy 'Nannie' C. RHEA born 1 Jan 1866,
      Sullivan Co. TN.
   vii   Ned RHEA born about 1867.
   viii   Joseph A. L. RHEA born 1870, Sullivan Co.
      TN.
170. ix   John Preston RHEA Jr. born 6-Feb-1872.
   x   Margaret 'Maggie' RHEA born 1873,
      Sullivan Co. TN, married Mr. DYKES, born about
      1873, died before 1917. Margaret died
      1917, Sullivan Co. TN. Brother J. A. L.
      Rhea was appointed administrator of her estate.
   xi   Josiah E. RHEA born 1 Jan 1877, Sullivan Co.
      TN.

xii   Norah Gammon RHEA born 1879, Sullivan Co. TN. 1900 census shows her living with Brother Robert and 1910 shows her still single (31) living next door from Robert with mother Matilda.

xiii   Matilda I. RHEA born 1 Jan 1879, Sullivan Co. TN.

53. Robert Campbell RHEA born 19-Apr-1837, Sullivan Co. TN, married Margaret Caroline MCQUEEN, born about 1836. Robert died 3-Nov-1911.

Children:

171. i   Samuel Robert RHEA born 22-Mar-1868.

172. ii   Mary Elizabeth RHEA born 21-Nov-1869.

173. iii   Nancy Matilda RHEA born 1871.

    iv   Margaret Belle RHEA born 1873, Sullivan Co. TN. Unmarried.

    v   Francis Preston RHEA born about 1875 Unmarried.

    vi   John Wayne RHEA born about 1877 Died young.

    vii   Charles Caldwell RHEA born about 1879

    viii   Edwin Bruce RHEA born about 1881

174. ix   Eleanor Campbell RHEA born 1885.

    x   Buelah Carolyn RHEA born 1890 Unmarried.

54. Margaret Jane RHEA born 25-Jan-1820, Sullivan Co. TN, married (1) 21-Jul-1848, Nicholas M. 'Col.' LONG, born about 1820, married (2) James Dysart RHEA, (See marriage to number 18). Margaret died 17-May-1880, Sullivan Co. TN, buried: Pleasant Grove Cemetery Sullivan Co. TN.

When Col. Long died Margaret married James D. Rhea. Margaret's sister Elizabeth married James D.'s brother John Rhea.

Children:

175. i   Nicholas M. LONG Jr. born 1849.

55. Elizabeth Looney RHEA (See marriage to number 21.).

56. Sarah Lucinda RHEA born 28-Feb-1828, Sullivan Co. TN, married (1) 28-Aug-1849, Alexander MILLER, born about 1828, TN?, married (2) 28-Aug-1849, S. A. MILLER, born 1-Oct-1823, died 28-Jan-1903. Sarah died 25-Aug-1892.

Children:
- i   Mary Jane MILLER born 6-Mar-1846, died 31-Dec-1927.
- 176. ii   S. A. MILLER Jr. born 24-Jan-1850.

57. John William RHEA born 1828, Sullivan Co. TN, married 12-Apr-1860, Italia G. PORTER, born about 1828, died 1929. John died 1873, Memphis TN. Died of yellow fever.

Children:
- i   Annie RHEA born about 1861.
- ii   William RHEA born about 1863, Memphis TN?
- iii   Pearl RHEA born about 1865 .
- iv   Lillian RHEA born about 1867.

58. Abram Looney RHEA born 25-Feb-1830, Sullivan Co. TN, married 10-Nov-1869, Emma CROSS, born 28-Apr-1846, died 7-Dec-1949. Abram died 9-Sep-1912.

Private in Co B 13th TN in C.S.A. infantry under Col. Vaughn. After fighting at Shiloh for 2 days was made surgeon in which place he served till close of the war.

Children:
- i   Matthew D. RHEA born about 1860, .
- ii   William RHEA born about 1862,.
- 177. iii   Jennie Lou RHEA born 3-Dec-1874.
- 178. iv   Richard Cary RHEA born 1877.
- v   Frank Preston RHEA born 14-Oct-1879.
- vi   Ellen C. 'Nellie' RHEA born 1881.
  married E. L. STEWART, born about 1881.

179. vii   Elizabeth 'Lizzie' RHEA born 1883.
     viii   Ruby F. RHEA born 14-Jan-1889, married Charles DUNCAN, born 9-Nov-1887, died 6-Feb-1955. Ruby died 18-Jan-1914.

59. Walter Preston RHEA born 28-Jul-1841, Sullivan Co. TN, married 29-Jun-1870, Jennie P. EDMONSON, born 1-Oct-1952, TN?, (daughter of William Campbell EDMONSON and Susan E. RHEA) died 1-Jul-1919. Walter died 30-Nov-1880.

Too young to join at the beginning of the war, in 1863 he raised a cavalry company and was mustered into the 14th TN Co A. Later Captain of 4th Tenn. Cavalry.

Children:
180. i   Hugh Preston RHEA born 1871.
    ii   William Edmondson RHEA born 1-Mar-1873, died 1910, Chattanooga TN?
181. iii   Susan Brown 'Susie' RHEA born 1-Feb-1875.
182. iv   Mary Looney 'Mamie' RHEA born 1877.
183. v   Walter Preston RHEA Jr. born 1879.

60. Ellen Preston RHEA born 2-Sep-1844, Sullivan Co. TN, married 1-May-1866, Hudson CARY, born about 1844. Ellen died Memphis TN?

Children:
i   Miles Fairfax CARY born about 1870
    ii   Rhea Preston CARY born 1871 married Charles EWING, born about 1871.
    iii   Eleanor Marion 'Nellie' CARY born 22-Dec-1884, TN, married 14-Jun-1902, Samuel Earnest RAGLAND, born about 1884.
    iv   Hudson Fairfax CARY born about 1886

61. Mary Frances Bell 'Fanny' RHEA born 13-Jun-1848, Sullivan Co. TN, married 20-May-1875, James Taylor RHEA, born 17-Jun-1847, The Elms, Bristol, Sullivan Co (son of

James Dysart RHEA and Elizabeth Juliet CARTER) died
5-Jul-1914. Mary died 12-Apr-1927.

Children:
184. i   Alfred Long RHEA born 5-Dec-1878.
185. ii   Mary Ellen RHEA born 1-Sep-1882.
186. iii James Dysart RHEA born about 1885.
187. iv   Howard Matthew RHEA born 22-Jan-1889.

62. Sarah Jane Gilliland PRESTON (See marriage to number
28.).

63. Alexander R. PRESTON born 8-Dec-1805, Washington Co.
VA, married Sarah SMITH, born 5-Jun-1815, Russell Co. VA,
(daughter of C. J. SMITH) died 26-Jan-1846.

Alexander died 3-Mar-1874, Washington Co. VA. Born at "Locust
Glen" the home of his father, 5 miles west of Abington VA. He
received his education at the Abington Academy and in medicine at
Transylvania College. Practiced in VA until his death. He was
elected to the General Assembly from Washington Co. in 1860 and
was clerk of the Circuit Court in 1870. His family is mentioned in a
letter his uncle Alex. Preston wrote in 1844 (contained in the
vertical file collection of the Washington Co. Virginia Historical
Society).

Children:
i   Henry Smith PRESTON born about 1830, Washington
     Co. VA.
ii   Robert PRESTON born about 1832, Washington Co.
     VA.

64. John Fairman 'Capt.' PRESTON (See marriage to number
40.).

65. Susan Smith PRESTON (See marriage to number 17.).

66. Robert Fairman PRESTON born 5-Dec-1804, Washington Co.

VA, married 5-Dec-1827, in Philadelphia PA, Sarah MARSHALL, born 1801, Philadelphia PA, (daughter of Charles MARSHALL and Mary WALLACE) died 10-Dec-1866, buried at Walnut Grove Cemetery, Washington Co. VA. Robert died 7-Jul-1889, Washington Co. VA.

Robert's father left him the plantation on which Robert lived and slaves namely: Hary, Viney and her family, Caine and Poly and her family. He was an eminent physician in Philadelphia but retired to his ancestral home in Virginia where he lived until his death. He had attended medical school in Philadelphia in 1824. Operated a drug and chemical store there for a time.

Children:

i   Mary Marshal PRESTON born about 1830, Washington Co. VA, married Edmund 'Capt.' WINSTON, born about 1830, VA?, died Washington Co. VA. Mary was born and later lived with her husband Edmund at 'Walnut Grove'.

188. ii   Elizabeth Virginia PRESTON born about 1832.

67. William Alfred PRESTON born 21-May-1808, Washington Co. VA, married (1) 30-Mar-1857, in Botetourt Co. VA, Elizabeth RADFORD, born 26-Jun-1832, Bedford Co. VA, (daughter of William RADFORD and Susanna Smith PRESTON) died 8-Feb-1898, married (2) 15-Sep-1828, Martha E. WYLEY, born about 1808 died Washington Co. VA, buried: Walnut Grove Cemetery. Washington Co. VA. William died 26-May-1862, Botetourt Co. VA.

His father left him land lying in Lee Co known as Wild Cat Valley place, also John's house in Kingsport TN, also a tract of land lying in Wise Co. called the Dysart Tract containing 375 acres. He was commissioned Justice of the County Court 18 July 1836 and qualified 26 Aug. 1836. In 1849 and 1850 he was one of the commissioners to supervise elections.

Children:

i   Alfred G. PRESTON born 24-Jan-1858, Washington Co. VA, married 28-Oct-1885, in Botetourt Co. VA, Alice BROCKENBROUGH, born 14-Nov-1865, Lynchburg, Campbell Co. VA, died 3-Apr-1936, Botetourt Co. VA. Alfred died 22-Jun-1933, Botetourt Co. VA. He was a student at Hampden-Sydney College 1874-76 and at Emory and Henry College 1875-77. He was one of the founders of the Chi-Psi fraternity at Hampden-Sydney. At age of 19 he became the owner of "Greenfield" where he lived the remainder of his life. He was elected Justice of the Peace of Botetourt Co. VA at age 21. Was chairman of county Democratic committee for many years. Commissioner of Revenue for 14 years. 1889-90 represented the county in VA House of Delegates. Had 11 children.

ii   William Moseley PRESTON born 20-May-1850, Washington Co. VA. Died young.

iii   John PRESTON born 23-Jul-1860, Washington Co. VA. Died young.

iv   Robert Moseley PRESTON born 8-Sep-1862, Washington Co. VA. Died young.

68. John PRESTON Jr. born 10-Feb-1811, Washington Co. VA, married 15-Jan-1852, in Lexington KY, Mary Howard WICKLIFFE, born about 1811, KY?, (daughter of Robert WICKLIFFE and Margaret Preston HOWARD) died 17-Nov-1892, Louisville, KY. John died 1-May-1882, KY?

Student at SC College in 1828 and graduated A.B. in 1830. After practicing law for a time in Washington Co. VA, he moved in 1836 to Helena Ark. where he lived for a number of years. In 1837 he was appointed judge of the circuit court and in 1838 was a candidate for the Arkansas Legislature. He again ran in 1840 but was defeated by 2 votes.

Children:

i   Robert PRESTON born 1860, died 1860.

69. Eleanor Fairman PRESTON born 7-Nov-1812, Washington Co.
VA, married 29-Dec-1835, in Washington Co. VA, James White
S. SHEFFEY, born 15-Mar-1813, Wythe Co. VA, (son of Henry L.
SHEFFEY and Margaret WHITE) died 27-Jun-1876, Richmond
VA.

Eleanor died 10-Jan-1887, Marion, Smythe Co. VA.

True noble Christian woman, managing her home and household
affairs well. A woman full of energy, instilling unto her children
habits of industry and morality. Lived to see all her children grow
married and settled in life and all professing Christians.
(W.L.Rhea-1895)

Born at "Walnut Grove" in Washington Co. VA. Her will dated 3
Nov. 1884 was proved 17 Jan. 1887 Smythe Co. VA Will Book 6
pp. 237-38.

Children:
189.i   Margaret SHEFFEY born 4-Oct-1836.
   ii   John Preston SHEFFEY born 12-Dec-1837, Marion,
           Smythe Co. VA, married 19-Jun-1863, in
           Wytheville VA, Josephine SPILLER, born about
           1836, VA? John died 20-Aug-1905, Marion,
           Smythe Co. VA. He attended Emory and Henry College
           and graduated with honors in 1858. Studied law
           at U. of VA. Began practice in Marion with his
           father in 1859. 25 May 1861 he enlisted as 1st
           Lt. Co. A 8th VA Cavalry. C.S.A. and May 14, 1862
           appointed Captain of the company. Captured at
           Moorfield WV and sent to Camp Chase OH until
           exchange at end of the war. House of Delegates
           1893-94. Circuit Court Judge.
   iii   Martha E. SHEFFEY born 15-Mar-1849, Marion,
           Smythe Co. VA, married 19-Oct-1875, in Smythe
           Co. VA, Robert James PRESTON, born 25-Jan-1841,

Washington Co. VA, (son of John Fairman 'Capt.'
PRESTON and Jane RHEA) died 20-Aug-1906,
Lewiston NY. Martha died 4-Nov-1898, Baltimore
Co. MD.

iv   Jane SHEFFEY born 31-Aug-1839, Marion, Smythe
Co. VA, died 11-Nov-1842, Marion, Smythe Co.
VA.

v   Elizabeth Madison SHEFFEY born 5-Jan-1842,
Marion, Smythe Co. VA, married 24-Oct-1872, in
Smythe Co. VA, James Albert Gallatin 'Maj.
PENDLETON, born 20-Feb-1836, Smythe Co. VA,
died 2-Mar-1901, Smythe Co. VA. Elizabeth died
10-May-1875, Marion, Smythe Co. VA.

190. vi   Ellen White SHEFFEY born 25-Aug-1843.

191. vii   Mary W. SHEFFEY born 8-Dec-1844.

viii   Virginia Watson SHEFFEY born 17-Aug-1850,
Marion, Smythe Co. VA, married Henry Bowen
HALLER, born 1-Apr-1849, Smythe Co. VA, died
1-Oct-1915, Richmond VA. Virginia died
31-May-1928, Richmond VA. in 1923 she donated
additional land for the Royal Oak Presbyterian
Church in Marion. She had no children.

70. Francis PRESTON born 26-Mar-1822, Washington Co. VA,
married (1) 6-Apr-1851, in Waverly, Loudon Co. VA, Martha
Virginia MOFFETT, born 1820, Loudon Co VA, died
23-Jun-1859, Washington Co. VA, buried: Walnut Grove
Cemetery. Washington Co. VA, married (2) Martha 'Mattie' Powell
FULTON, born about 1846, Smythe Co. VA, (daughter of Creed
FULTON and Mary TAYLOR) died 4-Jul-1927, Washington Co.
VA, buried: Walnut Grove Cemetery. Washington Co. VA. Francis
died 13-Jan-1892, Washington Co. VA, buried: Walnut Grove
Cemetery, Washington Co. VA.

He was a student at Caldwell Institute, Greensboro NC in 1840 and
at U of VA 1840-41. He was a farmer of Montgomery Switch,
Washington Co. VA. On 7 April 1862 he was mustered into

Confederate Service in the Washington Co. VA militia and served 9 days.

Children:
i   Mary Taylor PRESTON born 13-Nov-1877, Washington Co. VA, died 5-Sep-1894, Washington Co. VA, buried: Walnut Grove Cemetery. Washington Co. VA. A twin.
ii   Charles Fulton PRESTON born 13-Nov-1877, Washington Co. VA, died 3-Dec-1878, Washington Co. VA, buried: Walnut Grove Cemetery. Washington Co. VA. Mary's twin.

71. James Tecumseh 'Col.' PRESTON (See marriage to number 44.).

72. Margaret RHEA born 1823, Sullivan Co. TN, married Ezra Nuckolls SHEFFEY, born 13-Jul-1824, Wythe Co. VA, died 13-Feb-1891, Washington Co. VA, buried: Walnut Grove Cemetery, Washington Co. VA. Margaret died before 1855. First wife of Ezra Sheffey. (Second he married her cousin Elizabeth Preston.).

Children:
i   William SHEFFEY born about 1850.
ii   Elizabeth SHEFFEY born about 1852.
iii   John Preston SHEFFEY born about 1854.

73. Susan E. RHEA born 3-Aug-1828, Sullivan Co. TN, married 3-Aug-1848, in Marion, Smythe Co. VA, William Campbell EDMONSON, born 28-May-1816, Abington, Washington Co. VA, died 15-Jul-1883, Washington Co. VA, buried: Glade Springs Cemetery, Washington Co. VA. Susan died 13-Apr-1860.

Children:
i   John Preston EDMONSON born 1851, married (1) Flora HUMPHIA, born about 1850, Sommerville TN, married (2) Mary GRAHAM, born

about 1850, Memphis TN.
192. ii   Louise Smyth EDMONSON born 1857.
193. iii   Jennie P. EDMONSON born 1-Oct-1952.

74. James David RHEA born 7-Feb-1838, Pulaski, Giles Co. TN, married 1-May-1863, Mary Elizabeth 'Bettie' BUFORD, born about 1840, Giles Co TN, (daughter of Thomas BUFORD and wife of Thomas BUFORD). James died 16-Jan-1882, Pulaski, Giles Co. TN.

Served C.S.A as Capt. in 3rd TN Regiment, Infantry. Served through the war. Was in battles of Fort Donaldson TN, Shiloh, Missionary Ridge, Chicamauga, Resacca GA. Was commanding a Regiment at Bentonville NC when Southern army surrendered and surrendered with his regiment. He was a merchant before the war, and a farmer after. Fought with Gen. Hood throughout TN. Had been captured at Ft. Donaldson but escaped from Federal Camp Chase. Died January 16, 1882 by drowning while attempting to save a negro man. Lived at Buford Station.

Children:

i   James Buford RHEA born 1864 died 1864.
194. ii   Clifford RHEA born 1-Sep-1866.
195. iii   Annie RHEA born 1-Nov-1868.
196. iv   James David RHEA Jr. born 1-Oct-1870.
v   Frank Buford RHEA born 1-Jun-1873
vi   Bessie Buford RHEA born 1875 died 1877
197. vii   Joseph Campbell RHEA born 1-Sep-1877.
198. viii   Louise Jany RHEA born 1880.
ix   Mary Sumpter RHEA born 1881 Died young.

75. Mary Amanda RHEA born 1840, Pulaski, Giles Co. TN, married 27-Aug-1857, James Asher SUMPTER, born about 1840, Pulaski, Giles Co. TN, died 4-Aug-1885, Pulaski, Giles Co. TN. Mary died 1924.

Was only 17 when her mother died. She married in the same year
and took care of her husband, the house on Madison St. left by her
father, and her 2 younger siblings, Ellen Kate (14) and Willie (11).
Had six children of her own. Mary was a Sunday School teacher
for 25 years. Her granddaughter Mary Sumpter Long taught
for 17 years.

Children:

i   Edward Randolph SUMPTER born 13-Oct-1858,
Pulaski, Giles Co. TN, married Minnie WADE,
born about 1872, Pulaski, Giles Co. TN, (daughter
of Thomas Berryman WADE and Mary Ella
REYNOLDS). Edward died 1917.

ii   Catherine SUMPTER born 9-Aug-1860, Pulaski TN?,
died 26-Jan-1863, Pulaski TN?

199. iii   Buelah SUMPTER born 10-Feb-1863.

iv   James A. SUMPTER born 28-Nov-1868, Pulaski,
Giles Co. TN, died 15-Jan-1874, Pulaski, Giles
Co. TN.

200. v   William David SUMPTER born 28-Jun-1872.

vi   Joseph Rhea SUMPTER born 7-Dec-1874, Pulaski,
Giles Co. TN, married (1) Julia FLOURNEY, born
about 1874, died 1900, married (2) May
HAYES, born about 1874. Joseph died
1913. No children.

76. Ellen Catherine 'Kate' RHEA born 17-Dec-1846, Pulaski,
Giles Co. TN, married (1) 1-Feb-1868, Oscar ABERNATHY, born
about 1835, died 13-Jul-1892, (2) 17-Dec-1866, in TN, David O.
REYNOLDS, born about 1846 (son of Giles Alegree REYNOLDS
Sr.) died 1-Feb-1868 .

Children:

201. i   Catherine ABERNATHY born 1-Mar-1872.

ii   Mary ABERNATHY born 1-Sep-1874, married
Bayless FROMAN, born about 1874

iii   Nellie ABERNATHY born 1-Feb-1878, married Harry

Zohn LANDIS Jr., born about 1878.

  iv   Oscar ABERNATHY born 1-Sep-1881, married Annie ADAMS, born about 1881.

77. William Samuel RHEA born 16-Aug-1849, Pulaski, Giles Co. TN, married 1-Sep-1876, Ida Eudora OSBORN, born 20-Aug-1855, Giles Co TN, (daughter of Caleb OSBORN and Elizabeth Valena RASCKIN). William died 15-Sep-1894.

Civil engineer and county surveyor and also a farmer. It is said he should have been a minister of the Gospel for he was too good and noble to have been anything else. Presbyterian elder. He had attended Washington and Lee U. and became a surveyor. Married the daughter of the church deacon.

Children:

202. i   Caleb Osborne RHEA born 9-Jul-1877.
203. ii   Erma Valine RHEA born 1-Jun-1879.
204. iii Edward Sumpter RHEA born 1-May-1881.
205. iv William Samuel RHEA Jr. born 1-Aug-1884.
206. v   David Rankin RHEA born 19-Jul-1886.
    vi   Alwyn Porter RHEA born 20-Oct-1887, Pulaski, Giles Co. TN, died 1888. Died young.
    vii Alice Katherine RHEA born 20-Jun-1892, Pulaski, Giles Co. TN. Died young.

78. Elizabeth 'Bettie' RHEA born 22-Oct-1836, Sullivan Co. TN, married Beverly NORVELL, born about 1836. Elizabeth died Sullivan Co. TN, buried: Blountville Cemetery Sullivan Co. TN.

Children:

  i   Maude NORVELL born about 1852.
  ii   Margaret 'Maggie' Lou NORVELL born about 1852.
  iii Adah NORVELL born about 1854.
  iv Mary NORVELL born about 1856.
  v   Clara NORVELL born about 1858.
  vi Frank NORVELL born about 1860.

vii   Wade NORVELL born about 1862.

79. Margaret RHEA born 1841, The Elms, Bristol, Sullivan Co married Byron Giggs MCDOWELL, born about 1840, NC?, died about 1895, Bristol, Sullivan Co. TN?

Children:
i   James Rhea MCDOWELL born about 1860, Bristol,
        Sullivan Co. TN, died Knoxville TN. Had
        business in Knoxville in 1895 (W.L. Rhea-1895)
        No children.
ii   Elizabeth 'Lizzie' MCDOWELL born 1868,
        Bristol, Sullivan Co. TN, married 1-Oct-1893,
        in Sullivan Co. TN, James B. LYONS, born about
        1868, Bristol, Sullivan Co. TN.
iii   Albert Sidney MCDOWELL born 1870,
        Bristol, Sullivan Co. TN, married Inez CARTER,
        born about 1870. Albert died Knoxville TN?
        James and Bert ran business in Knoxville in
        1895 (W.L.Rhea-1895).
iv   Mary Eva MCDOWELL born 1875, Sullivan Co.
        TN, married William S. STUART, born about 1875,
        Sullivan Co. TN?
v   Margaret Rhea MCDOWELL born 1880,
        Sullivan Co. TN?, married William FERGUSON,
        born about 1880.

80. James Taylor RHEA (See marriage to number 61.).

81. Mary Ellen RHEA born 1849, The Elms, Bristol, Sullivan Co married Edward Anderson MCCLELLAND, born about 1845, (son of David 'Capt.' MCCLELLAND). Mary died 1882.

Children:
i   Samuel David MCCLELLAND born 1870,
        married Mary Effie SUGLE, born about 1870.
ii   James Nicholas MCCLELLAND born 1872,
        married Almira Levenie BENHAM, born about 1872,

81

TN?. James died 1912.

iii   John Looney MCCLELLAND born 1874,
married Myrtle BENNER, born about 1874.

iv   Margaret Elizabeth MCCLELLAND born 1877,
TN?, married William Edward COGSWELL, born about
1877.

v   Abraham Rhea MCCLELLAND born 1879,
married Georgia DESGRANGER, born about 1879.

vi   Edward Anderson MCCLELLAND born 1882,
TN?, married Grace Edric HELMS, born about 1882,

82. Harriet Netherland 'Hattie' RHEA born 10-Aug-1834,
Sullivan Co. TN, married 14-Jun-1855, in TN, John W. SEHORN,
born 1855, died 1-Aug-1884, Texas. Harriet died 1-Jun-1880,
Johnson City, Washington Co

Children:

i   James L. SEHORN born about 1859 married Miss
MCSWAIN, born about 1860. James died
1-Feb-1882.

ii   Charles Lee SEHORN born 1863 married
Rella AMOS, born about 1860.

iii   John SEHORN born about 1904, Sullivan Co. TN,
married Susan Addie SUSONG, born about 1904,
Sullivan Co. TN?.

83. Frances R. 'Fanny' RHEA born 1838, Sullivan Co.
TN, married 28-Oct-1863, by Rev. Joseph M. Huffmeister,
Oscar Marville LEWIS, born about 1838. Frances died
1904.

Children:

i   William Dulaney LEWIS born about 1860.

ii   Mary Cecelia LEWIS born 1866,
married John M. LYON, born about 1865.

iii   Harriet Elizabeth LEWIS born 1867,
married Riley PROFFITT, born about 1867.

iv   Ida Lee LEWIS born about 1870. Did not
marry.

v   Oscar Rhea LEWIS born 1872, married
Margaret W. RAY, born about 1872.

vi   Dora Lynn LEWIS born 1874, married
George W. ANGLON, born about 1874. Dora
died 1902.

vii   George Gertrude LEWIS born 1877,
married Samuel Clayton RIDDLE, born about 1877.

viii Charles Grant LEWIS born about 1879.

84. William Rockhold RHEA Jr. born 20-Oct-1840, Sullivan Co.
TN, married (1) 1-Apr-1869, in Sullivan Co. TN, Susan 'Sue'
NETHERLAND, born 19-Jan-1843, Kingsport, Sullivan Co TN,
(daughter of George Washington NETHERLAND and Nancy
RUTLEDGE) died 19-Jul-1882, Johnson City, Washington Co
married (2) 28-Apr-1891, Margaret 'Maggie' A. CARR, born
1879, Chattanooga TN, died 1933, Knoxville TN? William died
1-Jun-1903, Morristown, Polk Co. TN, buried: Jonesboro,
Washington Co.

Served the C.S.A - Company G 19th TN Infantry under Capt. Abe
L. Gammon. Was in several battles and in one in Resacca GA
5/13/1864 lost a leg. After marriage lived for a while in Johnson
City in business, in Knoxville in 1894. Clerked for brother Aaron,
and in the Pension Office. After the death of his brother,
did not enjoy very good health. Spent time with sister Jenny
in Washington Co. (W.L. Rhea-1895).

Children:

i   Nannie May Netherland RHEA born 19-Apr-1879,
Johnson City, Washington Co. TN married
7-Jan-1902, in TN, Robert Lee GALLAHER, born
25-Aug-1879, Roane Co. TN, died 8-Feb-1945,
Caryville, Campbell Co. TN. Nannie died
26-Mar-1879, Caryville, Campbell Co. TN. Was 3
when her mother died. Nannie died of
pneumonia.

ii   John Fain RHEA born 13-Jan-1893, Washington Co.
TN, died 13-Jan-1893, Washington Co. TN,

buried: Jonesboro, Washington Co.

85. John Adolphus RHEA born 1848, Sullivan Co. TN,
married 21-Dec-1880, in Texas, Lora Isabel ABERNATHY, born
about 1840, Texas?, died Morristown TN. John died
18-May-1913, Morristown, Polk Co. TN.

Belonged to the southern army but was not a regular. With home
Guards of TN and in the fight at Bull's Gap in the Fall of 1864. Put
to flight by Gen. Gillam's forces (Federals); their company much
scattered, many taken prisoner. After the War he came to
Knoxville and engaged in business until 1878, went to TX and
lived several years and married Miss Abernathy. Came back to
Knoxville in 1884 to work with Graves & Co. then moved to
Morristown keeping books at a flour mill.

Children:

207.	i	William Abernathy RHEA born 1881.
	ii	Mary RHEA born about 1885, Texas?
	iii	John RHEA born about 1887, Texas?

86. Charles Wells RHEA born 23-Jun-1853, Sullivan Co. TN,
married Emma Sarah ROBERTSON, born about 1853. Charles
died 6-Dec-1890.

Children:

208.	i	Hattie Mabel RHEA born 1883.

87. James Campbell RHEA born 2-Sep-1855, Sullivan Co. TN,
married Charlotte Jane 'Lottie' ROSS, born about 1855. James died
7-Feb-1900.

Children:

209.	i	George Sehorn RHEA born 1882.
210.	ii	William Rockhold Rhea born 1887.
	iii	Charles Lyon RHEA born 1889, married Willie Kate BLALACK, born about 1889.

88. Mary 'Mollie' Rhea IRVIN born 6-Jan-1846, married

11-Feb-1869, in Fayette Co. TN, William Abram RHEA, born
30-May-1844, Jonesboro, Washington Co (son of John RHEA
and Elizabeth Looney RHEA) died 24-Mar-1921, Memphis, Shelby
Co. TN. Mary died 19-Dec-1896, Sommerville, Fayette Co. TN.
Had 7 children with William A.

Children:
211.	i	Elizabeth 'Lizzie' RHEA born 27-Jan-1870.
	ii	Allie RHEA born 3-Jan-1872 died 22-Sep-1875
212.	iii	Frances 'Fannie' RHEA born 4-Apr-1874.
213.	iv	Harriet 'Hattie' RHEA born 4-Feb-1876.
	v	William RHEA born 22-Apr-1879 died 23-Sep-1881
	vi	John Montgomery RHEA born 22-Apr-1879, Jonesboro, Washington Co died 24-Mar-1906.

89. Sarah 'Sallie' Harriet IRWIN born 26-Jan-1848, Sullivan
Co. TN, married 1868, in Sullivan Co. TN, Samuel Wood
RHEA, born 12-Jun-1841, Sullivan Co. TN, (son of John Nancy
RHEA and Ruth M. ROCKHOLD) died 15-Jun-1927. Sarah died
30-Jun-1901, Sullivan Co., Tennessee?

Children:
214.	i	John Irwin RHEA born 24-May-1869.
215.	ii	Fannie Ruth RHEA born 1871.
216.	iii	Myra Bell RHEA born 1872.
217.	iv	Jenny Dysart RHEA born 1874.
218.	v	Mary Margaret RHEA born 22-Jan-1877.
	vi	Sarah Alice RHEA born 1880, Sullivan Co. TN.
219.	vii	Elizabeth 'Bessie' Breden RHEA born 18-Jan-1883.
220.	viii	Flavia Converse RHEA born 1885.
221.	ix	Samuel Wood RHEA Jr. born 5-May-1889.

90. William Abram RHEA born 30-May-1844, Jonesboro,
Washington Co married (1) 11-Feb-1869, in Fayette Co. TN, Mary
'Mollie' Rhea IRVIN, (See marriage to number 88) married (2)
1901, Louise Smyth EDMONSON, born 1857 VA?, (daughter of

William Campbell EDMONSON and Susan E. RHEA) died 1934.
William died 24-Mar-1921, Memphis, Shelby Co. TN.

Children:
222. vii   Jennie Edmonson RHEA born 6-Mar-1883.

91. Matthew Robert RHEA born 5-Jul-1846, Jonesboro,
Washington Co married 14-Dec-1870, Anna Adelaide 'Addie'
TUCKER, born 22-Jul-1850, died 10-Jun-1938, Florida?,
buried: Sommerville, Fayette Co. TN. Matthew died
21-Aug-1902, Sommerville, Fayette Co. TN, buried:
Sommerville, Fayette Co. TN.

Was in civil war as a young man. Died as a result of a logging
accident on the farm. Lived in Sommerville.

Children:
i   Thomas Tucker RHEA born 8-Oct-1872,
married 1908, Susan Mae THOMPSON, born
about 1872. Thomas died 18-Aug-1944.
ii   John William RHEA born 22-Jul-1874, died
28-Sep-1874.
223. iii   Lucy Mary 'Lula Mae' RHEA born 9-Aug-1876.
224. iv   Edward Francis RHEA born 30-Jan-1878.

92. James Samuel RHEA born 11-Feb-1849, Jonesboro,
Washington Co married 24-Feb-1880, Fannie Bell TROTTER,
born 27-Aug-1860, died 28-Jan-1928. James died 18-Sep-1898.

Children:
i   Benjamin Edward RHEA born 23-Jan-1881,
married Cleo ARNOLD, born about 1880. Benjamin
died 20-Apr-1923.
ii   Matthew RHEA born 20-Jan-1883, died
8-Oct-1883.
225. iii   James Wilson RHEA born 20-Jan-1883.
226. iv   John Edmondson RHEA born 1885.
227. v   Sarah Bell RHEA born 9-Aug-1889.

vi   Hudson Cary RHEA born 15-Feb-1894, died 1895.

vii   Mary Elizabeth RHEA born 1-Sep-1896, married 3-Jan-1929, Raymond Gill MCFADDEN, born 7-Oct-1891, died 23-Apr-1980. Mary died 16-Feb-1984.

viii   Robert Henry RHEA born 1-Sep-1896, died 1955.

93. Sarah Frances 'Fanny' RHEA born 6-Sep-1853, Jonesboro, Washington Co married 1875, Henry Harrison LEWIS, born about 1850. Sarah died 1924.

Children:

i   Bessie May LEWIS born 1876, married Thomas A. JAYROE, born about 1876.

ii   John Hampden LEWIS born 1878, married Lula May MORRIS, born about 1878.

iii   Maggie Lou LEWIS born 1881, married Arthur FLEMING, born about 1881.

iv   James Rhea LEWIS born 1883, married Rosa REVIERE, born about 1883.

v   Wiltshire M. LEWIS born 1885, married Margaret MACLIN, born about 1885.

vi   Gilley M. LEWIS born about 1889.

vii   Matthew H. LEWIS born 1891, married Louise Haynes MOORER, born about 1891.

viii   Gilly C. LEWIS born about 1893.

94. John Rufus Wells RHEA Jr. born 1855, Jonesboro, Washington Co married (1) Rebecca Jane 'Tillie' LOCKETT, born 22-Jul-1859, died 31-Dec-1901, married (2) Margaret Elnor LOCKETT, born 13-Nov-1863, died 19-Jan-1945. John died 1917.

Children:

228. i   Frank Lee RHEA born 1886.

ii   John Lockett RHEA born 1887, died

4-Dec-1887.
iii   Walter Howard RHEA born 18-Jun-1889, died
       29-Feb-1912.
iv   Oscar Preston RHEA born about 1890.
229. v   Elizabeth Susan RHEA born 1894.
vi   Anne Nona RHEA born 1897, married
       Harwell Lee PINKSTON, born about 1897, died
       30-Oct-1976. Anne died 1976.

95. Nancy ANDERSON born 1818, Blountville, Sullivan
Co. TN, married Abram Looney GAMMON, born about 1812,
Sullivan Co. TN, died about 1866. Nancy died 3-Feb-1837,
Sullivan Co. TN.

Died when only son was but two months old after an illness of 9
days. After that little Samuel's aunt 'Bettie' took care of him.

Children:
i   Samuel Rhea GAMMON born 1837,
       Blountville, Sullivan Co. TN, died 20-Aug-1879,
       Rodgersville TN. Capt., Hawkins Co. company.
       Read law with A.M. Looney at Columbia and
       graduated at the law school in Lebanon TN about
       the beginning of the war in 1861. Gave up the
       profession to and went into the service. Made
       Memphis his home and practiced law there. He
       had come to Rodgersville for a short time and
       there he died at the home of Elizabeth Fain
       (first cousin).

96. Joseph Rhea ANDERSON born 25-Oct-1819, Scott Co VA,
married 3-Jun-1845, in Sullivan Co. TN, Malinda Williams
KING, born 27-Jun-1821, Sullivan Co. TN, (daughter of James
KING and wife of Rev. James KING). Joseph died 18-May-1888,
Bristol, Sullivan Co. TN, buried: East Hill Cemetery. Bristol,
Sullivan Co. TN.

His memorial read ... Col. Joseph R. Anderson, who was nominated as the Prohibition candidate for governor by the Prohibition Convention in Johnson City Wed., died at his home in Bristol the following week. Those knowing him personally and having long been familiar with his character as a man of worth and great benevolence took pleasure in giving a sketch of his life. - His school education was quite limited but was a close and persevering student at home and managed in his leisure hours to store in his mind a vast amount of useful knowledge.

Before he was 15 years old, he began his long and prosperous business career as a clerk in the store of his uncle Samuel Rhea in Blountville TN at a salary of $50. and board fee allowance. At the end of 8 years he went into business for himself at Eden's Ridge TN. There he remained until March 1844 when he returned to Blountville TN and formed a partnership with his uncle Samuel Rhea taking charge of and conducting business until September 1853 when the firm was dissolved.

Col. Anderson previous to this had purchased of his father in law Rev. James King, 100 acres of land at "Sapling Grove" (Mr. King's home place) in Sullivan Co., Tennessee now the site of the town of Bristol in TN. and Goodson in Virginia. His land was situated on both sides of the VA and TN state lines, and now includes principal portions of the two towns. He founded the town in 1852 in which year he laid out lots and made a plot of the future city, naming the place Bristol after the great manufacturing city of Bristol, England, in hopes it might some day become a great manufacturing center. He removed his family from Blountville to Bristol in 1853 and resided there up to the time of his death being all the time in business except a short interval during the civil war.

He was actively engaged as a merchant and banker. He organized the National Bank of Bristol, of which he was the president at the time of his death. Throughout his life he conducted his business on the enduring side of honesty and truthfulness. He amassed great property consisting of real estate, and bank stock. He was a man of great staying power and his advice to young men was 'Keep to one business and make a success of it as you can no matter what the business is'. In 1838 he attached himself to the Presbyterian church in which he was an elder for about 30 years and a Sunday School teacher for nearly half a century.

Col. Anderson never knew the taste of brandy or whiskey, never drank a drop of any kind of intoxicants in his life, never tasted wine except at the communion table. He never used tobacco, in any form and as a consequence of his temperance and prudent habits he was never confined to bed by any sickness during his whole life of nearly 70 years. The principal work of his life outside the church has been the advocacy of Temperance which he pursued with great ardor, organizing societies, disseminating information bearing on the cause and emphasizing by precept and example the good results to flow from a life of total abstinence and self denial. The work in this field he loved best, was the organization into "Bands of Hope" of the young boys of this section; a work he engaged in and pursued with great ardor. Many of these boys grew to manhood and remember with gratitude this influence in setting them out in life on a temperance basis. They owe much of their prosperity and success to him. His personal appearance was pleasing and the expression of his countenance is well described as glad and grateful.

He was always a life long democrat but never aspired to office. The only position he ever held were those of mayor and alderman of Bristol. He was a man of high standing as a Knight Templar. Col. Anderson's life had been one of great simplicity and directness of manner and unimpeachable integrity to elevate the morals of the people and raise them to a higher standard.

As a rule he had few intimate friends outside of his family, although all who knew him entertained the highest regard and respect for him. His philanthropic life caused for him the reputation of a good man, and there is no higher or more honorable title than this. Died of Typhoid Fever at his home at 516 Anderson Street in Bristol

TN and rests on East Hill Cemetery. (Reported by W L Rhea -1895 Memorial Report to Holston Presbytery which met in Johnson City TN April 11, 1889 from the scrap book of his brother John L Rhea.)

Children:

i   James King ANDERSON born 14-Apr-1846, Blountville, Sullivan Co. TN, died Bristol, Sullivan Co. TN. Never married. Was always an invalid, not able to accomplish much in life though energetic and willing, yet his physical strength would not permit. A good kind man, member of Presbyterian Church in Bristol. (W.L. Rhea-1895) 1870 census shows him working as a bank clerk - probably for his father.

ii   Sarah Ann ANDERSON born 18-Aug-1847, Blountville, Sullivan Co. TN.

230. iii   John Campbell ANDERSON born 27-Mar-1850.

231. iv   Isaac Samuel ANDERSON born 9-Dec-1854.

232. v   Margaret 'Maggie' Micajah ANDERSON born 4-Nov-1857.

vi   Joseph King ANDERSON born 10-Aug-1861, Bristol, Sullivan Co. TN.

97. Audley ANDERSON born 28-Jan-1821, Scott Co VA, married (1) Cornelia ALEXANDER, born about 1825, (daughter of Dix ALEXANDER and Sarah GRAHAM) died before 1870, Rodgersville TN, married (2) Eliza C. RYLAND, born about 1830, Jonesboro, Washington Co married (3) Jane Rhea VANCE, born about 1830, Sullivan Co. TN. Audley died 18-Dec-1894, Scott Co VA.

He was born at the ancestral 'Blockhouse'. The 'Blockhouse' burned while it was occupied by Audley's family. He continued to live on the farm and built another house on the same spot where the Blockhouse formerly stood.

As a young man he clerked for his brother Joseph Anderson in
Bristol, and then for his uncle Samuel Rhea in Blountville TN.
Became a farmer and he and his family continued to live at the
Blockhouse. Audley ANDERSON, married Cornelia
ALEXANDER, had six children. 1st. Annie. 2nd. Alice and 3rd.
Audley. 4th. John P. 5th. Alexander. and 6th. Campbell. The
mother died, and he afterward married Eliza RYLAND she died
without children. He again married his cousin Jane Rhea VANCE.

He was quiet and retiring in disposition, loved his home and family.
His family were all Presbyterians. Audley ANDERSON the father
died of Paralysis Dec. 2, 1890. Sick but a week. Born 1821. See
No. 134.

His obituary read as follows: "At his residence, the
'Block House', or 'Lucille' in VA, at 4 p.m. Sabbath Dec.
3, 1894. Mr. Audley ANDERSON, departed this life. Blessed
day, to enter upon that rest. The subject of this notice, was born
on the old Anderson homestead, in Scott Co., VA Mar. 12, 1822.
He was the son of Isaac & Margaret Rhea Anderson of Scotch
Irish descent. With this death, only four of the twelve children are
living (1895). Mr. Anderson descended from a Presbyterian
ancestry. As a result of home training, as well as Church training
the old Anderson and Rhea families have given to the Church
ministers and wives of ministers 28 in number.

Before the war Mr. Anderson left his father's house and embarked
in the mercantile in Rodgersville TN. He carried with him his
church letter and at once united with the Old School
Presbyterian Church at that place having been converted in
youth under the ministry of Rev F. A. Ross in Kingsport.

He married the eldest daughter of Col. Dix and Sarah Graham
Alexander. The war ruined his business in Rodgersville and
after the death of his wife there he moved to Bristol and
went into business with his brother Joseph. He was made
deacon in the Bristol Presbyterian Church. He again
married, Eliza Ryland of Jonesboro. She died leaving no

children. In 1873 he married Jane Rhea Vance. He bought
the old homestead and passed the remaining days of his life.
He was made a ruling elder in the church.

Children:

i   Sarah ANDERSON born 1854, Rodgersville
TN.
233. ii   Alexander ANDERSON born 1856.
iii   Isaac Campbell ANDERSON born 1859,
Rodgersville TN.
234. iv   Annie ANDERSON born about 1860.
v   Alice ANDERSON born 1861, Rodgersville
TN, married A. S. NEWMAN, born about 1850.
vi   John P. ANDERSON born 1863, Rodgersville
TN, married Roxie MCCOSLAN, born about 1850.
vii   Audley S. ANDERSON Jr. born 1865,
Rodgersville TN.

98. Jane ANDERSON born 1833, Scott Co VA, married 1866,
William STEWART, born about 1833, VA?

Children:

235. i   Lynn STEWART born about 1870.

99. Samuel Audley RHEA born 23-Jan-1827, Blountville,
Sullivan Co. TN, married (1) 26-Apr-1860, in Jonesboro,
Washington Co Sarah Jane FOSTER, born 23-Jan-1827,
Blountville, Sullivan Co. TN, died Lake Forest, Ill, married
(2) Martha Ann HARRIS, born about 1827. Samuel died
5-Sep-1865, Alisheh Persia, buried: Mt. Seir. Persia.

Grew up and spent boyhood in Blountville with his father and
Aunt. Graduated from E. Tenn. University in Knoxville when
young. In 1846 went to Union Theological. Seminary. April 1860
married. After last visits and farewells, left for Bristol for the train
to Boston. Sailed from there on the 'Smyrniote' July 3, 1860 with
Mrs. Labone and the Cobbs. Reached chosen home on October 25,
1860. Died there in Persia.

Children:

236. i   Anna Dwight RHEA born 24-Aug-1861.

    ii   Foster Audley RHEA born 24-Jan-1863, Oroomiah, Persia. Came to America with his mother in 1869. Lived with his grandmother in Jonesboro, then moved with mother to Lake Forest Ill. His first job was cashier of Barb Wire Co. Then running transfer wagons through the city of Chicago about 30 miles.

    iii   Robert Leighton RHEA born 13-May-1864, Persia,

    died 21-May-1865.

237. iv   Sophia Perkins RHEA born 18-Apr-1866.

100. Fannie 'Fannie' Anderson RHEA born 6-Mar-1834, Blountville, Sullivan Co. TN, married 27-Oct-1858, in Sullivan Co. TN, John H. FAIN, born about 1834, Sullivan Co. TN?, died 5-Jul-1873, Jonesboro, Washington Co. Fannie died 26-Aug-1903, Jonesboro, Washington Co. Died at the home of her son-in-law in Jonesboro.

Children:

    i   Samuel Rhea FAIN born about 1858, Sullivan Co. TN?, died 4-Aug-1859.

238. ii   Martha Ellen FAIN born 19-Oct-1860.

239. iii   John Mitchell FAIN born 8-Nov-1861.

240. iv   James Rhea FAIN born 26-May-1863.

241. v   Mary Lynn FAIN born 11-May-1868.

101. Mary Martha RHEA born 14-Aug-1836, Blountville, Sullivan Co. TN, married 22-Dec-1868, Benjamin Franklin EARNEST, born 1821, died 4-Sep-1887. Mary died 11-Aug-1894. They lived on a farm on the 'Chucky' River where they reared their family. Mary was drowned at Afton in a swollen stream.

Children:

i   Samuel Rhea EARNEST born 1869, Sullivan
Co. TN?, married 1913, Margaret Eleanor
DOGGETT, born 1885, Sullivan Co. TN,
(daughter of James Polk DOGGETT and Ellen
NEWLAND).

242. ii   Nicholas Peter EARNEST born 15-Apr-1871.

iii   Eleanor Lynn EARNEST born about 1873. Never
married.

102. Joseph Brainard RHEA born 8-Apr-1838, Blountville,
Sullivan Co. TN, married 10-Oct-1866, in Marion, Smythe Co. VA,
Ellen White SHEFFEY, born 25-Aug-1843, Marion, Smythe Co.
VA, (daughter of James White S. SHEFFEY and Eleanor Fairman
PRESTON) died 8-Jan-1905, Marion, Smythe Co. VA. Joseph
died 7-Jul-1902, Smythe Co. VA.

Sold goods with brother John till 1872 when he moved with his
family to Marion Virginia. Served C.S.A in Co. A 60th Tenn.
Cavalry Regiment. Captured by the Yankees near Bristol Dec.
1864 and confined to Camp Chase, Ohio until May 1865.

Children:

i   James White Sheffey RHEA born 1869, VA?,
died 1918. Was a prominent educator.
Never married. Taught at the University School
in Memphis.

243. ii   Eleanor Lynn RHEA born 7-Aug-1871.

iii   Virginia Sheffey RHEA born 28-Jul-1880, VA?,
died 9-Nov-1883. Died in infancy.

244. iv   Margaret Preston RHEA born 1886.

103. Robert Morrison RHEA born 14-Oct-1842, Blountville,
Sullivan Co. TN, married 26-Oct-1870, in 2nd Presbyterian
Church, Bella W. COWAN, born about 1842, (daughter of
James COWAN and Lucinda DICKINSON). Robert died
11-Aug-1903.

Served as Orderly Sergeant in Co. F 63rd Tenn. Infantry for C.S.A. Was the highest ranking officer of 75 men in the Regiment at the surrender at Appomatox. Gave the last command to the 63rd. Regiment there - to surrender.

Children:
i   Mamie RHEA born 21-Aug-1871, died
       13-Feb-1872. Died young.
ii   Charles McLung RHEA born 14-Feb-1873, died
       10-Sep-1901.
iii   Lucy Foster RHEA born about 1874.
245. iv   Martha Lynn RHEA born about 1876.

104. Margaret Elizabeth RHEA born 24-Jul-1849, Blountville, Sullivan Co. TN, married 26-Oct-1870, in 2nd Presbyterian. Church, Knoxville, Perez D. COWAN, born about 1845, (son of James COWAN and Lucinda DICKINSON). Margaret and brother Robert married two Cowan siblings in a double wedding ceremony in Knoxville.

Children:
i   Margaret Mclung COWAN born 1876,
       died 8-Nov-1879, Wellesley, MA, buried:
       Knoxville, Knox Co. TN. Died at a young age of
       diptheria. In the year 1891 her remains were
       brought to Knoxville TN.
ii   Eleanor Rhea COWAN born 1878,
       married Allen DAVIES, born about 1877.
246. iii   James Dickerson COWAN born 17-Aug-1887.

105. Audley 'Doc' ANDERSON born 1826, Sullivan Co. TN, married (1) Margaret RHEA, born 1833, Sullivan Co. TN, (daughter of Robert 'Major' RHEA and Jane SCOTT) died Blountville, Sullivan Co. TN, married (2) Jane Preston RHEA, born 1829, Sullivan Co. TN, (daughter of Robert Preston RHEA and Sarah Jane Gilliland PRESTON) died after 1896. Audley died 1-Feb-1864, Sullivan Co. TN, buried: Blountville Cemetery Sullivan Co. TN.

Lived on Island Road 1.7 miles east of Junction of Island Road and
State Road 126. Audley was born in the Old Home 2 1/2 miles
from Blountville, Sullivan Co. TN. Grew up to manhood and when
the call came in 1847 to get volunteers for the Mexican War he was
among the number of Shavers Co. D, Col. George R. McClellen's
Regiment., Twiggs Brigade. This war did not last long. They were
discharged in the summer of 1848.

He returned to his father's house, and worked on the farm
until he married his cousin Margaret. After their marriage
they lived on the Island Road in the home of his father-in-law
who was dead. He was a farmer and there took charge of the
farm. He raised stock, being fond of it, and was a good judge of
stock.

Stayed on the farm until volunteers were called for from
East TN to go out to the Civil War. He volunteered in Capt.
McClellan's and served in the 4th Tennessee Cavalry. Was
wounded several times at Chattanooga. Was in several battles,
proved himself a brave, courageous soldier, never faltering. He fell
in the battle of Chicamagua, was carried from the field of battle. His
body was found to be pierced with seven bullets. He was brought
home to die. He suffered greatly from these wounds for some time
and finally died in Feb. 1864. He was buried in Blountville. A
salute of five or six guns was fired over his grave as the body was
lowered to its last resting place in honor of a brave and gallant
soldier.

Children:

i   Robert ANDERSON born about 1852, Blountville,
     Sullivan Co. TN, married Winnie BOY, born about
     1855, Sullivan Co. TN. Lived on the south bank
     of Beaver Creek a short distance below Thomas
     Mill.

ii   Joseph ANDERSON born about 1856, Blountville,
     Sullivan Co. TN, married Jane SMITH, born about
     1825, Sullivan Co. TN.

106. Fannie ANDERSON born about 1830, Sullivan Co. TN, married William EVANS, born 1819, Sullivan Co., Tennessee?, died 1894, Sullivan Co. TN. Fannie died Blountville, Sullivan Co. TN.

Children:
i   Ellen EVANS born about 1850, Blountville, Sullivan Co. TN.

107. Margaret E. ANDERSON born 1832, Sullivan Co. TN, married Jacob SMITH, born about 1830. Margaret died 21-Jul-1856, Sullivan Co. TN.

Her children were born and raised in the home 2 1/2 miles from Blountville on the road to Bluff City. In the west end of the house Frances Rhea, wife of Joseph made her home for many years and died there.

Children:
i   Alexander SMITH born about 1850, Sullivan Co. TN.
ii   Margaret 'Maggie' SMITH born about 1852, Sullivan Co. TN.

108. Samuel R. ANDERSON born 1834, Sullivan Co. TN, married Malissa BLEVINS, born about 1835, Sullivan Co. TN, died Gainsville TX? Samuel died Gainsville TX.

Attended school at the Rhea School house. He became a salesman for Samuel Rhea. Married and lived in Bristol when he went into the army in May 1861. Sent to Winchester VA and was in the first battle of Manassas July 12, 1861. Their regiment served in VA as the 3rd TN Infantry; later transferred to its successor regiment the 63rd Infantry. Was at the battle of Misty Ridge, Fort Saunder TN and became connected to Gen. Lee's army until the end of the war. After the war he moved to TX. Engaged in the lumber business.

Children:

i   Samuel ANDERSON born about 1868, Gainsville TX?
ii   Sallie ANDERSON born about 1870, Gainsville TX?
iii   Robert ANDERSON born about 1872, Gainsville TX?

109. Ann Peoples BACHMAN born 9-Mar-1827, Sullivan Co. TN, married (1) Joshua PHIPPS, born about 1835, Rotherwood TN, married (2) Rev. C. WATERBURY, born about 1825, New York, married (3) Mr. LYONS, born about 1825, Hawkins Co., Tennessee. Ann died 17-Nov-1901, Sullivan Co. TN, buried: Rotherwood TN.

When her first husband died she was left with and infant son, a large farm and many slaves to care for on the north fork, north bank of the Holston. The farm known as 'Rotherwood Farm' at one time belonged to F A Ross. She died at the home of her brother Rev. Jonathan W. BACHMAN.

Children:
247. i   Joshua 'Mack' Mckinney PHIPPS born 24-Feb-1853.

110. Jonathan Waverly BACHMAN DD, LDD. born 9-Oct-1837, Sullivan Co. TN, married 20-Oct-1863, Evalina DULANEY, born about 1836, died 9-Jun-1898. Jonathan died 1924.

Johnnie, when in his teens, came to Blountville to enter school in the year 1855 in Jefferson Academy. He made his home in the house of Samuel Rhea. After being in school for 2 years, he entered Emory and Henry College in the fall of '57 or '58. After he made a profession of Religion, he sobered down and began thinking of his life's work.

Having the ministry view and thought much about it, finally decided it to be his work. After finishing E & H he went to Union seminary NY to study theology and prepare for the ministry. He was there when Fort Sumpter fell, in 1861 and war was declared. He being in sympathy with the South, felt it his duty to return to his native land and do what he could for his country. When volunteers were called for he was among the number. He held ranks of 1st Lt., and

Captain and his men were in several battles. He stood by his men in all danger and they by him. They were in the siege of Vicksburg. Here he lost many of his men. He came near losing his life while swimming in Big Black River when Vicksburg was surrendered. 7/4/1863 went out as paroled prisoner. After this, Johnnie gave up his office as Capt. and determined to enlist men under the Banner of King Emanuel and was made Chaplain of the 60th Regiment to which he belonged. He had great influence over his men by example. Served under General Cooke in VA. Was later Chaplain in 16th Tennessee Cavalry.

Before the war was closed and while Johnnie was still a paroled prisoner, he and Eva Dulaney concluded to wed and were married at "Medical Grove", her father's house, in the fall of 1863. He and his wife taught school term in the "Female Institute" in Blountville. Pretty close to the end of the war they moved to Rodgersville, he took charge of the Female Institute and the Presbyterian Church there. In 1873 was called to Chattanooga to take charge of the 1st Presbyterian church there and was there in 1895. He was lovingly known as the Bishop of Chattanooga. (W.L. Rhea -1895)

Children:
- i   Frances 'Fannie' Taylor BACHMAN born 1857, Sullivan Co. TN, died 15-Oct-1887, Chattanooga TN.
- 248. ii   Mary BACHMAN born 1857.
- 249. iii   Annie Rhea BACHMAN born about 1864.
- iv   William BACHMAN born about 1866, Sullivan Co. TN.
- v   Margaret 'Maggie' Walker BACHMAN born about 1868, Sullivan Co. TN, married 20-Jun-1899, in Chattanooga TN, James L. CALDWELL, born about 1868, Sullivan Co. TN? Margaret died 11-Dec-1899.
- 250. vi   Nathan Lynn BACHMAN born about 1870.
- vii   Evalina Dulaney BACHMAN born about 1872, Sullivan Co., Tennessee?, married Charles Edward BUCK, born about 1870.

viii   Alfred BACHMAN born about 1875, Sullivan Co.
        TN?. Twin of Robert.
ix   Robert Rhea BACHMAN born about 1875, Sullivan
        Co. TN? Twin of Alfred.
x   Carrie VanDyke BACHMAN born about 1877,
        Sullivan Co. TN.

111. John Lynn BACHMAN born 23-Jan-1841, Sullivan Co. TN,
married Fannie ROGAN, born about 1845, Rodgersville TN, died
Kingsport, Sullivan Co. TN, buried: Kingsport Presbyterian
Cemetery. John died 1918, Sweetwater TN?

J. Lynn BACHMAN was a soldier in the Confederate Army,
belonged to 37th Virginia Infantry Regiment, under Col. Samuel
Fulkerson. This Regiment belonged to Stonewall Jackson's
Division. He was in all the engagements in which Jackson fought
and on many battlefields. He made a brave, fearless soldier.

After the battles were fought and the war ended in 1865 he,
with his brother Robert L. and his cousin C. E. Lucky, went to
Hamilton College, New York. After they were located thoroughly
in the College, some of the students thought they would try hazing
with them. As it happened, they were prepared for them; brought
out their pistols from their hiding places, laid them on the table.
Soon voices and footsteps were heard, then a loud blow upon the
door. The boys were interrupted from their studies and rose,
taking their pistols in hand. The intruders approached, and were
told " We are ready for you". Lynn being spokesman said "If
you don't leave here at once, we will let you have the contents of
the weapons we have been using for the past four years". They
retreated, feeling frightened and defeated. A few days after this,
these three new students were called up before the faculty on
charges of having firearms in their room, they were asked the
question and Lynn replied in the affirmative. He told the faculty
they had come to study and go on with their education. He said
one thing certain, they were not going to be run over. We would
certainly use them, if ever attacked in that way again, but if let
alone would fasten them by in their trunks. The faculty assured

them of no more annoyances of this kind. After this they made many warm friends.

Lynn graduated in 1872. Soon after graduation he came home and married Miss Fanny Rogan. He taught male school in the Academy, made a splendid teacher and good disciplinarian. He had not taught there long when a call came from Sweetwater to come and take charge of the male academy there. He moved there and built a fine flourishing school. He raised the school up step by step until his course of study ranked with any college. It came to be known by the name of Sweetwater College. He educated not only mentally but physically.

Later, the impression came to him "Woe is me, if I preach not the Gospel" and could not get rid of it until he gave himself up in theology, took the regular course, was examined by Presbytery and ordained a regular minister. Had charge of two churches in addition to his school work. (W.L.Rhea 1895)

Children:

i	James Rogan BACHMAN born 1874,	
	married Elizabeth EUBANKS, born about 1874.	
ii	Fanny Rhea BACHMAN born about 1875.	
251.iii	Annie Lynn BACHMAN born 1876.	
iv	Byers BACHMAN born about 1879.	
252.v	Bessie BACHMAN born 1881.	
vi	John W. BACHMAN born about 1883	
253.vii	Lilly Bell BACHMAN born 1886.	

112. Martha Fleming LYNN born 23-Feb-1827, Kingsport, Sullivan Co. TN, married 17-Jan-1856, John L. LAMPSON, born about 1825, Vermont, died 20-Apr-1877, Jonesboro, Washington Co. TN. Martha died 12-Apr-1882, Jonesboro, Washington Co, TN.

Bright and sprightly. She was a sufferer the last 2 or 3 years of her life. Fought cancer though she told no one, bore it quietly. Not until her last few days was an eating cancer on her right breast discovered.

Children:

i   John Lynn LAMPSON born 7-Feb-1853, Jonesboro, Washington Co. died 29-Nov-1900, Nashville, Davidson Co. TN. Boyhood spent in Jonesboro. A fine memory. His father furnished him a 'box of tools' at which he spent much of his leisure time. He loved to read. His father had a full and well selected library. In 1882 he graduated Hamilton College. Here he proved a fine linguist. Soon after college he received an appointment as Prof. of ancient languages in the State Normal at Nashville. There they prepared students as teachers. There in 1895 having been abroad in Germany twice. Never married. Died Thanksgiving night. (W.L. Rhea-1895).

ii   William Royal LAMPSON born 3-Mar-1860, Greeneville TN, married 4-Dec-1894, in Kansas City MO, Amanda Hopkins PARKER, born about 1860, Kansas City MO. Had advantages like his brother John, but perhaps not so quick. Loved to read, was splendid on dates, social, kind and conscientious. Clerked in fathers store and sold goods at Fall Branch. 1885 entered Hamilton College, graduating 1888. Was offered position in furniture manufacturing with Abonsathy & Son in Kansas City MO (He and his son Will were at Hamilton together). There he found a sweet little woman who became his wife. He brought her to East TN on their bridal tour.

iii   Lucy LAMPSON born 27-Oct-1862, Jonesboro, Washington Co. died 3-Mar-1869.

254. iv   Elenor 'Nellie' W. LAMPSON born 18-Jun-1864.

v   Nannie Rhea LAMPSON born 19-Mar-1867, Sullivan Co. TN, died 1-Aug-1873.

113. James LYNN born 9-Sep-1837, Kingsport, Sullivan Co. TN, married 5-Sep-1861, Sarah 'Sallie' ROGAN, born about 1840, Knoxville, Knox Co. TN, died 19-Mar-1920, Kingsport TN?. James died 23-Dec-1915.

Lived in Kingsport until his children were all but grown. During the war he could not take up arms against his country but preferred going through the lines, finally taking his family to Knoxville where he and W. L. Rhea opened up goods while waiting for the war to close. In the Spring of 1865 they brought their goods to Jonesboro. There they did business through the summer of 1865 when Jimmy thought best to return to Kingsport at the old stand with his father.

After his father had been dead some years he with his family moved to Knoxville. While there he was Superintendent of Schools and a Church Elder. In Sunday School he had the Infant Class of little boys, about 35 in number. Made a good and interesting teacher for them. Also Superintendent of the Mission School on Crojies(?) St. in the afternoon. (W.L. Rhea-1895)

Children:
i   Mary LYNN born 26-May-1870, Kingsport TN?
ii   Nancy Rhea 'Nannie' LYNN born 28-May-1870, Kingsport TN?
iii Perry Rogan LYNN born 1-Aug-1874, Kingsport TN?, died 15-Feb-1909. Served in Spanish American War as Sergeant of Company K, 3rd TN Volunteer Inf.

114. Samuel Alexander LYNN born 9-Jul-1839, Kingsport, Sullivan Co. TN, married 14-Dec-1865, Ofelia ROGAN, born 1849, Kingsport, Sullivan Co. TN, (daughter of Daniel ROGAN Jr. and Ann GAMBLE) died 18-Aug-1921. Samuel died 20-May-1884, Bristol, Sullivan Co. TN, buried: Kingsport, Sullivan Co. TN.

Samuel when a young man, went to school in Blountville, lived
with his uncle Samuel Rhea while there. About the middle of the
war, he concluded to go into the confederate Army though his
father preferred him not going. He went and was connected to the
commissary department. In that department it was not necessary
for him to go into battle, but he would not excuse himself from the
scene of battle. When he saw his comrades making ready and
marching into battle, he was up and ready. Went into the bloody
battle of Chicamagua. Unfortunately for him, in the early
part of the battle, he was disabled by a wound in the arm.

After the war he engaged in the mercantile business for
several years in Kingsport and Jonesboro finally moved to
Bristol with his family where he died in 1884; was taken
back to Kingsport for burial. Left widow and for children.
(W.L. Rhea-1895).

Children:

i   John Rogan LYNN born 21-Apr-1867, Kingsport,
Sullivan Co. TN, died 4-Jul-1883, Newport TN.
Drowned.

ii   William LYNN born 10-Apr-1869, Kingsport,
Sullivan Co. TN. Attended school in Bristol.
Father died when he was 16 and he went to work
to support family. Clerked in a store, now has
business of his own (1896).

iii   Annie Bell LYNN born 25-Jan-1871, Kingsport,
Sullivan Co. TN. Finished education in
Rodgersville and taught school in Public
Schools in Bristol TN.

iv   James LYNN born 23-Jan-1871, Kingsport,
Sullivan Co. TN. Went to work after his father
died. Went to Bristol Bank beginning on the
lowest round and went up year after year.
Assistant cashier in 1896.

v   Ada LYNN born 23-Sep-1873, Kingsport, Sullivan
Co. TN, died 1-Sep-1963.

115. Joseph RHEA III. born 12-Dec-1830, Virginia, married
Eliza Ann EARHART, born 25-Dec-1835, Virginia, (daughter of
George EARHART and Nancy TAYLOR) died 26-May-1919,
Sullivan Co. TN, buried: Blountville Cemetery Sullivan Co. TN.
Joseph died 13-Aug-1909, Sullivan Co. TN, buried: Blountville
Cemetery Sullivan Co. TN.

Born at the home of his father and grandfather, on Back Creek,
Sullivan Co., Joseph Rhea's education was limited, only attending
school in the log school house then near home. Not withstanding
these limited opportunities he has a strong good mind and well
stored with knowledge on all subjects, showed great love for books
and reading, read a great deal, retained it, could talk about it
fluently, dare say, we'd have made a brilliant man.

After he was grown had to take the management of the farm &
colored people on it, had to do this until the commencement of the
war, at which time he enlisted as a soldier in the Confederate Army,
went into it, was in several battles, but escaped all danger, all his
comrades say he was a splendid soldier, always at his post, ready
for duty, brave and fearless. Served in Company G. 19th Tennessee
Infantry.

After the War, returned to his fathers house, found things in a
dilapidated condition. The slaves all going, all had left the old
plantation but one family. The farm much wore out by long and
continued cultivation. But amid these discouraging features,
Joseph faltered not, he buckled on the harness, put his shoulders to
the that which with renewed strength and energy, determined ,by
divine help to bring things up again succeed, which he did.

All the children were born and raised on the Old Homestead of his
father R.P. Rhea. These children had been a great comfort and very
helpful to their parents. They were bright, quick, had habits of
neatness, good quiet dispositions, industry. The boys were musical
in their tastes, played the violin banjo and were mechanical, made
what they wanted. One of them told WL Rhea he intended to make
a "bicycle" before another year. Joe was very entertaining, loved

106

to talk and laugh, tell anecdotes very fond of his kindred. - W.L. Rhea (1895) 1870 census shows he and Eliza Ann living on the farm with his father Robert Rhea.

Joseph died at the age of 79 in the 4th District in Sullivan Co., Tennessee. The county records note senility as the cause.

Joseph died intestate and Robert E. was appointed administrator on 3/23/1910. Final distribution in 1911 widow E A Rhea $268, Mrs. Margaret Bullard $15, Ladie S. Rhea $15, Mrs. C Bullard $15.

Children:

255. i   Robert Earhart RHEA born 1-Jul-1870.

    ii   Alexander Preston RHEA born 1871, Sullivan Co. TN.

    iii   Joseph Anderson RHEA born 1873, Sullivan Co. TN.

    iv   Lady Sarah RHEA born 1874, Sullivan Co. TN. 1910 she was living in household of brother Robert with their mother as well.

256. v   Margaret David RHEA born 1876.

    vi   John RHEA born 1878, Sullivan Co. TN.

116. Frances "Frank" Elizabeth RHEA (See marriage to number 46.).

117. Margaret 'Peggy' Preston RHEA born 22-Jun-1835, Sullivan Co. TN, married 21-May-1862, in Sullivan Co. TN, John Taylor EARHART, born 31-Mar-1826, Blacksburg, Montgomery Co. VA, (son of George EARHART and Nancy TAYLOR) died 25-Mar-1896, Sullivan Co. TN, buried: Blountville Cemetery Sullivan Co. TN. Margaret died 25-Feb-1913, Sullivan Co. TN, buried: Blountville Cemetery Sullivan Co. TN.

Children:

    i   Charles Balfour EARHART I. born about 1860, Blountville, Sullivan Co. TN, died about 1864,

Blountville, Sullivan Co. TN.

ii   Robert R. EARHART born 1-May-1863, Sullivan Co.
        TN, married Maime Bell POWELL, born 1-Jul-1871,
        Sullivan Co. TN, (daughter of William POWELL
        and wife of Wm. POWELL) died 1920, Sullivan
        Co. TN, buried: Blountville Cemetery Sullivan
        Co. TN. Robert died 31-Jul-1915, Sullivan Co.
        TN, buried: Blountville Cemetery Sullivan Co.
        TN. No children living with them in 1900
        census. Obituary: 8/1/1915 Bristol: R R
        Earhart, 47 yr., pioneer businessman committed
        suicide at 529 Ala. by cutting his throat.
        Survived by brothers Joseph, Chas. John H.;
        sisters Mrs. Ed Carter, Mrs. Maggie Fain,
        Arizona.

257. iii   Charles Balfer EARHART II. born 23-Nov-1864.
258. iv   Sarah Ella EARHART born 1866.
259. v   Joseph Preston EARHART born 1-Dec-1869.
260. vi   Margaret Jane 'Maggie' EARHART born 1872.
261. vii   John Henry EARHART born 1-Mar-1874.

118. Sarah Jane LUCKY born 6-Feb-1834, Jonesboro, Washington
Co. married William Kirkpatrick MOORE, born about 1830,
Dalton GA, died 15-Nov-1895, Dalton GA, buried: Dalton GA.
Sarah died 17-May-1884, Dalton GA, buried: Dalton GA.

Educated in Jonesboro. Was an excellent student. Made a
profession of religion joining the church in 1849.

Children:
i   William Kirkpatrick MOORE Jr. born 1876,
        TN?

119. Ellen LUCKY born 18-Feb-1836, Jonesboro, Washington Co,
TN, married Jesse Hamilton GANT, born about 1835, Cleveland
TN. Ellen died Cleveland TN.

Raised and educated in Jonesboro. There when growing up was full of fun, a perfect tease. The boys were all afraid of her, but she sobered down, connected herself with the church early. After she married Mr. Gant, she took charge of his house and her step children (three boys). None of the children married.

Children:
i   Rhea GANT born about 1865, Cleveland TN.
262. ii   Sarah Lucky GANT born 1868.
iii   John Watson GANT born about 1871, Cleveland TN.
iv   Jessie Rhea GANT born about 1873, Cleveland TN.
263. v   Agnes Moore GANT born 1875.
264. vi   Luella Erwin GANT born 1875.
vii   Cornelius Lucky GANT born 1877, Cleveland
          TN, married Willa CLEVELAND, born about 1877.

120. John Rhea GAINES born 1827 married (1) Sarah RICE, born about 1830, married (2) Elizabeth BLAIR, born about 1830, married (3) Harriet Amanda CRAIG, born about 1830, TN?. John died 1911, Sweetwater TN.

Married Three times. Miss Rice, Miss Blair and Miss Craig. (W.L.Rhea-1895) Lived until the last three years of his life on his farm in Monroe Co. TN. He was distinguished for sterling honor and loyalty.

Children:
265. i   Annie Rhea GAINES born 1880.
266. ii   Susie Rice GAINES born 1883.
267. iii   Frances Louisa GAINES born 1888.

121. Robert J. GAINES born 1829 married Sarah 'Sallie' COOK, born about 1830 died Sweetwater TN? Robert died 1890, Sweetwater TN? Had 3 children in 1895. (W.L.Rhea-1895).

Children:
i   George W. GAINES born about 1860.
ii   John A. GAINES born about 1862.

iii   Allie GAINES born about 1864.

122. William Alexander RHEA born 23-Feb-1833, Loudon Co.
TN, married 16-Jul-1868, Ella FOOTE, born about 1833.
William died 26-Mar-1906. Captain in Co. D 6th Texas
Cavalry.

Children:
268. i   Jean Foote RHEA born 1872.
269. ii   William Alexander RHEA Jr. born 1874.
     iii   Lawrence Joseph RHEA born 1878. At
           the commencement of WWI Lawrence offered his
           services to the British Government. He was
           attached to the McGill Medical Staff as Lt. and
           sailed for France with the 2nd Canadian
           Contingent in 1915. Pending completion of the
           Canadian General Hospital Number 3 in Boulogne,
           he was stationed in London as purchasing agent
           for equipment. On its completion he assumed
           charge for of its pathological work. He was
           promoted to Major in 1916. His health failing
           from overwork, he was sent to England for
           complete rest but did not recuperate
           sufficiently to resume active duty and was sent
           to Canada in 1918. Major Rhea received many
           honors while in England and France. He was a
           member of the committee appointed by the
           British Government to inspect all Military
           Hospitals in France. He was selected to
           personally conduct the Queen of England on her
           inspection of hospitals.
     iv   Mary Elliot RHEA born 1880, married
           Lewis LINDEMUTH, born about 1880, TX?
270. v   John Edwin RHEA born 1883.

123. John W. RHEA born 1835, Sullivan Co. TN, married
24-Nov-1857, Veronica Slaughter MAYES, born about 1835, TX?
John died 1-Oct-1862, Corinth MS, buried: Near McKinley,

Texas. Served C.S.A. in Company D 6th TX Cavalry with 2
brothers, as a orderly Sergeant. Taken prisoner to a Federal
Hospital where he died of his wounds.

Children:
i   Joseph E. RHEA born 1858, TX?, married
Florence BASS, born about 1858, TX? Joseph died
1917.
271.ii   John W. RHEA Jr. born 1864.

124. James Calvin RHEA born 11-Apr-1837, Sullivan Co. TN,
married 14-Sep-1875, Mary A. GOSSETT, born 4-Mar-1854, TX?,
died 7-Jul-1920. James died 19-Mar-1937, Collin Co. Texas.
Served in Company D 6th TX Cavalry.

Children:
i   Lula May RHEA born 1876, TX?, died
1877.
272.ii   William Joseph RHEA born 10-Nov-1877.
iii   Hattie Emma RHEA born 2-Oct-1879, TX?, died
26-Sep-1883.
iv   John Alexander RHEA born 25-Jul-1881, TX?, died
21-Sep-1883.
273.v   Robert Lee RHEA born 10-Oct-1882.
vi   James Long RHEA born 13-Sep-1884, TX?, died
4-Apr-1907.

125. Mary Elizabeth RHEA born 2-May-1840, Sullivan Co. TN,
married 3-Sep-1873, William MILLER, born about 1840, Lee Co
VA, died Collin Co. Texas. Mary died 29-Dec-1913.

Children:
274.i   Rhea MILLER born 1874.
ii   Mary Erma MILLER born about 1876, Collin Co.
Texas?
iii   Joseph W. MILLER born about 1878, Collin Co.
iv   Stella Ella MILLER born about 1880, Collin Co.
Texas?

275. v   Lula Alexander MILLER born 1880.

126. Elizabeth M. ANDERSON born 1840, Sullivan Co. TN, married James HUFF, born about 1840. Elizabeth died 1881.

Children:

    i   Elizabeth K. HUFF born 1868, Sullivan Co. TN?, married Dr. JUMP, born about 1870.
276. ii   William E. HUFF born 1872.
    iii   James Alexander HUFF born 1875, Sullivan Co. TN?, married Mabel WILSON, born about 1875, Sullivan Co. TN?.
    iv   Mamie HUFF born 1877, Sullivan Co. TN?, married James C. MILLER, born about 1877.

127. Alexander Dodson RHEA born 16-Jun-1841, Louden TN, married Mary Frances HATCHETT, born 14-Jul-1843, died 13-Mar-1908. Alexander died 16-Nov-1917, Whitney TX, buried: Trasebeck TX.

Inherited the farm from his father. Was said to be the best farmer in Louden. Clever and hard working be became entangled in some Commission merchants and lost what he had inherited from his father, gave all up, even to his watch. This was great trouble to him.

Major 11th TN Cavalry, Union Army and his comrades say he was a brave soldier and always on his post. After the War he moved to TX but then moved back to TN with is family. In bad health in 1895. (WL Rhea 1895) Died of pneumonia.

Children:

    i   John RHEA born about 1861 TX?
    ii   Sam RHEA born about 1863, Louden TN.
277. iii   Adeline RHEA born 1866.
278. iv   Robert RHEA born 24-Jul-1868.
279. v   Joseph RHEA born 1871.
    vi   Elizabeth RHEA born about 1873 TX?

112

   vii   Louise RHEA born 1877 TX?, married
          Lillan Lester DAVIS, born about 1877 TX?
   viii   Francis Rodgers RHEA born 1879 TX?,
          married Annie WRIGHT, born about 1879 TX?
          Served as Corporal in Company L, 2nd TX
          Volunteer Inf. during Spanish American War.
          While encamped in Florida he suffered an attack
          of Typhoid fever.
280. ix   Cleaves RHEA born 1882.
281. x   Alexander Dodson RHEA Jr. born 1885.

128. Sarah Elizabeth 'Bettie' RHEA born 1843, married
10-May-1863, Samuel Andrew RODGERS, born 5-Mar-1830,
Loudon TN, died Loudon TN. Sarah died 1893, Louden TN.

Children:
   i   Mary Bell RODGERS born about 1846, married Jasper
        Porter STEPHENSON, born about 1840.
   ii   Annie Eliza RODGERS born about 1847, married
        Ulrich ITA III., born about 1870.
   iii   California 'Callie' Elizabeth RODGERS born
        1869, married Joseph Marion GREER,
        born about 1869, Blount Co. TN.
   iv   Alice RODGERS born about 1870, Louden TN.
   v   Samuel Rhea RODGERS born about 1874, Louden TN.
        During the Spanish American War served as 2nd
        Lt. in Company B, 4th TN Inf. Served in Cuba.
   vi   May Belle RODGERS born about 1876, Louden TN.
282. vii   Arthur RODGERS born 1879.
283. viii Jean Rhea RODGERS born 1885.

129. John R. CRAWFORD born 1831, Sullivan Co. TN,
married Mary 'Mollie' BACHMAN, born about 1831, Sullivan Co.
TN?, died aft 1895, Blountville, Sullivan Co. John died 1891,
Blountville, Sullivan Co. TN, buried: Blountville Cemetery Sullivan
Co. TN.

Lived on a farm a half mile from his father and mother; carried on farming in connection with his profession. Practiced medicine many years very successfully He was not very long lived, his work was soon done and he called 'up higher' leaving his little family, sad and lonely.

Children:
i   Fanny Powell CRAWFORD born about 1860, Blountville, Sullivan Co. TN.
ii   Bessie CRAWFORD born about 1870, Blountville, Sullivan Co. TN.

130. Seraphine 'Sarah' CRAWFORD born 1833, Sullivan Co. TN, married William CRAWFORD, born about 1830, Blountville, Sullivan Co. TN. Seraphine died before 1895.

Children:
i   William CRAWFORD born about 1874, Blountville, Sullivan Co. TN. Graduated at East TN Univ. Knoxville TN in 1894.

131. Samuel H. CRAWFORD born 1835, Sullivan Co. TN, married Fanny O. BACHMAN, born about 1840, Sullivan Co. TN. Served in C.S.A. Co. F, 63rd Tennessee Infantry.

Children:
i   Cornelia Daisy CRAWFORD born about 1860.
ii   Joseph R. CRAWFORD born about 1863, Sullivan Co., Tennessee?
284. iii   John Kerr CRAWFORD Jr. born 10-Dec-1877.

132. Elizabeth Crawford 'Lizzie' RHEA born 23-May-1839, Blountville, Sullivan Co. TN, married 19-Mar-1857, in Sullivan Co. TN, Samuel Patton SPURGEN, born 1837, Sullivan Co. TN, (son of Joseph and Ann SPURGEN). Elizabeth died 6-Oct-1860, Sullivan Co. TN, buried: Blountville Cemetery Sullivan Co. TN.

Children:
285.i   Alice Ann SPURGEN born 11-Mar-1858.
  ii   Olivia J. SPURGEN born about 1862, Sullivan Co.
TN.

133. Samuel Wood RHEA (See marriage to number 89.).

134. John M. RHEA born 9-May-1848, Blountville, Sullivan Co.
TN, married Elizabeth SMITH, born 1849, Sullivan Co.,
Tennessee?. John died Blountville, Sullivan Co. TN, buried:
Muddy Creek Cemetery. 1880 Sullivan Co. TN census shows John
as head of household. Mother Ruth and siblings Mollie, Joe, and
Margaret were also in household in 1880.

Children:
  i   Carrie May RHEA born 1879, Blountville,
       Sullivan Co. TN. 1880 census shows her as
       'Casy M.'
  ii   Cora Lee RHEA born about 1882, Blountville,
       Sullivan Co. TN, died by 1932.
  iii   John William RHEA born about 1884, Sullivan Co.,
       Tennessee?, died by 1932.
  iv   William Plummer RHEA born about 1888, Sullivan
       Co., Tennessee?
  v   Joseph Chalmers RHEA born about 1890, Sullivan
       Co., Tennessee?
  vi   Maggie Pearl RHEA born about 1892, Sullivan Co.,
       Tennessee?.
  vii   John Lynn RHEA born about 1894, Sullivan Co.,
       Tennessee?

135. Harriet Nancy RHEA born 15-Jul-1851, Blountville,
Sullivan Co. TN, married 23-Oct-1873, Lemuel Milburn
CARTRIGHT, born 11-Aug-1849, Sullivan Co. TN, (son of
William CARTRIGHT Jr. and Elizabeth SHIPLEY) died
14-Jun-1942, Rockwood, Roane Co. TN. Harriet died
31-Jul-1939, Spring City, Rhea Co. TN.

In 1939 the 'Holston Annual' quotes Rev. Lavens M. Thomas II:

The brevity of the paper can but faintly reveal the wealth of Christian patience, fortitude and love which God for over three score years and ten, released through the life of his now sainted daughter. Harriet Nancy Rhea, daughter of John N. Rhea and Ruth M. Rhea of Sullivan Co. TN, was born June 15, 1851 and died at her home in Spring City TN on July 31, 1939 aged 78 years. On October 23, 1873 she was married to Rev. Lemuel M. Cartright of Sullivan Co. TN. To this happy union were born 8 children, four sons and four daughters, five of whom survive her, namely Rev. N. Rhea Cartright, Mrs. Lena M. Blair, Miss Frances M. Cartright, Robert C. Cartright, and Miss Elizabeth Cartright.

Mrs. Cartright having been born of Christian parents and reared in a Christian home, professed religion in her early girlhood and united with the Southern Presbyterian Church. Some few years after her marriage, when her husband entered the itinerant ministry, she joined the M. E. Church South. From that time forward, covering a period of 45 years, she share the joys and sorrows of itinerant life with remarkable fortitude. In all these eventful years of stress and strain, her faith in prayer and in God's willingness to answer was simply sublime.

During the past few years of her life she was a great sufferer and but for her remarkable power of endurance and resolute will power she would never reach this age. Just a few days before her death she said to her husband "I am doing my best to get well but if I do not it will be all right." All that medical skill and careful nursing could do were done to save her life, but to no avail. Her life's work was done. The weary, tired heart ceased to function, her immortal spirit stepped out of the frail suffering body and was borne by angels across the mystic river into that celestial country where the inhabitants know no sickness.

Her funeral was held at the M.E. Church, South, in Spring City TN. Dr. J. A. Burrow, Rev. P. H. Horner being in charge.

Children:

i   Nancy Rhea CARTRIGHT born about 1874.

286. ii   Nathan Rhea CARTRIGHT born 28-Aug-1875.

iii   Lena May CARTRIGHT born 15-May-1877, Sullivan
Co. TN, married 3-Aug-1911, in Russell Co. VA,
William Munsey BLAIR, born about 1900. Lena died
13-Jun-1969, Spring City, Rhea Co. TN. Had no
children.

iv   Joseph W. CARTRIGHT born 27-Jul-1879, Sullivan
Co. TN, died 17-Sep-1906, Sullivan Co. TN.
Died after being kicked by a horse. Unmarried,
had no children.

v   Frances 'Fanny' Grant CARTRIGHT born
25-Aug-1882, Sullivan Co. TN, died 10-Aug-1923,
Spring City, Rhea Co. TN. Never married.

287. vi   Robert Carlock CARTRIGHT born 11-Oct-1884.

vii   Elizabeth 'Lizzie' R. CARTRIGHT born
8-May-1888, died 29-Apr-1973, Knoxville,
Knox Co. TN, buried: Spring City, Rhea Co. TN.
Never married.

viii   Bertha Weaver CARTRIGHT born 8-Sep-1889
died 1890.

ix   Arthur Shield CARTRIGHT born 2-Aug-1893

136. Mary A. 'Mollie' RHEA born 1854, Blountville, Sullivan Co.
TN, married 15-Mar-1882, W. R. SMITH, born about 1860. Mary
died 19-Oct-1891, Blountville, Sullivan Co.

Children:

i   Hattie May SMITH born about 1880, died
1891.

ii   Lydia Anderson SMITH born about 1880.

137. Joseph S. RHEA born 25-Nov-1861, Blountville, Sullivan
Co. TN, married 22-Sep-1886, in TN?, Adeline 'Addie' SMITH,
born about 1865. Joseph died 21-Nov-1906, Sullivan Co. TN?
Died at 11:05 am of pneumonia.

Children:
i   Elizabeth RHEA born about 1885.
ii   John Walker RHEA born about 1887.
iii   Asa RHEA born about 1892, Sullivan Co.,
       Tennessee?, married Joseph Erskin RHEA, born
       about 1892.
iv   Mary RHEA born about 1894, Sullivan Co.,
       Tennessee?

138. Margaret R. 'Maggie' RHEA born 15-May-1865,
Blountville, Sullivan Co. TN, married William Rodgers HULL,
born 28-Feb-1845, Sullivan Co. TN, died 16-Apr-1921, Sullivan
Co. TN, buried: Muddy Creek Cemetery. Margaret died
13-Dec-1905, Sullivan Co. TN, buried: Muddy Creek Cemetery.
Died at 4:00 of pneumonia.

Children:
i   John Houston HULL born 24-Jun-1888, Sullivan
           Co. TN, died 7-Sep-1968, CA. No children.
288. ii   Minnie Lucinda HULL born 3-Jun-1891.
iii   Elbert Miller HULL born 14-Apr-1896. Co. TN, died
           21-Sep-1950, Sullivan Co. TN. Had no children.

139. Rhoda RHEA born 1833, Blountville, Sullivan Co. TN,
married John 'Capt.' PIERCE, born about 1830. Rhoda died
1-Sep-1849, GA?

Children:
i   Nola PIERCE born about 1855.
ii   John PIERCE born about 1858.
iii   Ethel PIERCE born about 1870.
iv   Rhea PIERCE born about 1872.
v   Henry PIERCE born about 1872.
vi   Rhoda PIERCE born about 1874.

140. Archibald W. 'Archie' RHEA born 1838, Blountville, Sullivan Co. TN, married 1861, Mary E. SMITH, born about 1845, Newport TN.

When small he was taken by his parents to Watauga Bend in Washington Co. TN. He attended the academy at Jonesboro and also attended Washington College. He studied medicine with Dr. Carson. Received Medical education at University of VA. Began to practice shortly thereafter at Newport TN. Surgeon for the 62nd TN C.S.A. during he war. Married Mary and had two children.

Children:
i   Archibald W. 'Archie' RHEA Jr. born about 1870.
ii   Lucia M. RHEA born about 1875 married
       Charles MIMS, born about 1870. Lived in
       Newport TN.

141. Samuel RHEA born 1850, Blountville, Sullivan Co. TN, married Ella D. CARTER, born about 1850, Sullivan Co. TN? Samuel died Bristol, Sullivan Co. TN.

Children:
i   Joseph Carter RHEA born about 1880.
ii   James Wendell RHEA born about 1882.
iii   Janie RHEA born about 1884.

142. James Brainard PRESTON born 3-Dec-1845, Washington Co. VA, married 20-Oct-1920, Hattie B. TINSLEY, born 18-Feb-1861, Richmond VA, died 1-Jul-1898. James died 21-Oct-1922.

Children:
289. i   Seaton Tinsley PRESTON born 29-Mar-1892.

143. Cynthia Lodoville SNAPP born 1844, Green Co. TN, married Wendall Daniels SNAPP, born about 1844, Washington Co. TN. Cynthia died 1917.

Children:

290. i   Abraham Lawrence SNAPP born 1870.
291. ii   John Pemberton SNAPP born 1872.
     iii   Hawkins Wendell SNAPP born 1874
          married Laura BAYLE, born about 1874.
292. iv   Rhea McIlwaine SNAPP born 1880.

144. Anna Cornelia RHEA born about 1850 married Thomas Humes WILLIAMS Jr., born about 1850.

Children:
   i   Copeland Rhea WILLIAMS born about 1880.
   ii   Thomas H. WILLIAMS III. born about 1882.

145. Wright Smith RHEA born 1848 married Jennie RICE, born about 1850. Wright died 1917.

Children:
   i   Walter Preston RHEA born about 1880.
   ii   Houston RHEA born about 1882.
   iii   Grover C. RHEA born about 1882.
   iv   Wright Smith RHEA Jr. born about 1884.
   v   Alexander RHEA born about 1888.

146. James RHEA III. born 1850, Sullivan Co. TN, married Eugenia COCHRAN, born about 1855. James died Dennison TX?

Children:
   i   Willa RHEA born 1890, Dennison Texas.
   ii   Elizabeth RHEA born 1899, Dennison TX?

147. Bryant Whitefield RHEA born 1854, Sullivan Co. TN, married Sadie ROSENBERRY, born about 1855.

Children:
   i   Raymond RHEA born about 1880.
   ii   Rubie RHEA born about 1882.
   iii   Wilber RHEA born about 1884.
   iv   Losley RHEA born about 1886.

148. Florence RHEA born 1859, Sullivan Co. TN, married John C. LOCKE, born about 1855. Florence died 1893.

Children:
i   Charles L. LOCKE born about 1885.
ii   David Rhea LOCKE born about 1887.

149. David M. RHEA born about 1862, Sullivan Co. TN, married (1) Janice HARRIS, born about 1865, married (2) Margaret HASTON, born about 1862, TX?

Graduated at Lebanon Law School TN, with marked distinctions, was Assistant Prosecuting Attorney for Commonwealth of TX for three years and was practicing in Oklahoma Chancery court in 1895. (W.L. RHEA, Genealogy of Rhea Family 1895) Divorced Janice Harris - no children by her.

Children:
i   Flora RHEA born about 1890, TX?

150. Thomas B. RHEA born 1873, Sullivan Co. TN, married May LEGG, born about 1873.

Children:
i   Robert L. RHEA born about 1900, Sullivan Co. TN?

151. John PRESTON born 21-Jul-1851, Washington Co. VA, married 16-Apr-1876, Annie Lewis WHITE, born 12-Apr-1861, Seguin, Guadalupe Co., TX (daughter of John Preston WHITE and Annie Stuart LEWIS) died 27-Nov-1946. John died 27-Jun-1938, Austin TX.

Married a cousin. He was a student at University of VA 1871-72 and received M.D. He also graduated from Belleveue Hospital. Medical College in New York City 1873 and began practice in Washington Co. VA. In 1878 he moved to TX and located in Seguin. In 1887 he was appointed 1st Assistant Physician at TX

State Lunatic Asylum at Austin. Superintendant of NorthTX Hospital for the insane in 1890 and then Superintendant of the TX State Epileptic Colony at Abilene. 1906 President and Superintendent of TX State Lunatic Asylum till 1925.

Children:

293. i   Walter White PRESTON born 1880.

294. ii   John Lewis PRESTON born 1883.

    iii   James Rhea PRESTON born 1885, Feoral, Texas?

    iv   Frances 'Fanny' Rhea PRESTON born 1890, Feoral, Texas?

    v   Robert White PRESTON born 1892, Feoral, Texas?. Served in Quartermasters Department, Camp McArthur Texas during WWI.

    vi   Annie Lewis PRESTON born 1898, TX?

    vii   Margaret Lynn PRESTON born 1904, TX?

152. James Copeland RHEA born 1862, Sullivan Co. TN, married Anna Louisa OWENS, born about 1860. James died 1889, Beancoy, Ill, buried: Rock Hill S.C. Was a stock dealer in Columbia S.C. He was killed in a railroad wreck at Beancoy, Ill. Was buried in Rock Hill SC far away from his kindred and people. His widow erected a monument to his memory. His death was deeply deplored by all who knew him (WL Rhea 1895).

Children:

    i   James Copeland RHEA Jr. born about 1890.

153. Samuel Williams RHEA born 1864, Sullivan Co. TN, married Dora WELSH, born about 1864.

Children:

    i   Frances RHEA born about 1890, Sullivan Co. TN?

154. Thomas Humes RHEA born 1866, Sullivan Co. TN, married Mrs. LATHAM, born about 1866, Sullivan Co. TN?

Children:
i   Thomas Humes RHEA Jr. born about 1890.

155. Mary Lucy RHEA born 1868, married Jacob W. DENNY, born about 1868, Sullivan Co. TN.

Children:
i   Lucy DENNY born about 1890, Sullivan Co. TN, married Charles WORLEY, born about 1890, Sullivan Co. TN?
ii   Maxie Owens DENNY born about 1892, Sullivan Co. TN, married Wilbur HANNER, born about 1892, Sullivan Co. TN?
iii   Mary DENNY born about 1894, Sullivan Co., Tennessee?, married Scott PATTON, born about 1894, Sullivan Co. TN?

156. Kate RHEA born 1873, Sullivan Co., Tennessee?, married John H. ANDERSON, born about 1874, Sullivan Co. TN, died 2-Jun-1940. They lived on the William Anderson farm.

Children:
i   George Rhea ANDERSON born about 1900.
ii   Lucy ANDERSON born about 1902.

157. Elizabeth 'Bettie' Dysart RHEA born 1856, Blountville, Sullivan Co. TN, married Alexander ANDERSON, born 1856, Rodgersville TN, (son of Audley ANDERSON and Cornelia ALEXANDER).

Children:
295.i   Audley Rhea ANDERSON born 1881.

158. Robert Preston RHEA born 6-Mar-1859, Blountville, Sullivan Co. TN, married Nannie Belle GILLISPIE, born 22-Jan-1851, Texas, died 17-Apr-1932, Texas. Robert died 1930, Wichita Falls, Forney, TEXAS.

Moved to Forney TX. Married Bell in TX. He had gone there, started in business and identified himself with all her public interests of church and state. Was made an elder in the church.

Children:
296. i   Joseph Earhart RHEA born 3-Aug-1882.
297. ii   Frank Bland RHEA born 1884.
    iii   Lillian Buris RHEA born 1889, Forney TX.
    iv   Robert Preston RHEA Jr. born 1894, Forney Texas.

159. James Theodoric RHEA born 1860, Blountville, Sullivan Co. TN, married Caroline Lee 'Carrie' RIGGS, born about 1860, TX? James died Forney Texas.

Bookkeeper for his brother Robert in Forney TX. Had the management of two stores and did the buying for both. 1880 Sullivan Co. TN census shows him in TN living alone at age 20.

Reported in the Bristol Herald Courier July 9, 1909:
Mrs. Bettie Rhea Anderson of this city is in receipt of a letter from Forney Texas telling of a thrilling automobile accident in which James T Rhea formerly of this county was seriously injured.

Mr. Rhea and a partner were returning from a trip to a nearby point when the large automobile in which they were riding ran over a bridge and all were hurled into a deep ravine below. Mr. Rhea suffered two broken ribs and was internally injured...It is thought all will recover.

Children:
    i   Clarence Ward RHEA born 1890, TX?
    ii   William Edwin RHEA born 1894, TX.
    iii   James Theodoric RHEA Jr. born 1902, TX.

160. Sarah 'Sally' Gilleland RHEA born 1862, Sullivan Co. TN, married 1888, in TX?, Frank Milton ADAMS, born about 1862, Texas?, died Forney Texas. Sarah died Forney Texas.

Children:
i   Frank Milton ADAMS Jr. born 1888, Forney Texas, married Jessie Lee FRENCH, born about 1888, TX?
ii   Leta Rhea ADAMS born about 1892, TX.
iii   Yancey Dailey ADAMS born about 1894, TX.

Fifth Generation

161. Joseph Rhea WOLFORD born 18-Apr-1834, Sullivan Co. TN, married 30-May-1861, in Salem, Fulton Co. AR, Sarah Ann Carrigan WALKER, born 20-Jun-1844, Hawkins Co. TN, (daughter of Joshua WALKER and Louise HUGHES) died 14-Nov-1922, Purdin, Linn Co. MO, buried: Purdin Cemetery. Purdin, Linn Co. Missouri. Joseph died 31-Aug-1895, Texas Co. MO, buried: Big Creek Cemetery. Texas Co. MO. Died 3 weeks after he was stricken with a stoke.

Children:
i   Louise Jennet WOLFORD born 9-Aug-1862, Texas Co. Missouri, died 18-Aug-1863, Texas Co. Missouri.
ii   William Henry WOLFORD born 30-Apr-1864, Texas Co. Missouri, died 9-Jul-1890, Texas Co. Missouri. Died of typhoid fever.
298. iii   Margaret Alice WOLFORD born 30-Apr-1867.
iv   Elkanah Walker WOLFORD born 1-Dec-1869, Texas Co. Missouri, died 18-Jan-1870, Texas Co. Missouri.
299. v   Rodney Ross WOLFORD born 18-May-1879.
vi   Grace WOLFORD born 18-Jan-1879, Texas Co. Missouri, died 18-Jan-1879, Texas Co. Missouri. Stillborn.
300. vii   Lettie Escott WOLFORD born 28-Feb-1883.
301. viii   Howard Frank WOLFORD born 24-Feb-1886.

162. William Owen WOLFORD born 17-Dec-1838, Sullivan Co.
TN, married (1) 9-Jan-1862, in Sullivan Co. TN, Martha Eleanor
DECK, born 28-May-1837, Sullivan Co. TN, died 17-Apr-1871,
Texas Co. Missouri, buried: Old Wolford Cemetery. Texas Co.
Missouri, married (2) Alice Odell WALKER, born 9-Jul-1849,
Independence Co. ARK, (daughter of Joshua WALKER and Louise
HUGHES) died 1912, Springfield, Greene Co. Missouri,
buried: Maple Grove Cemetery. Springfield MO. William died
27-Jun-1917, Springfield MO, buried: Maple Grove Cemetery.
Springfield MO.

Served in Co. F 63rd Reg. TN Infantry. Captured at Shiloh.

Children:

302. i   Jennet 'Jennie' Elizabeth WOLFORD born 1-Oct-1865.
ii   Joseph Walter WOLFORD born 28-Mar-1866, Texas
      Co. Missouri.
iii   Ida Lee WOLFORD born 10-Jul-1873, Springfield,
      Greene Co. MO, died 1955, Springfield,
      Greene Co. MO. Never married.
iv   Thomas White WOLFORD born 22-Sep-1875, Texas
      Co. Missouri, married (1) 22-Sep-1901, Bird
      WATERMAN, born about 1875, Mo?, died about 1914,
      married (2) 19-Feb-1914, Ertie MCFALL, born
      4-Jul-1892, Mo? Thomas died 1960,
      Springfield, Greene Co. MO. No children by
      either marriage. Worked installing cooling
      systems in US and Canada. Fell in 1932 and was
      permanently disabled. Retired and lived as a
      semi-invalid for over 30 years.
v   Charles Ross WOLFORD born 26-Jan-1878, Texas
      Co. Missouri, died 1921, St. Joseph MO.
      Never married. Served in WWI. While serving
      in France doing construction he fell and
      crushed his skull. He was discharged from the
      army on full disability with a silver plate in
      his head. He lived at home a few years before
      he became violent and had to be placed in the

State Hospital for the Insane, St. Joseph MO.
He died there.

vi   Lula Preston WOLFORD born 22-Nov-1881,
Missouri, died 1966, Springfield, Greene
Co. MO. Never married.

163. Joseph Rhea MILLARD born 24-Jan-1856, Sullivan Co. TN,
married 1889, Anna Lee ELLIOTT, born about 1860, Chester
Co. SC.

Graduated King College 1885 and from Theological Seminary,
Columbia SC 1888. Minister and pastor of Richburg Church,
Richburg SC.

Children:
i   J. R. M. MILLARD born 1890, SC?, died
1-Dec-1894.

164. Laura Ella RHEA born 1856, married R. A. ROBBINS, born
about 1856.

Children:
i   Maude ROBBINS born about 1888.
ii   Ethel ROBBINS born about 1890.
iii   Lillian ROBBINS born about 1892.
iv   Bernice Preston ROBBINS born about 1894.
v   Sarah ROBBINS born about 1896.
vi   Neil ROBBINS born about 1898.
vii   Pauline ROBBINS born about 1898.
viii   Elizabeth ROBBINS born about 1900.
ix   Alfred Gerald ROBBINS born about 1902.

165. Joseph Matthew RHEA born 1862, Sullivan Co. TN, married
Alice POWELL, born about 1862.

Children:
i   Preston RHEA born about 1890.
ii   David RHEA born about 1892.

iii   Samuel RHEA born about 1894.

iv   Virginia RHEA born about 1896.

166. Margaret Lillian RHEA born 1862, married A. W. ELLIS, born about 1862.

Children:

i   Eula Maude Rhea ELLIS born about 1890.

ii   Margaret Lee Rhea ELLIS born about 1892.

167. Oscar Lee RHEA born 1876, married Jane RAND, born about 1878.

Children:

i   Orion RHEA born about 1900.

ii   Lucille RHEA born about 1902.

iii   Walter Preston RHEA born about 1904.

168. Holmes Gans RHEA born 1878, married Ethel WATERS, born about 1878.

Children:

i   Lelia RHEA born about 1905.

ii   Hugh RHEA born about 1907.

iii   Edmund RHEA born about 1909.

169. Robert Orestes RHEA born 3-May-1864, Sullivan Co. TN, married 1889, Barsheba M. GAMMON, born 7-Oct-1867, Sullivan Co. TN, died 14-Nov-1945, Sullivan Co. TN?, buried: Weaver Cemetery., Weaver Pike, Sullivan Co. TN. Robert died 28-Dec-1938, Sullivan Co. TN?, buried: Weaver Cemetery, Weaver Pike, Sullivan Co. TN.

1900 census shows Robert's household included 4 children and his mother, sisters Maggie and Nora and bother John. 1910 census shows mother Matilda and Nora enumerated next door.

Children:

i   Margaret Gammon RHEA born about 1890, Sullivan Co. TN, died Sullivan Co. TN?, buried: Weaver

Cemetery, Weaver Pike, Sullivan Co. TN. No dates on
her tombstone.
ii   Bertha RHEA born 1-Mar-1891, Sullivan Co. TN.
iii   Clara B. RHEA born 1-Jul-1892, Sullivan Co. TN.
iv   Belmont R. RHEA born 1-Dec-1897, Sullivan Co.
TN.
v   Carl O. RHEA born 1-Oct-1900, Sullivan Co. TN.
vi   Laura N. RHEA born 1902, Sullivan Co. TN.

170. John Preston RHEA Jr. born 6-Feb-1872, Sullivan Co. TN,
married 1902, Ada Texanna CARMACK, born 10-Jul-1878,
Paperville TN, (daughter of John 'Honest' CARMACK and Mary C.
R. HAGY) died 4-Jan-1924. John died 27-Jul-1915, Sullivan
Co. TN, buried: Weaver Cemetery, Weaver Pike, Sullivan Co. TN.

Graduated from University of Chattanooga Medical School in
1902. Master of the Masonic Lodge at Zollicoffer and a renowned
checkers player. One death records show cause as Brights Disease
and another record shows fall from second story window.

Children:
i   Matthew Wendell RHEA born 1904, Sullivan
Co. TN, buried: Weaver Cemetery, Weaver Pike,
Sullivan Co. TN.
ii   Mary Beuloxia RHEA born 1907, Sullivan
Co. TN.
303. iii   Eva Preston RHEA born 25-Feb-1910.

171. Samuel Robert RHEA born 22-Mar-1868, married Nellie
HENDRICKSON, born about 1868. Samuel died 28-Sep-1930.

Children:
i   Caroline RHEA born about 1900, Sullivan Co. TN?
ii   Robert Randolph RHEA born about 1902, Sullivan
Co. TN?
iii   Margaret RHEA born about 1904, Sullivan Co. TN?

172. Mary Elizabeth RHEA born 21-Nov-1869, Sullivan Co. TN?,

married Joseph Shoun DONNELLY, born 30-Dec-1869, Sullivan Co. TN?, died 12-Mar-1915. Mary died 16-May-1924.

Children:
i   Irene DONNELLY born about 1900, Sullivan Co. TN?
ii   Harrison Rhea DONNELLY born about 1902, Sullivan Co. TN?
iii   Margaret Edith DONNELLY born about 1904, Sullivan Co. TN?

173. Nancy Matilda RHEA born 1871, Sullivan Co. TN, married Charles Meigs DULANEY, born about 1871, Sullivan Co. TN.

Children:
i   Charles Meigs DULANEY Jr. born about 1895, Sullivan Co. TN.
ii   Robert Nathan DULANEY born about 1897, Sullivan Co. TN?
iii   William Davis DULANEY born about 1897, Sullivan Co. TN?
iv   Mary Elizabeth DULANEY born about 1899, Sullivan Co. TN?
v   John Jay DULANEY born about 1901.
vi   Laura DULANEY born about 1903, Sullivan Co. TN?.
vii   James Rhea DULANEY born about 1905, Sullivan Co. TN?

174. Eleanor Campbell RHEA born 1885 married William C. WRIGHT, born about 1885, Mountain City.

Children:

i   Charles Mcqueen WRIGHT born about 1910.

175. Nicholas M. LONG Jr. born 1849 married Shirley WILSON, born about 1849. Nicholas died Memphis TN?

Children:

Descendants of Rev. Joseph Rhea

i   Richard LONG born about 1880.
ii   Margaret Rhea LONG born about 1882.
iii   Shirley Wilson LONG born about 1884.
iv   Walter Preston LONG born 1889.
v   Phelps W. LONG born 1891.
vi   Frances M. LONG born about 1893.
vii Emma Law LONG born about 1895.

176. S. A. MILLER Jr. born 24-Jan-1850, married Annie, born 1848, died 1920. S. A. died 14-Sep-1896.

Children:
i   Allie Frank MILLER born 17-Aug-1890, died 23-Jun-1891.

177. Jennie Lou RHEA born 3-Dec-1874, married George T. WEBB, born about 1874. Jennie died 21-Dec-1917.

Children:
i   Abram Rhea WEBB born about 1900.
ii   Virginia WEBB born about 1902.

178. Richard Cary RHEA born 1877, married Mattie Lou ANDERSON, born 1879, died 1933. Richard died 1933.

Children:
i   Louise RHEA born 1907, married Joseph T. ALFORD, born 1906, died 1982. Louise died 1982.
ii   Richard Cary RHEA Jr. born about 1912.

179. Elizabeth 'Lizzie' RHEA born 1883, married G. L. RHODES, born about 1883.

Children:
i   Albert H. RHODES born about 1905.

180. Hugh Preston RHEA born 1871, married Louise BROWN, born about 1871. Hugh died 1901, Oakland FLA.

Children:
i Hugh Preston RHEA Jr. born about 1895.

181. Susan Brown 'Susie' RHEA born 1-Feb-1875, married Thomas BUFORD, born 1-Jul-1871, died 1-Oct-1949. Susan died 1-Mar-1950, Pulaski TN?

Children:
i John Edmondson BUFORD born 12-May-1896, died 2-Mar-1897.
ii Clara May BUFORD born about 1902.
iii Thomas Edmondson BUFORD born about 1906.

182. Mary Looney 'Mamie' RHEA born 1877, married Lunnsford Y. WILLIAMSON, born about 1877.

Children:
i Jean Rhea WILLIAMSON born about 1900.

183. Walter Preston RHEA Jr. born 1879, married (1) Mazie SALE, born about 1879, died 1921, married (2) June GROVE, born about 1888, died 4-Mar-1982. Walter died 1921.

Captain in the A.E.F in Frances during WWI. He was gassed and shell shocked. Both he and his wife died in 1921. Another source notes he died in Feb. 20, 1940.

Children:
304. i Walter Preston RHEA III. born about 1910.
305. ii Henry Sale RHEA born about 1913.

184. Alfred Long RHEA born 5-Dec-1878 married Mary Armstrong WAUNCHOPE, born 25-Jun-1884, died 8-May-1948. Alfred died 22-Jul-1925.

Children:
306. i   James Taylor RHEA born 29-Apr-1908.
   ii   Mary Frances RHEA born about 1910.
307. iii   Katherine Wanshope RHEA born 5-Jul-1911.
308. iv   Ellen Preston RHEA born 31-Dec-1918.
309. v   Josephine Wauchope RHEA born 5-Jul-1921.

185. Mary Ellen RHEA born 1-Sep-1882 married 1907, John Kerr CRAWFORD Jr., born 10-Dec-1877, Sullivan Co., Tennessee?, (son of Samuel H. CRAWFORD and Fanny O. BACHMAN) died 7-Aug-1936. Mary died 14-Jan-1949.

Children:
   i   Mary Rhea CRAWFORD born about 1908.
310. ii   Mary Frances CRAWFORD born 3-Mar-1909.
   iii   Louise Edmonson CRAWFORD born about 1912.
311. iv   John Kerr CRAWFORD III. born 9-Jun-1914.
   v   Eleanor Cary CRAWFORD born about 1915
312. vi   James Taylor CRAWFORD born 1-Dec-1917.

186. James Dysart RHEA born about 1885, Sommerville, Fayette Co. TN, married Jessie HEARN, born about 1885. James died October 30, Nashville, Davidson Co. TN at the age of 45.

A native of Sommerville, he left Sommerville to attend law school at Cumberland University and practiced at Memphis until the outbreak of trouble with Mexico. He was a member of the Chickasaw Guards at the time and was ordered with that unit to the border. He returned to Memphis with a 2nd Lt.'s commission and shortly thereafter World War I began. He went to Fort Oglethorpe and with a captain's commission was acting major in the 6th Division when it was ordered to France. The division was abroad 7 months but Captain Rhea was confined to the hospital with influenza much of the time and never reached the front. After the war he was continuously in Government service.

In 1917 he married Miss Jennie Hearn. They lived at 3709 Meadowbrook Av. in Nashville. He was a chief estate tax

officer of the Nashville division, United States Internal Revenue
Service for the last 6 years of his life.

Although he had not been in exceptionally good health for 2 years,
he was apparently unaware of an impending illness when on
Saturday afternoon he took his two sons George Hearn Rhea 10,
and Bunn Sumpter Rhea 4, to see the Vanderbilt-Tulane football
game. He was very ill Sunday morning and was taken to Barr's
Infirmary where he died of pneumonia with complications at age
45. His obituary appeared in the he Nashville Tennessean October
30.

At the time of his death he held a commission as a 1st Lt. in the
55th field artillery and was a member of the personal staff of
General Robert Travis, commander of all filed artillery units
attached to the 30th Division.

Children:
i   Jessie Hearn RHEA born about 1918.
ii   George Hearn RHEA born about 1920, Sommerville,
       Fayette Co. TN? 10 years old when he father
       died.
iii   Bunn Sumpter RHEA born about 1926, Nashville,
       Davidson Co. TN. Was 4 years old when his
       father died.

187. Howard Matthew RHEA born 22-Jan-1889 married
11-Jun-1913, Wilhelmina Blackman LITTERMER, born
15-Sep-1892, died 3-Oct-1978. Howard died 24-Feb-1958.

Children:
i   Abel RHEA born 22-Jan-1890, died 5-Jul-1891.
313. ii   Elizabeth Weaver RHEA born 30-Aug-1915.
iii   Howard Matthew RHEA Jr. born 28-Apr-1921.
       Married June 26, 1949
314. iv   Karl Byington RHEA born 2-Nov-1931.

188. Elizabeth Virginia PRESTON born about 1832, Washington

Co. VA, married 1855, Ezra Nuckolls SHEFFEY, born
13-Jul-1824, Wythe Co. VA, died 13-Feb-1891, Washington Co.
VA, buried: Walnut Grove Cemetery. Washington Co. VA.
Second wife of E. N. Sheffey.

Children:
315. i   Robert Preston SHEFFEY born 1868.
   ii   Charles Marshall SHEFFEY born about 1860, VA?,
      married Carrie WINSTON, born about 1860.
   iii   Sarah SHEFFEY born about 1862, VA?, married Mr.
      BIDDLE, born about 1862.
   iv   Henry SHEFFEY born about 1866, VA?, married Faith
      FULKERSON, born about 1866.

189. Margaret SHEFFEY born 4-Oct-1836, Marion, Smythe Co.
VA, married 8-Sep-1829, in Smythe Co. VA, William Elisha
'Col.' PETERS, born 18-Aug-1829, Bedford Co. VA, died
22-Mar-1906, Charlottesville, VA. Margaret died 29-Aug-1869.

Children:
  i   James White Sheffey PETERS born about 1865, VA,
     died Kansas City MO.
  ii   William Edgar PETERS born about 1867, VA.

190. Ellen White SHEFFY (See marriage to number 102.).

191. Mary W. SHEFFY born 8-Dec-1844, Marion, Smythe Co.
VA, married 14-Jul-1873, in Smythe Co. VA, William Elisha 'Col.'
PETERS, born 18-Aug-1829, Bedford Co. VA, died 22-Mar-1906,
Charlottesville, VA. Mary died 1906, Charlottesville, VA.

Children:
316. i   Don Preston PETERS born 1887.

192. Louise Smyth EDMONSON (See marriage to number 90.).

193. Jennie P. EDMONSON (See marriage to number 59.).

194. Clifford RHEA born 1-Sep-1866 married Delia DONOVAN, born 1867, Washington D.C., died 1-Sep-1945, Kansas City MO, buried: Calvary Cemetery. Kansas City, MO. Clifford died 3-Sep-1921, Kansas City MO, buried: Calvary Cemetery. Kansas City, MO.

It was said he was the largest hog dealer in that part of the country. Office was at 312 American Bank Bldg. - C. Rhea Serum Co.

Children:
i Margaret RHEA born 1898.
ii Clifford Campbell RHEA born 1900.
iii David RHEA born 1901.
iv Mamie Louise RHEA born 1902.
v Annie Delia RHEA born 1905.
vi Joseph RHEA born 1908.
vii Edward Buford RHEA Sr. born 15-Aug-1910, Kansas City MO, married Dorothy CORLESS, born 2-Feb-1911, Kansas City MO, died 6-Jul-1989, Kansas City MO, buried: Calvary Cemetery. Kansas City, MO. Edward died Kansas City MO, buried: Calvary Cemetery. Kansas City, MO. Served in the US Navy in WWII. Served on the island of Guam and at in Manila.

195. Annie RHEA born 1-Nov-1868 married William Presley DABNEY, born about 1868.

Children:

i William Rhea DABNEY born 1892
 Captain in WWI.

196. James David RHEA Jr. born 1-Oct-1870 married Sadie GARDNER, born about 1870. James died 1952.

Children:
i Joseph Campbell RHEA born about 1889

ii   James David RHEA III. born 13-Dec-1899 died 14-Jan-1971. Attended Vanderbilt as a Medical Student. As a first year man, received Founders Medal for Oratory.

iii   William Gardner RHEA born 20-Nov-1901 married 24-Jan-1929, Marian Travis GREEN, born about 1901.

197. Joseph Campbell RHEA born 1-Sep-1877 married Addie Martha BOOTH, born about 1877. Graduated in Law at Harvard University.

Children:

i   Buford Booth RHEA born about 1900. Was a student at Leland Stanford University.

198. Louise Jany RHEA born 1880 married Harry H. CHANDLER, born about 1880.

Children:

i   Elizabeth 'Bettie' Buford CHANDLER born 1905.

ii   Annie Rhea CHANDLER born 1913.

199. Buelah SUMPTER born 10-Feb-1863, Pulaski, Giles Co. TN, married 1887, Edgar F. ANDERSON, born about 1863, died 1911.

Children:

i   James Sumpter ANDERSON born 1893. He was a noted Nashville physician.

ii   Mary Frances ANDERSON born 1903

200. William David SUMPTER born 28-Jun-1872, Pulaski, Giles Co. TN, married 1902, Tommie WRENN, born about 1872, Nashville, Davidson Co. TN. Prominent surgeon and member of the board of Protestant Hospital in Nashville TN.

Children:
i   Clara SUMPTER born 1903.
ii   Thomas SUMPTER born 1906.
iii   Mary Rhea SUMPTER born 1910.

201. Catherine ABERNATHY born 1-Mar-1872, married Will FARMER, born about 1872.

Children:
317. i   Katherine FARMER born 1913.

202. Caleb Osborne RHEA born 9-Jul-1877, Pulaski, Giles Co. TN, married 15-Dec-1909, in Robertson Forks TN, Margaret Ellen DONALDSON, born about 1877, died 4-Feb-1964, Nashville, Davidson Co. TN?, buried: Woodlawn Cemetery. Caleb died 1953, Nashville, Davidson Co. TN.

Children:
i   Caleb Osborne RHEA Jr. born 1912,
        Nashville, Davidson Co. TN.
318. ii   Barclay Donald RHEA born 1914.

203. Erma Valine RHEA born 1-Jun-1879, Pulaski, Giles Co. TN, married 20-Nov-1901, in Pulaski, Giles Co. TN, George REED, born about 1870, died Nashville, Davidson Co. TN. Erma died 7-Jan-1944, Nashville, Davidson Co. TN, buried: Maplewood Cemetery. Pulaski, Giles Co.

Nashville Obituary: Mrs. Erma Rhea Reed, Nashville civic and church leader died at her home, 1928 21st Av S. yesterday at 12:15 pm. She had been critically ill for a month. Funeral services-chapel of Westminster Presbyterian Church of which she was a member. Burial will be in Pulaski TN, cemetery at 2 pm tomorrow.

Born in Pulaski TN daughter of W S Rhea and Ida Osborn Rhea. She received her early education in the Pulaski Public schools and in Martin College there. She later attended the Philadelphia Art Academy and then came to Nashville where she finished her

Descendants of Rev. Joseph Rhea

education in Ward's seminary and Peabody College. For many
years she followed painting as a hobby.

In 1902 she married George Reed.

Mrs. Reed was active in the affairs of the Moore Memorial
Presbyterian church on Broadway near 15th Av. before the
congregation became the Westminster Presbyterian church.
She was also a charter member of Sunset Park club a civic
and literary organization.

She was survived by two daughters, Miss Katherine Reed,
teacher in the industrial arts department of Peabody and Mrs.
Matthew T. White of Topeka KS., four brothers Dr. C O Rhea
Sr. of Nashville, Ed Rhea of Shepardsville KY, Will S. Rhea
and Rankin Rhea both of Pulaski and three grandchildren.

Children:
i   Ida Kathleen REED born 1902, Nashville,
       Davidson Co. TN. Taught in the industrial arts
       department of Peabody College Nashville.
ii   Erma REED born 1912, Nashville, Davidson
       Co. TN, married about 1930, Matthew T. WHITE,
       born about 1902, KS?. Erma died Topeka KS?
       The obituary of her mother includes reference to 3
       g-children who must have been of this the only married
       daughter. She is not named in the article.

204. Edward Sumpter RHEA born 1-May-1881, Pulaski, Giles Co.
TN, married 4-Sep-1907, in Shepherdsville KY, Hannah
Shanklin SMITH, born about 1881. Edward died Shepherdsville
KY.

Children:
i   Robert RHEA born 1908.
ii   Alice Cordelia RHEA born 1910. Died
       young.
iii   Helen Pearl RHEA born 1912.

iv   David Osborne RHEA born 1914.

205. William Samuel RHEA Jr. born 1-Aug-1884, Pulaski, Giles
Co. TN, married 31-Dec-1907, in Pulaski, Giles Co. TN, Hattie
Cornelia MILLER, born about 1884. Bridges were his engineering
specialty.

Children:
i   William Samuel RHEA III. born 1912.

206. David Rankin RHEA born 19-Jul-1886, Pulaski, Giles Co.
TN, married Vernon Louise PORTER, born about 1886, died
after 1964. David died 9-Feb-1964, Pulaski, Giles Co. TN,
buried: Maplewood Cemetery. Pulaski, Giles Co. Lived in the
old William Rhea home on Crestview Rd and raised their
daughter and son there. He was an elder in the Presbyterian
Church.

Obituary - Pulaski TN David Rankin Rhea 77, long time civic
and church leader was buried in Maplewood Cemetery. He
died Sunday at Giles Co. Hospital.

Funeral services will be held at First Presbyterian Church where he
had been a member for 61 years. Body is at the home of
brother-in-law Eddie Roe of Pulaski.

He received his education at Giles College and Washington
and Lee University. He was director of the Union Bank in Pulaski
for 26 years and served on the Giles Co. Board of Education for 16
years. He was very active in the First Presbyterian Church having
been ordained a deacon in 1920 and a ruling elder in 1938. From
1925 to 1942 he was superintendent of Sunday School. He was the
oldest continuous male member of the church. His grandfather
Caleb Osborn was builder of the sanctuary.

He is survived by his wife the former Miss Vernon Porter, a
daughter Mrs. Jack Tannehill, of Philadelphia, Miss, a son Porter
Rhea, Pulaski, two bothers W. S. Rhea, Pulaski, Ed Rhea of

Shelbyville KY, 3 grandchildren and 2 great grandchildren.

Children:
i   Robert Porter RHEA born 1914, Pulaski,
Giles Co. TN.
ii   Courtney RHEA born about 1915, Pulaski, Giles Co.
TN, married Jack Long TANNEHILL, born
21-May-1913, Winnfield LA.
iii   Alwyn Porter RHEA born about 1917, Pulaski, Giles
Co. TN. Died in infancy.
iv   Alice Catherine RHEA born about 1919, Pulaski,
Giles Co. TN. Died in infancy.

207. William Abernathy RHEA born 1881 married Daisy Vaughn
HUSSON, born about 1881. William died 1913.

Was killed in Morristown TN in a tragic accident when he was
struck by a Southern Railroad Engine. Served in 3rd TN Inf.
during Spanish American War.

Children:
i   Dooley RHEA born about 1910, Morristown, Polk Co.
TN.

208. Hattie Mabel RHEA born 1883, married Claude BENNETT,
born about 1883.

Children:
i   Rhea Worth BENNETT born about 1910.
ii   Sarah Bess BENNETT born about 1912.

209. George Sehorn RHEA born 1882, married (1) Alma PETTY,
born about 1882, married (2) Emma JONES, born about 1882.

Children:
i   James Clarence RHEA born about 1910.
ii   Charles William RHEA born about 1912.
iii   George Hunter RHEA born about 1914.

iv   Eldridge RHEA born about 1916.

210. William Rockhold Rhea born 1887, married Elva BLALACK, born about 1887.

Children:
i   Roger Jackson Rhea born about 1910.
ii   Rita Aline Rhea born about 1912.
iii   Elizabeth Lloyd Rhea born about 1914.

211. Elizabeth 'Lizzie' RHEA born 27-Jan-1870, Jonesboro, Washington Co. Married 10-Jun-1903, in Ruxby TN, Thomas Delaney COBB, born about 1870. Elizabeth died 1916.

Children:
319. i   Mary Rhea COBB born about 1900.
ii   Delaney COBB born about 1902.

212. Frances 'Fannie' RHEA born 4-Apr-1874, Jonesboro, Washington Co. Married (1) 9-Jun-1897, Samuel TAYLOR, born about 1874; married (2) Samuel DAY, born about 1874.

Children:
i   Matthew Edmund TAYLOR born 1899.
320. ii   Jennie Belle TAYLOR born about 1900.
iii   Rhea Venable TAYLOR born about 1902.
iv   Mary Louise TAYLOR born about 1904.
v   Lois TAYLOR born about 1908, died 1971.
vi   Samuel Chunn TAYLOR born about 1912, married Opal Lawson MATHENY, born about 1912.

213. Harriet 'Hattie' RHEA born 4-Feb-1876, Jonesboro, Washington Co. Married 23-Dec-1897, Arthur Peter WINFREY, born 23-Apr-1867, died 29-Nov-1938. Harriet died 23-May-1960.

Children:
321. i   Mattie Sweeney WINFREY born 25-Feb-1900.

ii	Elizabeth King WINFREY born 15-Jan-1902.
322. iii	John Allen WINFREY born 5-Oct-1903.
323. iv	Montgomery Rhea WINFREY born 15-Apr-1906.
324. v	Arthur Peter WINFREY born 20-Dec-1908.
325. vi	William 'Col.' Rhea WINFREY born 1-Sep-1916.
vii	Harriet Gray WINFREY born 13-Aug-1918, married 2 1945, Roger Pitkin ELSER PhD., born about 1918.

214. John Irwin RHEA born 24-May-1869, Sullivan Co. TN, married 1905, Retta Catherine SLAGLE, born 6-Oct-1878, Sullivan Co. TN?, died 13-May-1967, Sullivan Co. TN, buried: Blountville Cemetery Sullivan Co. TN. John died 12-Apr-1933, Sullivan Co. TN?, buried: Blountville Cemetery Sullivan Co. TN.

Children:

326. i	Alpha Josephine RHEA born 1908.
327. ii	John Irvin RHEA Jr. born 1910.
328. iii	Sarah Harriet RHEA born 1912.
329. iv	Thomas Clarke Rye RHEA born 2-Nov-1914.
330. v	Retta Katheryn RHEA born 1917.
vi	Margaret Frances RHEA born 1920, died 1925.

215. Fannie Ruth RHEA born 1871, Sullivan Co. TN, married John J. HICKS, born about 1870, Sullivan Co. TN?

Children:

i	Velma HICKS born about 1890, Sullivan Co. TN?

216. Myra Bell RHEA born 1872, Sullivan Co. TN, married Daniel A. WITCHER, born 1866, Sullivan Co. TN, (son of James 'Capt.' WITCHER and Mary Jane RUTLEDGE) died 1903. Myra died 1920.

Children:

i	Mary Irvin WITCHER born 5-Mar-1900, Sullivan Co. TN, married 25-Dec-1921, Henry Allen

GLOVER, born 9-Oct-1889, Sullivan Co. TN, died
28-Jan-1964. Mary died 6-Jan-1962. Henry and
Mary lived on a farm about a quarter mile from
Fairview School. The house had only four
rooms. In winter the family would warm around
the fireplace in the main room. Meals were
cooked in the fireplace and bread baked in a
baker in the kitchen which was too cold for the
family to dine in. She was a teacher in Bristol
but gave up the profession to become a
housewife and mother.

ii   James Rhea WITCHER born about 1902.
iii   John Daniel WITCHER born about 1904.

217. Jenny Dysart RHEA born 1874, Sullivan Co. TN,
married James I. A. HUGHES Jr., born 1867, Sullivan
Co. TN.

Children:
i   James Rhea HUGHES born about 1900.
ii   Samuel Dysart HUGHES born about 1902.
iii   Allen Campbell HUGHES born about 1904.

218. Mary Margaret RHEA born 22-Jan-1877, Sullivan Co. TN,
married 1901, in Sullivan Co. TN, Charles Lee COOPER,
born 9-Jun-1875, Blountville, Sullivan Co. TN, died 1952 Sullivan
Co. TN, buried: Blountville Cemetery Sullivan Co. TN. Mary died
22-Mar-1952, Piney Flats, Sullivan Co. TN, buried: Blountville
Cemetery Sullivan Co. TN.

Children:
i   Sarah 'Sallie' Lavine COOPER born about 1900,
        Sullivan Co. TN.
331.ii   Perry Carson COOPER born about 1901.
iii   Carl Lee COOPER born about 1904, Sullivan Co. TN.
iv   Ardine COOPER born about 1906, Sullivan Co. TN.

219. Elizabeth 'Bessie' Breden RHEA born 18-Jan-1883,

Sullivan Co. TN, married 2-May-1915, Henry Allen GLOVER,
born 9-Oct-1889, Sullivan Co. TN, died 28-Jan-1964. Elizabeth
died 8-Dec-1918, Sullivan Co. TN, buried: Blountville Cemetery
Sullivan Co. TN. Cause of death not shown in the county records
but occurred just ten months after the birth of her only daughter.

Children:

332. i   Edith Thyra GLOVER born 6-Feb-1918.

220. Flavia Converse RHEA born 1885, Sullivan Co. TN,
married Monroe J. BROYLES, born about 1885, Sullivan Co. TN?
Flavia died Sullivan Co. TN. W L Rhea indicates she died as
an infant. Other sources indicate she married. Possible another
daughter of this name.

Children:

i   Sallie Kate BROYLES born about 1910.
ii   Nannie Bess BROYLES born about 1912.
iii   Lillian Ruth BROYLES born about 1914.
iv   Irvin Lewis BROYLES born about 1916.

221. Samuel Wood RHEA Jr. born 5-May-1889, Sullivan Co. TN,
married (1) Minola LINDENWOOD, born about 1889, Sullivan
Co. TN?, married (2) Margaret HARR, born 2-Feb-1892, Sullivan
Co. TN?, died 24-Jul-1950, Sullivan Co. TN, buried: Blountville
Cemetery Sullivan Co. TN. Samuel died 25-Jun-1948, Sullivan Co.
TN, buried: Blountville Cemetery Sullivan Co. TN.

Children:

i   Glena Leota RHEA born about 1915.
ii   Kenneth D. RHEA born about 1917.

222. Jennie Edmonson RHEA born 6-Mar-1883, Jonesboro,
Washington Co married 14-Jun-1911, Herman A. BUTTS,
born 21-Dec-1882, died 1-Sep-1966. Jennie died
22-Feb-1973.

Children:

i   Herman A. BUTTS born 5-Oct-1917, died

5-Oct-1917.
333. ii   Sarah Winfrey BUTTS born 18-Jan-1919.
334. iii   Willouise BUTTS born 24-Jul-1921.

223. Lucy Mary 'Lula Mae' RHEA born 9-Aug-1876, married George M. SHAW, born about 1876. Lucy died 6-Mar-1912.

Children:
i   Lucy Adelaide SHAW born 1-Nov-1911.

224. Edward Francis RHEA born 30-Jan-1878, Sullivan Co. TN, married 27-Mar-1909, Mary Adele HERBERT, born 30-Oct-1885, Mississippi, died 20-Dec-1969. Edward died 10-Jun-1957, Memphis, Shelby Co. TN.

Was a station agent, telegrapher with the Railroad. Was sent to Mississippi where he met and married his wife. Moved back to Sommerville in 1925. His daughter Frances contracted typhoid when visiting relatives in Memphis. After her 3 month hospital stay in Sommerville, Edward's brother convinced him to move back to TN and go into his retail coal business.

Children:
335. i   Frances Adele RHEA born 27-Oct-1916.
336. ii   Thomas Edward RHEA born 6-Jan-1920.
337. iii   Stephen Herbert RHEA born 18-Aug-1922.

225. James Wilson RHEA born 20-Jan-1883, married 20-Jan-1904, Mary Lou CROSS, born 15-May-1884, died 16-Jul-1947. James died 12-Nov-1965.

Children:
i   Frances Elizabeth RHEA born 7-Sep-1905,
      died 26-Aug-1908.
ii   Marion Overton RHEA born 23-Jul-1909,
      married (1) Fred P. HALLUM, born about 1909,
      married (2) C. M. WILKINSON, born about 1909,
      married (3) Harry GASSAWAY, born about 1909.

Marion died 18-Oct-1977.
iii   Sarah Bell RHEA born 2-Jun-1911, married
8-Jun-1941, Charles Tyrone MCNAMEE, born
17-Jan-1910, died 7-Sep-1978.
338. iv   James Samuel RHEA born 7-Jun-1913.
339. v   Betty Cross RHEA born 15-Aug-1917.
vi   William Cross RHEA born about 1918.
340. vii   Mary Louise RHEA born 18-Jan-1925.

226. John Edmondson RHEA born 1885, married 26-Nov-1902, Fannie Kemp WATKINS, born 7-Feb-1883, died 2-Mar-1966. John died 18-Apr-1925.

Children:
i   Addie Frances RHEA born 4-May-1908.
341. ii   Thomas Watkins RHEA born 14-Feb-1910.

227. Sarah Bell RHEA born 9-Aug-1889, married 16-Mar-1915, Sidney A. BAYNES, born 1885, died 1976. Sarah died 20-Jun-1976.

Children:
i   Mary Virginia BAYNES born 12-Mar-1922.

228. Frank Lee RHEA born 1886, married Mary TEALL, born about 1886, died 1-Feb-1966.

Children:
i   John RHEA born about 1910.
ii   Patricia RHEA born about 1912.
iii   Gerald RHEA born about 1914. Twin.
iv   Geraldine RHEA born about 1914. Twin.

229. Elizabeth Susan RHEA born 1894, married Egbert SMITH, born about 1894.

Children:
i   Egbert Franklin SMITH born about 1920.

230. John Campbell ANDERSON born 27-Mar-1850, Blountville, Sullivan Co. TN, married (1) 22-Sep-1876, Annie ANDERSON, born about 1860, Rodgersville TN, (daughter of Audley ANDERSON and Cornelia ALEXANDER) died about 1880, Bristol, Sullivan Co. TN, married (2) Frances ' Fannie' WILLIAMSON, born about 1850, TN? John died 1913, Bristol, Sullivan Co. TN.

An extraordinary man. Followed in the footsteps of his father. Gave strict attention to business, was a merchant for many years in Bristol, then the President of the bank founded by his father. Did all his business on an honest and truthful basis. Made elder on the death of his father whose place he took. (W.L.Rhea-1895)

John attended school at Blountville and spent 2 years at Princeton University. After returning from college he entered the general mercantile business in Bristol with his father, being a member of the firm Joseph A. Anderson and Co. This firm was founded in Blountville and moved to Bristol in 1852. He continued in business with his father until Joseph retired in the 1870's. The firm of Anderson and Carr was then formed with Aaron Carr. He continued in business until 1886 when he entered the First National Bank, of which his father was president. Upon the death of his father in 1888, he was elected President and held the position until his death in 1913.

He married twice. Gave generously to the church and to various causes for the relief of the poor. He served as member of the Board of Mayor and as Mayor.

Children:
i   Audley King ANDERSON born 1878, Bristol, Sullivan Co. TN.
ii   Joseph Rhea ANDERSON born about 1880, Bristol, Sullivan Co. TN.
iii   Alice Melinda ANDERSON born about 1882, Bristol, Sullivan Co. TN, married Herman BLACKLEY, born

about 1882.

iv   Florence Alexander ANDERSON born about 1884, Bristol, Sullivan Co. TN.

v   John Campbell ANDERSON Jr. born about 1885, Bristol, Sullivan Co. TN.

vi   Margaret Williamson ANDERSON born about 1887, TN?.

vii   John Campbell ANDERSON III. born about 1889, Sullivan Co. TN.

viii   Thomas Parish ANDERSON born about 1891, Sullivan Co. TN.

ix   Robert Banks ANDERSON born about 1893, Sullivan Co. TN.

231. Isaac Samuel ANDERSON born 9-Dec-1854, Bristol, Sullivan Co. TN, married Alice GIBSON, born about 1855, Lee Co. VA., died Lee Co. VA. Isaac died Lee Co VA? In charge of a Presbyterian Church in Lee Co VA (1895).

Children:

342. i   Nancy Melinda ANDERSON born 1894.

232. Margaret 'Maggie' Micajah ANDERSON born 4-Nov-1857, Bristol, Sullivan Co. TN, married 25-Aug-1880, John Henderson CALDWELL, born about 1857, Bristol, Sullivan Co. TN, (son of George CALDWELL) died Bristol, Sullivan Co. TN. Margaret died Bristol, Sullivan Co. TN.

Children:

i   Margaret Melinda CALDWELL born about 1880, Bristol, Sullivan Co. TN.

343. ii   John Henderson CALDWELL Jr. born 1882.

344. iii   Joseph Anderson CALDWELL born 1884.

iv   George Aiken CALDWELL born 1887, Bristol, Sullivan Co. TN, married Harriet PARRISH, born about 1887.

v   Walter McFarland CALDWELL born about 1891, Bristol, Sullivan Co. TN.

vi   Mable CALDWELL born 1893, Bristol,
Sullivan Co. TN.

vii   Almedia Brooks CALDWELL born 1896,
Bristol, Sullivan Co. TN.

233. Alexander ANDERSON (See marriage to number 157.).

234. Annie ANDERSON (See marriage to number 230.).

235. Lynn STEWART born about 1870, GA?, married Hugh
Mitchell NEWLAND, born 1870, GA?, (son of Isaac Anderson
NEWLAND and Martha LEWIS).

Children:
i   Emmett NEWLAND born 1893, GA?
ii   Joseph Anderson NEWLAND born 1895, GA?
iii   Maxie Jayne NEWLAND born 1896, GA?,
married Joseph Dorton COX, born about 1896, GA?
iv   Samuel Rhea NEWLAND born 1898, GA?
v   Hugh Lynn NEWLAND born about 1900, GA?
vi   Vernon Ross NEWLAND born about 1902, GA?
vii   Mabel Angeline NEWLAND born about 1906, GA?
viii   Robert Rhea NEWLAND born about 1908, GA?

236. Anna Dwight RHEA born 24-Aug-1861, Mt. Sair, Persia,
married 16-Sep-1886, in Lake Forest Ill, Samuel Graham
WILSON, born about 1860, Indiana PA.

Graduated from Lake Forest U. in 1881, then went to Wesley
College in Mass. and took special courses. Fine in languages,
mathematics. Returned to Lake Forest and was elected teacher of
Ancient Languages in the college where she graduated.

Children:
i   Samuel Rhea WILSON born 6-Mar-1890, Tabiz,
Persia, died 23-Nov-1891, Tabiz, Persia. Died
of membranous croup.
ii   Mary Agnes WILSON born 10-Dec-1892, Tabiz,

Persia.
iii   Rose Dulles WILSON born 25-Jul-1894, Lake
     Forest Ill.
iv   Esther Foster WILSON born 21-Sep-1899, Tabiz,
     Persia, died 16-Jun-1901.
v   Andrew WILSON born 15-Aug-1899, Tabiz, Persia,
     died 1-Oct-1902.
vi   Annie Rhea WILSON born 15-Jun-1901, Tabiz,
     Persia.
vii   Robert Leighton WILSON born 26-Jul-1903, Tabiz,
     Persia.

237. Sophia Perkins RHEA born 18-Apr-1866, Oroomiah, Persia,
married 18-Jan-1891, in Lake Forest, Ill, William DULLES
Jr., born about 1860, Philadelphia PA, died Englewood NY.
Sophia died 1907, NY.

Moved with her mother to Lake Forest and attended school there.
Went to Wesley College and stayed with Uncle Perry and Aunt
Meg while there. Afterward taught school in Lake Forest. In 1891
married and left to make home in NY.

Children:
i   Mabel Rutledge DULLES born about 1890, New York
     City NY. Died young.
ii   Dorothy DULLES born 24-Nov-1893, New York City
     NY.
iii   Edith Rutledge DULLES born 20-Mar-1897,
     Englewood NJ.
iv   Foster Rhea DULLES born 24-Jan-1900, Englewood
     NJ.
v   Winslow DULLES born 9-Dec-1903, Englewood NJ.

238. Martha Ellen FAIN born 19-Oct-1860, Washington Co. TN,
married 27-Jun-1889, in Jonesboro, Washington Co Robert N.
DOSSER, born about 1860. Martha died 1-Jul-1910, Washington
Co. TN.

Children:
i   Frances 'Fannie' Rhea DOSSER born 14-Aug-1892, Jonesboro, Washington Co.
ii   Margaret Cowan DOSSER born 14-Nov-1893, Jonesboro, Washington Co.
iii   Mary Nell DOSSER born 10-Jan-1896, Jonesboro, Washington Co.
iv   Robert N. DOSSER Jr. born 2-Oct-1897, Jonesboro, Washington Co.

239. John Mitchell FAIN born 8-Nov-1861, Bluff City, Sullivan Co. TN, married (1) Margaret 'Maggie' A. CARR, born 1879, Chattanooga TN, died 1933, Knoxville TN?, married (2) 23-Nov-1893, in Bluff City, Sullivan Co. TN, Gertrude WORLEY, born about 1860. The family was in Boseman, Montana in 1906 due to the health of Gertrude.

Children:
i   Worley FAIN born 22-Mar-1895, Bluff City, Sullivan Co. TN. 1st Lt. in Virginia Coast Artillery during WWI.
ii   James Rhea FAIN born 1-Jul-1897, Bluff City, Sullivan Co. TN. Was sent by the Government to teach in a Military School in South Carolina during WWI.
iii   Martha Ellen FAIN born 21-Mar-1900, Bluff City, Sullivan Co. TN.
iv   John Mitchell FAIN Jr. born 13-Oct-1904, Bluff City, Sullivan Co. TN.

240. James Rhea FAIN born 26-May-1863, Sullivan Co. TN?, married 15-Jun-1904, in Norfolk, Nebraska, Lillian Mae LINKHEART, born 26-Nov-1880.

During Spanish American War was 2nd Lt. of Engineers, Company F 3rd TN Infantry as a U.S. government employee, he had to move his family around a lot.

Children:
i   Margery Cowan FAIN born about 1904.
ii   Margaret Luikart FAIN born 26-Mar-1905,
     Nebraska?.

241. Mary Lynn FAIN born 11-May-1868 married 20-Sep-1892, Samuel Decatur STUART, born about 1868, died 8-Nov-1893, Washington Co. TN. Mary died 21-Jun-1894.

Her husband died in 1893. The next year Mary died and 3 hours after her funeral their only son Samuel D. Jr. died.

Children:
i   Samuel Decatur STUART Jr. born about 1890,
     Washington Co. TN, died 25-Jun-1894, Washington
     Co. TN.

242. Nicholas Peter EARNEST born 15-Apr-1871, married 23-Sep-1896, in Jonesboro, Washington County, Lida Beatrice DOGGETT, born 1873, Sullivan Co. TN, (daughter of James Polk DOGGETT and Ellen NEWLAND). Lived on the farm that belonged to his father.

Children:
i   Mary Eleanor EARNEST born 2-Nov-1897,
     Jonesboro, Washington Co
ii   James Doggett EARNEST born 23-Nov-1898,
     Jonesboro, Washington Co
iii Joseph Rhea EARNEST born 16-Feb-1903,
     Jonesboro, Washington Co.
iv   Benjamin Foster EARNEST born 14-Sep-1904,
     Jonesboro, Washington Co.
v   Charles Edward EARNEST born about 1906,
     Jonesboro, Washington Co.
vi   Katherine Louise EARNEST born about 1908,
     Jonesboro, Washington Co.

243. Eleanor Lynn RHEA born 7-Aug-1871, VA?, married (1)

26-Dec-1895, William H. ADAMS, born about 1871, Bristol, Sullivan Co. TN, died 5-Jul-1899, married (2) Steven W. CARSON, born about 1871, Atlanta GA. Eleanor married twice. Had 2 sons by her first husband.

Children:

i   Charles Linwood ADAMS born 14-Dec-1896.
ii   Brainard Rhea ADAMS born 26-Jul-1898.

244. Margaret Preston RHEA born 1886, VA?, married 23-Jun-1898, in Marion, Smythe Co. VA, Henry Boyd STANLEY, born about 1886, Marion, Smythe Co. VA.

Children:

i   Ellen Sheffey STANLEY born 25-May-1899, Marion, Smythe Co. VA.
ii   Pauline Hill STANLEY born 6-Jul-1900, Marion, Smythe Co. VA.
iii   Henry Boyd STANLEY Jr. born 5-Jan-1903, Marion, Smythe Co. VA.

245. Martha Lynn RHEA born about 1876, married 18-Oct-1899, in 2nd Presbyterian Church, Knoxville, Fayette Flannary VANDERVENTER, born about 1876.

Children:

i   Christopher VANDERVENTER born 17-Jun-1901.
ii   Robert Rhea VANDERVENTER born 15-Feb-1903.
iii   Letitia VANDERVENTER born 30-Aug-1905.
iv   Isabella VANDERVENTER born about 1908.

246. James Dickerson COWAN born 17-Aug-1887, married Elsie BAILEY, born about 1879. In 1906 was living in Canastola, New York.

Children:

i   James Dickerson COWAN Jr. born about 1905.

247. Joshua 'Mack' Mckinney PHIPPS born 24-Feb-1853,
Sullivan Co. TN, married Mary MCKINNEY, born about 1855,
Rogersville died Kingsport TN? Joshua died Kingsport,
Sullivan Co. TN. Member of Presbyterian Church in Kingsport.

Children:
345. i   Charles McKinney PHIPPS born 1877.
346. ii   James Gaines PHIPPS born 1881.
347. iii   Annie PHIPPS born 1884.
     iv   Kenneth Logan PHIPPS born about 1884, Kingsport
          TN?, died 14-Dec-1901. Died at his parents
          home.
     v   Joshua McKinney PHIPPS Jr. born about 1886,
          Kingsport TN?
348. vi   Frances 'Fannie' PHIPPS born 1889.
     vii   Mary PHIPPS born about 1890, Kingsport TN?

248. Mary BACHMAN born 1857, Sullivan Co. TN, married
8-Oct-1888, in Chattanooga TN, Charles ANDERSON, born about
1860, Chattanooga TN, died 1902, Chattanooga TN. Mary
died 15-Oct-1897, Chattanooga TN, buried: Chattanooga TN.

Her obituary read: DEATH OF MRS. CHAS. C. ANDERSON -
One Or the Best Beloved and most popular ladies of Chattanooga
died unexpectedly yesterday. Mrs. Mary BACHMAN
ANDERSON, the wife of Charles C. ANDERSON and daughter or
Dr. and Mrs. J. W. BACHMAN, died yesterday afternoon at 1
o'clock after a brief illness at her home on McCallie Avenue. The
news of this lamentable event spread rapidly, and plunged the
community into profound sorrow, for there are no home in
Chattanooga where Dr. BACHMAN, pastor or be first Presbyterian
Church, and his esteemed family are respected and beloved. The
death of a good, noble woman lady is a loss to the entire city, and
in this case is particularly sad. Mrs. Anderson had been ill only four
weeks, and at no time had her physicians or family anticipated
death. A robust constitution and a cheerful disposition, Mrs.
Anderson herself did not fear the result, and though she suffered
intensely the end was entirely unexpected. The direct cause of

death was the rupture of a blood vessel on the brain, precipitated by nervous prostration. Mrs. Anderson began to sink only two hours before she died, but the end came peacefully simple passing out of a Christian life, rich in good deeds, without even the consciousness of the parting from her loved ones. Surrounding her death bed were the members of her own family and Dr. Bachman. It was a bitter trial for that divine, who has brought solace to so many departing souls, to minister in the last and hour to his daughter, cut off in the prime of her womanhood, taken from a devoted husband, three little children, a happy, unbroken family chain, and a good work, constantly her labor of love. The melancholy intelligence was telegraphed to her sisters, Mrs. Anne Bachman Hyde, at Richmond, and Misses Fannie and Eva D. BACHMAN, at Spartanburg, S.C., and to her brother, M. Nathan Bachman, who was out of the city - Until they are heard from no definite arrangements for the funeral will be made. All day yesterday there was a stream of people passing into the Aldine to express their condolence and to leave cards for the bereaved family.

The Deceased was the historian of the Daughters of the Confederacy, a position she had held for a year with credit and honor to herself and the society; and by none will her death be more deeply deplored than by her associates in that benevolent organization. Mrs. Anderson was the third daughter of Dr. and Mrs. Bachman; she was married nine years ago last Saturday at the age of 21, to Charles C. Anderson, and was the mother of three children two boys and one girl the eldest is 8, the youngest 2 years of age.

Children:

349. i   Jonathan Waverly ANDERSON born1890.
    ii   William Dulaney ANDERSON born 1892, Chattanooga TN.
    iii   Mary Margaret ANDERSON born 1895, Sullivan Co. TN, married Charles Shelby COFFEY, born about 1897.

249. Annie Rhea BACHMAN born about 1864, Sullivan Co. TN, married 29-Jan-1889, Charles R. HYDE, born about 1860, died Richmond VA?

Children:
350. i   John Bachman HYDE born 1890.

250. Nathan Lynn BACHMAN born about 1870, Sullivan Co. TN, married Pearl DUKE, born about 1870, Sullivan Co. TN? An attorney and a member of the Supreme Court of Tennessee.

Children:
   i   Martha Dulaney BACHMAN born about 1895.

251. Annie Lynn BACHMAN born 1876 married 22-Nov-1899, in Sweetwater TN, William A. MCCLAIN, born about 1876.

Children:
   i   William A. MCCLAIN Jr. born 1-Apr-1901
  ii   Frances MCCLAIN born about 1902.
 iii   Lynn MCCLAIN born about 1904.
 iv   Annie MCCLAIN born about 1906.

252. Bessie BACHMAN born 1881 married 16-Jan-1902, in Sweetwater TN, James R. PATTON, born about 1881.

Children:
   i   James H. PATTON born about 1905.

253. Lilly Bell BACHMAN born 1886, married James M. HARRIS, born about 1886.

Children:
   i   James M. HARRIS Jr. born about 1910.
  ii   Frances 'Fannie' HARRIS born about 1912.

254. Elenor 'Nellie' W. LAMPSON born 18-Jun-1864,

Jonesboro, Washington Co. married 8-Jun-1893, in Jonesboro, Washington Co. Elbridge James BAXTER, born about 1860.

When young did her mothers canning & preserving. Attended Western Seminary, Oxford. Mother died before she could finish. Kept up her music and taught in class in Franklin TN and at Wytheville VA for 2 or 3 years.

Children:
i   Martha Lampson BAXTER born 20-Apr-1894, Jonesboro, Washington Co.

255. Robert Earhart RHEA born 1-Jul-1870, Sullivan Co. TN, married 1905, in Sullivan Co. TN, Margaret Rebecca RHEA, born 1873, Sullivan Co. TN, (daughter of Robert Bruce RHEA and Sarah E. SELLS).

1910 census shows family with 3 children and mother Eliza A. living in the household. Born on his grandfathers farm.

Children:
i   Margaret RHEA born 1907, Sullivan Co., Tennessee? Twin.
        1910 census shows she is twin of Mary E.
ii   Mary Eleanor RHEA born 1907, Sullivan Co., Tennessee?
iii   Helen Bruce RHEA born 1909, Sullivan Co. TN.

256. Margaret David RHEA born 1876, Sullivan Co. TN, married Chester BULLARD, born about 1876. Appears from settlement of her fathers estate that she married a Bullard by 1911.

Children:
i   Willie Margaret BULLARD born about 1900, married Cameron MCCUE, born about 1900.
ii   Joe Rhea BULLARD born about 1902.

257. Charles Balfer EARHART II. born 23-Nov-1864, Bristol, Sullivan Co. TN, married 6-Mar-1884, in Blountville, Sullivan Co. TN, Etta Emma POWELL, born 1-Aug-1866, Blountville, Sullivan Co. TN, (daughter of John "Jack" POWELL and Margaret Emaline 'Emma' ROLLER) died 1935, Blountville, Sullivan Co. TN, buried: Blountville Cemetery Sullivan Co. TN. Charles died 1-Nov-1932, Bristol, Sullivan Co. TN, buried: Blountville Cemetery Sullivan Co. TN.

Infant Charles hidden by his mammie when Union came through valley, burned future wife's family house and store in Blountville TN. He raised his family in a 2 story house on part of the original Rhea farm across from the Little Red Schoolhouse. Property borders Sperry View Rd.

Children:
351. i   John 'Powell' EARHART born 1-Jul-1885.
352. ii   Samuel Pearce EARHART born 5-Dec-1887.
353. iii   Margarita R. EARHART born 1-Apr-1893.
     iv   Charles B. EARHART born 1-May-1896, Blountville, Sullivan Co. TN, died before 1920. Died of diptheria.
354. v   Violet Etta EARHART born 29-Oct-1898.
     vi   Robert Rhea EARHART born 1-May-1900, Blountville, Sullivan Co. TN, died 1912, Sullivan Co. TN. Died at age of 12 years from diptheria.
     vii   Nellie Roller EARHART born about 1900, Sullivan Co. TN. Died of scarlet fever at the age of 3.
     viii   Ralph Preston EARHART born 1905, Bristol, Sullivan Co. TN, married Lillian HOUSTON, born about 1905, Bluff City, Sullivan Co. TN, died Florida. Ralph died about 1950. In 1920 census he is the only child living with parents at home. Had no children.

258. Sarah Ella EARHART born 1866, Sullivan Co. TN, married 16-Sep-1896, William Edgar 'Ed' CARTER, born 1867, Sullivan

Co. TN. 1910 Sarah, William and family were enumerated near her brother Joseph's family.

Children:
i   Joseph E. CARTER born 1898, Sullivan Co. TN.
ii   William Hubert CARTER born 1900, Sullivan Co. TN.
iii   Cara 'Carrie' P. CARTER born 1903, Sullivan Co. TN.

259. Joseph Preston EARHART born 1-Dec-1869, Bristol, Sullivan Co. TN, married 10-Jun-1901, in Sullivan Co. TN, Sarah Ann 'Sadie' BOY, born 1871, Sullivan Co. TN. Joseph died 1933, Sullivan Co. TN, buried: Blountville Cemetery Sullivan Co. TN.

In 1896 inherited 260.5 acres from his parents, including the old Rhea homestead, the 'Elms' farm on Sperry View Road Blountville, Sullivan Co. 1900 census Joseph is living at home with mother and brother John. 1901 mother Margaret still living with the family at age 75.

Children:
i   Mary Lillian EARHART born 1904, Sullivan Co. TN.
ii   John Sidney EARHART born 9-Mar-1906, Sullivan Co. TN, died 8-Aug-1909, Sullivan Co. TN, buried: Blountville Cemetery Sullivan Co. TN.
iii   Phillip Boy EARHART born 30-Nov-1910, Blountville, Sullivan Co. TN, married Katharyn BROWN, born 20-Aug-1922, died 25-Apr-1980, Sullivan Co. TN, buried: Blountville Cemetery Sullivan Co. TN. Phillip died 13-Mar-1967, Blountville, Sullivan Co. TN. Left 125 acres of the family farm to his family on his death in 1967. Farming of tobacco and silage for the Holstein cattle continue to this day.

260. Margaret Jane 'Maggie' EARHART born 1872, Sullivan Co. TN, married 25-Apr-1899, in Sullivan Co. TN, Thomas J. FAIN, born about 1870, Sullivan Co. TN, died Montana?

Children:
i   William FAIN born about 1900, Sullivan Co. TN.
ii   Ruth FAIN born about 1902, Sullivan Co. TN.
iii   Thomas J. FAIN II. born about 1905, Sullivan Co. TN.
iv   Florence FAIN born about 1907, Sullivan Co. TN.
v   Margaret Preston FAIN born about 1909, Sullivan Co. TN.

261. John Henry EARHART born 1-Mar-1874, Bristol, Sullivan Co. TN, married 25-Dec-1900, in Sullivan Co. TN, Frances Susan FLEENOR, born 1880, Bluff City, Sullivan Co. TN, died 1959, buried: Blountville Cemetery Sullivan Co. TN. John died 1940, buried: Blountville Cemetery Sullivan Co. TN.

Children:
i   Clarence Wade EARHART born 1903, Sullivan Co. TN.
ii   Hazel Etta EARHART born 1905, Sullivan Co. TN.
iii   Charles Henry EARHART born 6-Sep-1906, Sullivan Co. TN, died 22-Feb-1907, Sullivan Co. TN, buried: Blountville Cemetery Sullivan Co. TN.
355. iv William Herman EARHART born 1909.
v   Martha Evelyn EARHART born 1909, Sullivan Co. TN. Twin of William Herman Earhart.
vi   John Howard EARHART born 1911, Sullivan Co. TN.

262. Sarah Lucky GANT born 1868, Cleveland TN, married James G. DEARMOND, born about 1868. Sarah died 1902.

Children:

161

i   Cornelius Hamilton DEARMOND born about 1890.
ii   Margaret Eleanor DEARMOND born about 1892.

263. Agnes Moore GANT born 1875, Cleveland TN, married Hugh Montgomery KNOX, born about 1875.

Children:
i   Agnes Moore KNOX born about 1900.
ii   Thomas Jefferson KNOX born about 1902.

264. Luella Erwin GANT born 1875, Cleveland TN, married Thomas Oscar MARSHALL, born about 1875.

Children:
i   Orlando Gant MARSHALL born about 1890.
ii   Agnes Lucky MARSHALL born about 1902.

265. Annie Rhea GAINES born 1880, Monroe Co. TN, married Charles Leonidas CLARK, born about 1880.

Children:
i   James William CLARK born about 1910, Monroe Co. TN.
ii   John Craig CLARK born about 1912.
iii Charles Palmer CLARK born about 1914.
iv Mary CLARK born about 1916.

266. Susie Rice GAINES born 1883, Monroe Co. TN, married Frank Knox HUTCHESON, born about 1883.

Children:
i   John Gaines HUTCHESON born about 1910.
ii   Frank HUTCHESON Jr. born about 1912.
iii Susan Craig HUTCHESON born about 1914.
iv Charles Strother HUTCHESON born about 1918.

267. Frances Louisa GAINES born 1888, Monroe Co. TN, married John Cotton OATES, born about 1888.

Children:
i   Jack Cotton OATES Jr. born about 1910.
ii   Catherine Craig OATES born about 1912.

268. Jean Foote RHEA born 1872, married Clifton EMERSON, born about 1872, TX?

Children:
i   James Fredrick EMERSON born about 1894.
356. ii   Ella EMERSON born 1895.
iii Clifton Alexander EMERSON born about 1896, TX?

269. William Alexander RHEA Jr. born 1874, married Mary HERNDON, born about 1874, TX?

Children:
i   Lawrence Herndon RHEA born 1897, TX?
     Was a 2nd Lt. in the Coast Artillery during WWI.
     Was under orders to sail when the Armistice
     was signed.
ii   Alexander Foote RHEA born 1899, TX?

270. John Edwin RHEA born 1883, married Ida DOWELL, born about 1883.

Children:
i   John Edwin RHEA Jr. born about 1905, TX?
ii   Mary Ida RHEA born about 1907, Sullivan Co. TN.

271. John W. RHEA Jr. born 1864, TX?, married Winfield LEDBETTER, born about 1864, TX?

Children:
i   Olivia RHEA born about 1890, TX?
ii   John W. RHEA III. born about 1892, TX?
iii Veronica RHEA born about 1894, TX?
iv   Winfield RHEA born about 1896, TX?

272. William Joseph RHEA born 10-Nov-1877, TX?, married 10-Mar-1909, Elizabeth GROVES, born 2-Aug-1879, TX?, died 23-Feb-1951. William died 18-Jul-1952.

Children:
357. i William Joseph RHEA Jr. born 17-Oct-1916.

273. Robert Lee RHEA born 10-Oct-1882, TX?, married Margaret BUCKHOLZ, born about 1882, TX? Robert died 1965.

Children:
i Robert Lee RHEA Jr. born about 1905, TX?

274. Rhea MILLER born 1874, Collin Co. Texas?, married May MCKAMEY, born about 1874, TX?

Children:
i Truman MILLER born about 1900, TX?
ii William Fredrick MILLER born about 1902, TX?
iii Sarah Elizabeth MILLER born about 1904, TX?

275. Lula Alexander MILLER born 1880, Collin Co. Texas?, married Fred J. SMITH, born about 1880, TX?

Children:
i Rhea Marsh SMITH born about 1900, Collin Co. Texas?
ii Fred J. SMITH Jr. born about 1902, Collin Co. Texas?

276. William E. HUFF born 1872, Sullivan Co. TN?, married Lucy GALLAHER, born about 1872, Sullivan Co. TN?

Children:
i James Gallaher HUFF born 1898.
ii Hugh McCroskey HUFF born 1901.

277. Adeline RHEA born 1866, TX, married Lee E. BURGESS, born about 1866, TX? Adeline died 1909.

Children:
i   Addie Lee BURGESS born 1891, TX?, married Joseph A. RUDNICK, born about 1891, TX?
ii   Rhea BURGESS born about 1893, TX?

278. Robert RHEA born 24-Jul-1868, Greeneville TN, married 10-Feb-1891, Rhoda Maude LOVE, born 8-Nov-1870, Texas, died 7-Jun-1914. Robert died 7-Mar-1939, Whitney TX. Died from hypertensive cardiovascular disease.

Children:
358. i   John Love RHEA born 19-Nov-1891.

279. Joseph RHEA born 1871 TX?, married Anna B. PEEPLES, born about 1871.

Children:
i   Frances Anne RHEA born 1906.

280. Cleaves RHEA born 1882, married Mae B. LOWDON, born about 1882.

Children:
i   Mary Alice RHEA born about 1905.
ii   Helen Louise RHEA born about 1907.

281. Alexander Dodson RHEA Jr. born 1885, married Annie L. BOESCH, born about 1885.

Children:
i   Elizabeth RHEA born about 1910, TX?
ii   Alexander Dodson RHEA III. born about 1912, TX?

282. Arthur RODGERS born 1879, Louden TN, married Dean Stuart PENLAND, born about 1879, Loudon TN.

Children:
i   James Penland RODGERS born about 1892, Loudon TN?
ii   Samuel Andrew RODGERS born about 1894, Loudon TN?
iii   Jasper Rhea RODGERS born about 1896, Loudon TN?
iv   Arthur RODGERS Jr. born about 1900, Loudon TN?

283. Jean Rhea RODGERS born 1885, Louden TN, married George Steel DEWEY, born about 1885.

Children:
i   Elizabeth Rhea DEWEY born about 1910, Loudon TN?
ii   George Steele DEWEY Jr. born about 1912.
iii   Mary Alice DEWEY born about 1914, Loudon TN?
iv   Samuel Rodgers DEWEY born about 1916.
v   Charles DEWEY born about 1918, Loudon TN?

284. John Kerr CRAWFORD Jr. (See marriage to number 185.).

285. Alice Ann SPURGEN born 11-Mar-1858, Sullivan Co. TN, married 15-Jul-1875, William Henry FAIN, born 24-May-1842, Sullivan Co. TN, (son of Thomas FAIN and Rachel ANDERSON) died 3-Feb-1897, Sullivan Co. TN. Alice died 1-Dec-1922, Sullivan Co. TN.

Children:
i   Rachel FAIN born about 1880, Sullivan Co. TN.
ii   Hanna FAIN born about 1882, Sullivan Co. TN.
iii   Margaret E. FAIN born about 1884, Sullivan Co. TN, died Johnson City, Washington Co. TN. Died unmarried.
iv   Lella Lynn FAIN born about 1886, Sullivan Co. TN.
v   Carrie Ruth FAIN born about 1888, Sullivan Co. TN, married S. T. MOSER, born about 1880, Johnson City, Washington Co
vi   Samuel Patton Spurgen FAIN born about 1890,

166

Sullivan Co. TN, died 4-Apr-1859.

286. Nathan Rhea CARTRIGHT born 28-Aug-1875, Sullivan Co.
TN, married 29-Mar-1899, in Spring City, Rhea Co. TN, Grace
Bell WATKINS, born 22-Mar-1877, Montgomery Co. OH, died
10-Feb-1923, Miami FL, buried: Chattanooga TN. Nathan died
28-Feb-1931, Dayton, Rhea Co. TN, buried: Chattanooga TN.
Died of pneumonia.

Children:

359. i   Harriet Eleanor CARTRIGHT born 18-May-1900.
    ii   Nathan Rhea CARTRIGHT Jr. born 3-Jun-1900,
           Pocahontas, Tazwell Co. VA, died 25-Jan-1967,
           Nashville, Davidson Co. TN, buried: National
           Cemetery. Nashville TN. Married 6 times. No
           children by any of his wives. Last wife was
           Eva Norman. Died in Veterans Hospital.
    iii   Amy Frances Lois CARTRIGHT born 21-May-1911,
           Bristol, Washington Co., Virginia, married
           21-May-1936, John ROBINSON Jr., born
           29-Sep-1891, Pittsburgh, PA, died 14-Oct-1967,
           Dayton, Rhea Co. TN. In 1972 her address
           was PO Box 7564 St. Petersburg Fl. Born on
           Goodson St. in the Mary St. Methodist Parsonage.
           Dedicated genealogist. Donated 300 museum
           articles to the Netherland Inn at Kingsport TN.
           Has no children.

287. Robert Carlock CARTRIGHT born 11-Oct-1884 married
1913, Lucille Hogue 'Lucy' BROWN, born about 1884, Radford
VA. Robert died 2-Aug-1959.

Children:

360. i   Milburn Jonathan CARTRIGHT born 25-Aug-1914.
361. ii   Dorothy Ruth CARTRIGHT born 27-May-1917.

288. Minnie Lucinda HULL born 3-Jun-1891, Sullivan Co. TN,
married 30-Jun-1912, Simon William COLE, born 15-Oct-1889,

Sullivan Co. TN, (son of Henry Thomas COLE and Amanda K. BARR).

Children:
i   Irl Dennis COLE born 22-Mar-1913, Bristol, Sullivan Co. TN, married 20-Jun-1941, Iris Lucille HIGGINS, born about 1913.

ii   Margaret Kathryn COLE born 13-Nov-1914, Bristol, Sullivan Co. TN, married 16-Aug-1950, Edward Feegua SUMNER, born about 1914.

362. iii   Dorothy Lucille COLE born 20-Mar-1917.

iv   Claude Clayton COLE born 2-Aug-1920, Sullivan Co. TN, married 8-Jul-1948, Vivian Iris WEDDLE, born about 1920.

v   Herman Dulaney COLE born 9-Oct-1922, Sullivan Co. TN, married 20-Dec-1952, Mary Nell STANLEY, born about 1922.

289. Seaton Tinsley PRESTON born 29-Mar-1892, married 20-Jul-1920, Sara Kathryn BARBER, born about 1892. Lived in Florida. Had 3 sons.

Children:
363. i   Seaton Tinsley PRESTON Jr. born 29-Aug-1921.

364. ii   James Brainard PRESTON born 30-Mar-1923.

365. iii   Frederick Leigh PRESTON born 27-Jan-1930.

290. Abraham Lawrence SNAPP born 1870 married Flora C. MARLIN, born about 1870.

Children:
i   Tennie SNAPP born about 1890.

ii   John Wendell SNAPP born about 1892.

iii   Hawkins Sevier SNAPP born about 1894.

iv   Elmer E. SNAPP born about 1896.

v   Elizabeth Rachel SNAPP born about 1898.

291. John Pemberton SNAPP born 1872 married Julia Adah SHEILDS, born about 1872.

Children:

i   Lecta Pemberton SNAPP born about 1900.
ii   Ivan Sheilds SNAPP born about 1902.

292. Rhea McIlwaine SNAPP born 1880 married Dora ROWE, born about 1880.

Children:

i   Onell Rhea SNAPP born about 1905.
ii   Lester Wiseman SNAPP born about 1907.
iii   Alta Junetta SNAPP born about 1909.
iv   Janeva Florena SNAPP born about 1911.

293. Walter White PRESTON born 1880, Feoral, Texas?, married Annie Marie BONHAN, born about 1880, TX?

Children:

i   Walter Bonhan PRESTON born about 1910, TX.
ii   John Courtney PRESTON born about 1912, TX.
iii   Fredrick Lewis PRESTON born about 1914, TX. Twin of Frances.
iv   Frances PRESTON born about 1914, TX.

294. John Lewis PRESTON born 1883, Feoral, Texas?, married Leonora MCKELLAR, born about 1883.

Children:

i   John Lewis PRESTON Jr. born about 1920.

295. Audley Rhea ANDERSON born 1881, Sullivan Co., Tennessee?, married Bertha Eleanor SHORT, born about 1881.

Children:

i   Audley Rhea ANDERSON Jr. born about 1910.

296. Joseph Earhart RHEA born 3-Aug-1882, Forney TX, married
(1) 4-Jun-1921, in Pittsburgh, PA, Mabelle Benjamin LARSEN,
born 8-May-1894, Chicago, Cook Co, IL, died 6-Jul-1977,
Chicago, Cook Co, IL, married (2) Jeanette MCNABB, born about
1882, TX? Joseph died 12-Jan-1978, Maywood, IL.

Children:
i   Mabelle Lenox RHEA born 17-Jul-1922, Chicago,
     Cook Co, IL, married 27-Apr-1946, in Chicago,
     Cook Co, IL, Wallace John EWALD, born about 1920.

297. Frank Bland RHEA born 1884, Forney Texas, married Nell
HILL, born about 1884.

Children:
i   Sara Carolyn RHEA born about 1910, TX?

Sixth Generation

298. Margaret Alice WOLFORD born 30-Apr-1867, Texas Co.
Missouri, married (1) 5-Dec-1888, in Texas Co. Missouri, Joshua
Cole DAVIS, born 29-Oct-1849, Clinton Co. KY, died
14-Nov-1906, Texas Co. Missouri, married (2) George HARMON,
who died 1918, Purdin, Linn Co. MO. Margaret died
26-Aug-1955, Little Rock, Pulaski Co. AR.

After the death of her second husband George, she lived near
her children in Cartney and Little Rock ARK.

Children:
i   Edward Earnest DAVIS born 25-Nov-1889, Kennet,
     Dunklin Co. Missouri, died 6-Aug-1890, Kennet,
     Dunklin Co. Missouri.
366. ii   William Rhea DAVIS born 1-Aug-1891.
367. iii   Henry Otis DAVIS born 5-Jun-1893.
iv   Rufus Atley DAVIS born 30-Sep-1895, Bugg,

Hickman Co. KY, died 29-Apr-1920, Kansas City
MO. Married but had no children.

368. v   Mary Carrigan 'Carrie' DAVIS born 2-Apr-1898.

369. vi   Herschel S. DAVIS born 2-May-1900.

299. Rodney Ross WOLFORD born 18-May-1879, Texas Co.
Missouri, married 4-Apr-1904, in Texas Co. Missouri, Cora
Mae SCOTT, born 31-Jul-1881, Brown Co. OH, died Taft, Kings
Co. CA. Rodney died 23-Oct-1940, Texas Co. MO. Twin of
Grace. Started the Wolford Monument Company in Houston Mo.
with his brother Howard. Worked together until 1921. His
grandson operated the business in 1992. Elected Judge of Texas
Co. Court and served a number of years.

Children:

370. i   Verna WOLFORD born 4-Oct-1911.

371. ii   Joseph William WOLFORD born 15-May-1915.

300. Lettie Escott WOLFORD born 28-Feb-1883, Texas Co.
Missouri, married 9-Dec-1914, in Houston, Texas Co. MO,
Walter Clifton URBACK, born 13-Oct-1877, Browning, Linn Co
MO, died 9-Dec-1959, Browning, Linn Co. MO, buried:
11-Dec-1959, Purdin Cemetery. Purdin MO. Lettie died
20-Aug-1949, Manhattan, Riley Co. KS.

Attended Nagle School and Houston Business College graduating
in 1908. 1914 Moved to Linn Co. MO after marriage. Living in
Purdin in 1949. After that berry season, she went to visit her
daughter in Manhattan where she died of a heart attack.

Children:

372. i   Lulu Faye URBACK born 28-Sep-1915.

    ii   Walter Wolford URBACK born 1-Dec-1916, Purdin,
Linn Co. MO, died 1-Aug-1917, Purdin, Linn Co
MO.

373. iii   Alice Marie URBACK born 9-Jul-1919.

301. Howard Frank WOLFORD born 24-Feb-1886, Texas Co.

Missouri, married 11-Apr-1909, in Houston, Texas Co.
Missouri, Eunice Mae STARK, born about 1886, Houston, Texas
Co. Missouri, (daughter of Ephraim STARK and Minnie
SIMMONS) died 4-Sep-1961, Batesville, Independence Co. AR.
Howard died 30-Jun-1960, Batesville, Independence Co. AR.

With his brother started Wolford Monument Company in Houston
Mo. 1913. Moved to Nevada Mo. to work a quarry for marble. In
1921 moved his family to Cartney Ark. There the family lived in
a tent house for a few weeks until they built a regular house. In
1928 they moved to Guion Ark. to be near the quarry and remained
there until 1933 when they move to Batesville 20 miles away for
the better schools. Supplied the marble for the famed Lincoln
Cenotaph in the Lincoln Monument, Oak Ridge Cemetery.
Springfield IL (Abe is buried behind the stone).

Children:

i   Infant WOLFORD born 29-May-1910, Texas Co.
Missouri, died 29-May-1910, Texas Co. Missouri.
Stillborn.

ii   Dana Francis WOLFORD born 12-Mar-1912, Tyrone
MO, died 27-Oct-1914, Nevada MO.

iii   Leonard WOLFORD born 6-Mar-1914, Cabool, Texas
Co. Missouri, married 29-May-1937, in
Batesville, Independence Co. AR, Venita PAINTER,
born 16-Apr-1916, Cassville, Boone Co. MO,
(daughter of Thomas Q. PAINTER and Delphia
TOWE). Leonard died 1-Oct-1933, Batesville,
Independence Co. AR. Graduated Batesville HS
1936. Worked at Wolford Marble Company. Later
flight instructor for Navy Cadets during WWII;
associated with Arkansas College.

374. iv   Inez Hazel WOLFORD born 25-Apr-1917.

375. v   Treva Mae WOLFORD born 25-Mar-1919.

376. vi   Reva WOLFORD born 25-Mar-1919.

vii   Henry Stark WOLFORD born 13-Feb-1921, Houston,
Texas Co. Missouri, died 8-Jul-1921, Houston,
Texas Co. Missouri.

377. viii   William Earnest WOLFORD born 23-Mar-1924.

    ix   Howard Frank WOLFORD born 9-May-1926, Cartney, Baxter Co. ARK. Graduated Batesville HS in 1944. Joined the Navy. At the end of his first year at Arkansas College he and a group of friends went swimming in White River to celebrate the end of school. He dived too deeply in shallow water and hit his head on the bottom. He has been almost totally paralyzed ever since. In 1994 he was in Fort Roots Veterans Administration Hospital, Little Rock Ark.

378. x   Charles Richard WOLFORD born 14-Feb-1929.

302. Jennet 'Jennie' Elizabeth WOLFORD born 1-Oct-1865, Sullivan Co. TN, married Francis Smith HUGHES, born 1-Feb-1857, Pleasant Grove, Jackson Co. ILL, (son of Jerimiah HUGHES and Margaret BIBLE). Jennet died 14-Aug-1938, Marion, Williamson Co. ILL.

Jennie's father William objected to any of his daughters marrying anyone. Jennie was determined and started to ride away on a horse with Smith Hughes. Her father relented and accompanied them to the courthouse in Houston Mo. Jennie's her step-mother was only 14 years older than she.

Children:

379. i   Bert HUGHES born 3-Mar-1888.

    ii   Fred HUGHES born about 1890, ILL?

    iii   Jack HUGHES born about 1892, ILL?

303. Eva Preston RHEA born 25-Feb-1910, Sullivan Co. TN, married 30-May-1938, Claude J. BUCKLES, born 10-Jul-1904, Sullivan Co. TN, died 17-Jul-1968, Sullivan Co. TN.

Graduate of VA Intermount College, King College and East Tennessee State U. Taught school in Sullivan Co. and Bristol City school systems for 30 years.

Children:

380. i   Jane Preston BUCKLES born 11-Feb-1944.

304. Walter Preston RHEA III born about 1910, married. Walter died 1978.

Children:

i   Anne RHEA born about 1940.
ii   Walter Preston RHEA IV born about 1942.
iii   William B. RHEA born about 1944.

305. Henry Sale RHEA born about 1913, married Sara, HARRELL, born about 1913.

Children:

i   Carol Louise RHEA born about 1940.
ii   Maizie RHEA born about 1942.
iii   Henry Sale RHEA Jr. born about 1944.

306. James Taylor RHEA born 29-Apr-1908, married 28-Dec-1933, Louise RALSTON, born 4-Feb-1907. James died 11-Sep-1961.

Children:

381. i   Jill RHEA born 1936.
382. ii   Jacqueline Ralston RHEA born 6-Apr-1938.

307. Katherine Wanshope RHEA born 5-Jul-1911, married 11-Sep-1934, Mayes Lyle WEBB, born 2-Oct-1905.

Children:

383. i   Mayes Rhea WEBB born 13-Jun-1935.
384. ii   John Weber WEBB born 1937.

308. Ellen Preston RHEA born 31-Dec-1918, married 6-Apr-1942, Jasper Leland BARKER, born 15-Jan-1903.

Children:

    i   Mary Josephine BARKER born 5-Feb-1954.

309. Josephine Wauchope RHEA born 5-Jul-1921, married
William Allen THOMAS, born 17-Feb-1922.

Children:

385. i   James Robert THOMAS born 10-Nov-1856.
  ii   William Robert THOMAS born 1951, died
         1951.
  iii   William Allen THOMAS Jr. born 27-Sep-1952.

310. Mary Frances CRAWFORD born 3-Mar-1909 married
3-Sep-1932, Arthur Peter WINFREY, born 20-Dec-1908,
(son of Arthur Peter WINFREY and Harriet 'Hattie' RHEA) died
11-May-1985.

Children:

386. i   Arthur Peter WINFREY III. born 7-Oct-1934.
387. ii   John Crawford WINFREY born 2-Jul-1936.

311. John Kerr CRAWFORD III. born 9-Jun-1914, married
19-Dec-1950, Jean BASS, born about 1914. John died
13-Jun-1952.

Children:

    i   Jean Kerr CRAWFORD born 23-Jul-1952, married
         20-Apr-1985, Donald Carleton LEE, born about
         1952.

312. James Taylor CRAWFORD born 1-Dec-1917, married
14-Dec-1941, Jane Coleman GOWEN, born 1-Aug-1920.

Children:

388. i   Constance Avalyn CRAWFORD born 1943.
389. ii   James Taylor Rhea CRAWFORD Jr. born 1946.
390. iii   Cathryn Ann CRAWFORD born 1953.

313. Elizabeth Weaver RHEA born 30-Aug-1915, married

(1) 3-Feb-1935, Julius Benjamin SUMMERS, born about 1915, married (2) Robert Earl SEIBOLD, born about 1915. Elizabeth died 9-Oct-1978.

Children:
i   Mary Anne 'Bunny' SUMMERS born 10-Aug-1935, married 24-Jun-1955, Ronald W. HARVEY, born about 1935.
ii   Julius Benjamin 'Bud' SUMMERS Jr. born 13-Oct-1938.

314. Karl Byington RHEA born 2-Nov-1931, married 11-Jun-1959, Mary Elizabeth BORUM, born 13-Nov-1937.

Children:
i   Karl Byington RHEA Jr. born 25-Jul-1961, married 7-Dec-1985, Lisa Kay COLEMAN, born 29-Sep-1964.
ii   Robert Howard Matthew RHEA born 27-Apr-1961.
iii   William Scott RHEA born 29-Dec-1967.

315. Robert Preston SHEFFEY born 1868, Washington Co. VA, married wife of Robert SHEFFEY, born about 1856, VA? Robert died 1941, Washington Co. VA, buried: Walnut Grove Cemetery, Washington Co. VA. Inherited Walnut Grove homeplace from his aunt Mary Preston Winston.

Children:
i   Robert Preston SHEFFEY Jr. born about 1880, Washington Co. VA.
ii   Margaret SHEFFEY born about 1884, VA?

316. Don Preston PETERS born 1887, VA?, married Rhetta GHANGH, born about 1887, VA?

Children:
i   Mary PETERS born about 1915, VA?
ii   Don Preston PETERS Jr. born about 1917, VA?

317. Katherine FARMER born 1913, married Dennis CAMPBELL, born about 1918.

Children:
i   William CAMPBELL born 1937.
ii   Dennis Rhea CAMPBELL born 1944.

318. Barclay Donald RHEA born 1914, Nashville, Davidson Co. TN, married wife of Barclay RHEA, born about 1902. Barclay died Pensecola FL?

Children:
i   Barclay Donald RHEA Jr. born about 1930, FL?
ii   William H. RHEA born about 1932, Pensecola FL?

319. Mary Rhea COBB born about 1900, married FRITZ EGGERS, born about 1900.

Children:
i   Rhea EGGERS born about 1930.

320. Jennie Belle TAYLOR born about 1900, married Marshall CROSS, born about 1900.

Children:
391. i   June CROSS born 14-Jun-1936.

321. Mattie Sweeney WINFREY born 25-Feb-1900, married 25-Oct-1919, Junius Galloway WALKER, born 2-Aug-1893, died 1973. Mattie died about 1995.

Children:
392. i   Mary Pricilla WALKER born 4-Mar-1926.
393. ii   Arthur Winfrey WALKER born 24-Jan-1928.
394. iii Elizabeth Winfrey WALKER born 19-Jun-1931.
395. iv Junius Galloway WALKER Jr. born 6-Aug-1934.
396. v   Patsy Louise WALKER born 7-Nov-1935.

322. John Allen WINFREY born 5-Oct-1903, married (1) Betty CULPEPPER, born 1906, died 1944, married (2) Virginia CORBIN, born about 1905. John died 12-Jan-1983.

Children:
i   John Allen WINFREY Jr. born 7-Jun-1929.
ii   Brice Corbin WINFREY born 15-Sep-1949.
iii   Allen Mont WINFREY born 29-May-1955.
v   Roger Rhea WINFREY born 3-Mar-1957, died 1-May-1995.

323. Montgomery Rhea WINFREY born 15-Apr-1906, married Margaret Letitia WILKINSON, born about 1906. Montgomery died 21-Apr-1984.

Children:
i   Whitson Wilkinson WINFREY born 4-Mar-1934.
ii   Mary Margaret WINFREY born 20-Nov-1936.

324. Arthur Peter WINFREY (See marriage to number 310.).

325. William 'Col.' Rhea WINFREY born 1-Sep-1916, married 11-Sep-1945, Marguerite MASON, born about 1916.

Children:
i   William Rhea WINFREY Jr. born 8-Nov-1946.

326. Alpha Josephine RHEA born 1908, Sullivan Co. TN?, married James OLIVER, born about 1908. Alpha died 1983.

Children:
i   Billie Rhea OLIVER born about 1930, married James HOOD, born about 1930.
ii   Nancy Ruth OLIVER born about 1932, Blountville, Sullivan Co. TN, married Chester HOOD, born about 1932. Served as Church Elder in the Blountville Presbyterian Church and as Asst. Sunday School

Superintendent. Retired after 33 years of teaching in
Sullivan Co. and Bristol City schools.

iii   James Graham OLIVER born about 1934, married
Sandra LINKOUS, born about 1934.

327. John Irvin RHEA Jr. born 1910, Sullivan Co. TN?, married
Rosetta HUND, born about 1910.

Children:

i   Mary Judith RHEA born about 1940, married David
WILEY, born about 1940.

328. Sarah Harriet RHEA born 1912, Sullivan Co. TN?, married
Charles TYREE, born 1914, died 1975.

Children:

i   Lillie Kathryn TYREE born about 1940, married
John MCFADDEN, born about 1940.

ii   Pauline Bernice TYREE born about 1942, married
George DEVAULT, born about 1940.

329. Thomas Clarke Rye RHEA born 2-Nov-1914, Sullivan Co.
TN, married 4-Apr-1940, Bobbie BAKER, born about 1914.

Graduated from King College and Louisville Theological
Seminary. He and his brother followed their g-g-g-grandfather
Joseph and became Presbyterian Ministers. Tom was on the board
of trustees for King College for 14 years and received and honorary
doctorate degree there in 1954. In 1982 he was elected moderator
of the Synod of the Mid South. He retired to Louisville KY

Children:

i   Thomas Clarke Rye RHEA Jr. born about 1940,
married Karen HENDRIX, born about 1940.

ii   Robert Peter RHEA born about 1942, married Patti
WILSON, born about 1942.

iii   John Irvin RHEA born about 1944, married
Christine ANTES, born about 1944.

330. Retta Katheryn RHEA born 1917, married Ted Earl TATE, born about 1917.

Children:
i Ted Rhea TATE Jr. born about 1940.

331. Perry Carson COOPER born about 1901, Sullivan Co. TN, married 17-Aug-1921, Ina Jean FICKLE, born 16-Aug-1901, Sullivan Co. TN, (daughter of Samuel Bruce FICKLE and Ellen Akard CROSS) died 28-Apr-1983.

Children:
i Sally Lavine COOPER born about 1891, Sullivan Co. TN, married 29-Apr-1939, Marvin Diggs FICKLE, born 11-Aug-1891, Sullivan Co. TN, (son of Samuel Bruce FICKLE and Ellen Akard CROSS) died 21-Feb-1974, Sullivan Co. TN. Had no children.
397. ii Carl Lee COOPER born 11-May-1908.
398. iii Wanda Blake COOPER born 1-Apr-1922.
399. iv Donald Weems COOPER born about 1925.

332. Edith Thyra GLOVER born 6-Feb-1918, Sullivan Co. TN, married 17-Apr-1938, Ralph MASSEY, born 1 1919, Sullivan Co. TN?, (son of William David MASSEY and Emma Rachel BERRY).

Children:
400. i Danny Rhea MASSEY born 6-Oct-1948.

333. Sarah Winfrey BUTTS born 18-Jan-1919, married 30-Mar-1941, Charles Edwin CROUSE, born 1918.

Children:
401. i Charles Edwin CROUSE Jr. born 20-Sep-1946.
402. ii Karen Rhea CROUSE born 26-Jan-1950.
403. iii Linda Louise CROUSE born 15-Sep-1951.
iv Sarah Lynn CROUSE born 14-Mar-1956, married 7-Jun-1980, Randal Wayne CRIST, born about 1965.

v   James Herman CROUSE born 24-Sep-1957, died
24-Sep-1957.

334. Willouise BUTTS born 24-Jul-1921, married 29-Jun-1946,
George Edgar LUCE, born 28-May-1921.

Children:
404. i   Helen Rhea LUCE born 7-Aug-1947.
    ii   Sarah Louise LUCE born 22-Sep-1950.

335. Frances Adele RHEA born 27-Oct-1916, Mississippi,
married (1) 9-Feb-1938, Richard Hanslow HARRISON, born
1-Apr-1911, died 29-Nov-1989, married (2) 8-Oct-1949, in TN,
James Albert MURPHY, born 10-Aug-1910. Lives in Memphis
1995.

Children:
405. i   Lynn HARRISON born 16-Sep-1941.
406. ii   Richard Hanslow HARRISON Jr. born 23-Jun-1944.
    iii   Gene Lee HARRISON born 25-Feb-1946, Brownwood
        TX, married (1) 20-Jun-1970, Ellen SIMON, born
        about 1946, married (2) 20-Jun-1970, Suzanne
        Marie OLSON, born about 1946. Married twice
        but has no children. Flys search and rescue.
        His father had been living in Leesburg and he
        came to the area and lives there (1995).
        Graduated with degree in electrical engineering
        from Virginia Tech. Works at Mitre Corp.

336. Thomas Edward RHEA born 6-Jan-1920, Mississippi, married
(1) 5-Feb-1944, Helena Annette CARD, born 11-Aug-1918, died
31-May-1990, married (2) 25-Nov-1991, Josephine TOWNSEND,
born 18-Feb-1943.

Received medical training at UT in Memphis. After his time in the
service a friend asked if he would like to come to Oklahoma and
work as the company doctor for Dirks Paper company. Moved to

Oklahoma and also had his own private practice. Lives in Idabell OK (1995).

Children:

407. i   Thomas Edward RHEA Jr. born 1945.
408. ii   Allene Adele RHEA born 23-Sep-1946.
    iii   Catherine RHEA born 28-Jan-1949, died 28-Jan-1949.
409. iv   George Matthew RHEA born 6-Oct-1950.
410. v   Sarah Elizabeth RHEA born 27-Dec-1951.
411. vi   Richard Card RHEA born 20-Feb-1956.
412. vii Herbert Card RHEA born 20-Feb-1956.
413. viii Robert Eugene RHEA born 6-Nov-1958.

337. Stephen Herbert RHEA born 18-Aug-1922, Mississippi, married 7-Sep-1945, Sarah Linda WILLIAMS, born 4-Oct-1923, TN?

General partner of the Private Investment Consortium and president of Rhea Financial Corp. A CPA. Founder of Rhea & Ivy CPA's in 1954. 1973 started SSM Corp., a financial consulting business. Stepped down in 1983. Member of board of trustees of Rhodes College and elder of Second Presbyterian. Church. President of TN Society of CPA's.

Children:

414. i   Stephen Herbert RHEA Jr. born 3-Jul-1949.
    ii   Suzanne McCleish RHEA born 16-Oct-1951, married 30-Mar-1984, Paul BURGAR, born 28-Oct-1948, GA?. 1995 working as PA for 3 kidney specialists in Macon.
    iii   Linda Lavenia RHEA born 8-Jun-1956, died 8-Jun-1956.
    iv   Marilyn Baird RHEA born 31-Aug-1959.

338. James Samuel RHEA born 7-Jun-1913, married 14-Jun-1939, Annie Marie CRAWFORD, born about 1913. James died 24-Jul-1973.

Children:
i   Ann Crawford RHEA born 30-Oct-1940.
415. ii   James Samuel RHEA Jr. born 6-Sep-1943.
416. iii   David Charles RHEA born 18-May-1951.

339. Betty Cross RHEA born 15-Aug-1917, married 28-Nov-1940, Claude Powell SNOWDEN Jr., born 24-Aug-1917.

Children:
417. i   James Wilson SNOWDEN born 27-Jun-1941.
ii   Mary Lou SNOWDEN born 29-Oct-1950.

340. Mary Louise RHEA born 18-Jan-1925, married 17-Nov-1956, Arthur Frank SPENGLER Jr., born about 1925.

Children:
418. i   Sarah Ann SPENGLER born 2-Sep-1957.
ii   Mary Margaret SPENGLER born 22-Aug-1960.

341. Thomas Watkins RHEA born 14-Feb-1910, married 15-Nov-1933, Lillie Boyd HIGHTOWER, born 10-Dec-1909. Thomas died about 1982.

Children:
419. i   Thomas Watkins RHEA Jr. born 28-Nov-1934.

342. Nancy Melinda ANDERSON born 1894, VA?, married John Frank KINCAID, born about 1894, VA?

Children:
i   John Frank KINCAID Jr. born about 1920, VA?

343. John Henderson CALDWELL Jr. born 1882, Bristol, Sullivan Co. TN, married Genevieve RICE, born about 1882.

Children:
i   Margaret Rice CALDWELL born about 1905.

ii   Genevieve CALDWELL born about 1907.

344. Joseph Anderson CALDWELL born 1884, Bristol, Sullivan Co. TN, married Isabella HAWLEY, born about 1884.

Children:
i   Joseph Anderson CALDWELL Jr. born about 1905, Sullivan Co. TN, married Virginia BYARS, born 21-May-1901, (daughter of Cloyd J. BYARS and Jane Preston BAILEY).
ii   John Henderson CALDWELL born about 1907.

345. Charles McKinney PHIPPS born 1877, Sullivan Co. TN, married 14-Jun-1905, in Lovedale Annie Sevier MORRISON, born about 1877.

Children:
i   Mary McKinney PHIPPS born about 1900.
ii   Margaret Sevier PHIPPS born about 1902.

346. James Gaines PHIPPS born 1881, Sullivan Co. TN, married Mabel Sevier MORRISON, born about 1881.

Children:
i   Kenneth Logan PHIPPS born about 1905, Sullivan Co. TN?
ii   James Gaines PHIPPS Jr. born about 1907, Sullivan Co. TN?

347. Annie PHIPPS born 1884, Kingsport, Sullivan Co TN, married 6-Jun-1894, in Sullivan Co. TN, Samuel Lee KING, born 1863, Sullivan Co. TN. Married at her home Rotherwood TN by her grand uncle Rev. Jonathan Bachman.

Children:
i   Samuel Lee KING Jr. born about 1900, Sullivan Co. TN. 2nd Lt. in the Army during WWI. After

going overseas was loaned to Great Britain and
assigned to 21st London Rifles.
ii   John G. KING born about 1902, Sullivan Co. TN?
iii   Charles Logan KING born about 1904, Sullivan Co.
TN?

348. Frances 'Fannie' PHIPPS born 1889, Sullivan Co. TN, married
Arthur S. COSLER, born about 1887.

Children:
i   Arthur S. COSLER Jr. born about 1910.

349. Jonathan Waverly ANDERSON born 1890, Chattanooga
TN, married Dorothy MORGAN, born about 1890.

Children:
i   Dorothy Dulaney ANDERSON born about 1915.

350. John Bachman HYDE born 1890, married Willia FOSTER,
born about 1890.

Children:
i   Rose HYDE born about 1915.

351. John 'Powell' EARHART born 1-Jul-1885, Bristol,
Sullivan Co. TN, married Kate Viola SANDERS, born 1888.

Children:
i   Charles Sanders EARHART born 1914,
Sullivan Co. TN.
420. ii   Lawrence S. EARHART born 29-Aug-1918.

352. Samuel Pearce EARHART born 5-Dec-1887, Blountville,
Sullivan Co. TN, married 16-Jun-1914, in Bristol, Sullivan
Co. TN, Eveleen Bryley MAUK, born 1894, Morristown TN,
(daughter of John Samuel MAUK and Etta MCCRARY) died
1965, Bristol, Sullivan Co. TN. Samuel died 3-Aug-1977, Sullivan
Co. TN.

Traveled a good bit on the railroad. Met Mr. Moore who had leather goods business and became partner. When Moore died Pierce ran the bus. Brother Ralph also worked there at Moore-Earhart Co. on State Street in Bristol. (1900-1976) Manufactured harnesses on second and third floor. Retailed on first floor. Sold shoe fittings and athletic goods. Named after uncle Sam Pearce (husband of Bettsy Roller).

Children:

421. i   Margaret Kathleen EARHART born 24-Nov-1915.
422. ii   Etta Elizabeth EARHART born 1-Mar-1917.

353. Margarita R. EARHART born 1-Apr-1893, Blountville, Sullivan Co. TN, married Archie DOANE, born circa 1900.

Children:

i   Balfer DOANE born circa 1930.
ii   Violet Helen DOANE born circa 1930.

354. Violet Etta EARHART born 29-Oct-1898, Blountville, Sullivan Co. TN, married 22-Apr-1919, James O'dell BOUTON, born 1-May-1893, Emmitt (Sullivan) TN, (son of Daniel Arthur BOUTON and Frances 'Fannie' George ODELL) died 8-Jun-1978, Dennisville, Cape May Co., NJ, buried: 10-Jun-1978, Cold Spring Presbyterian Cape May NJ. Violet died 23-Jul-1949, Sibley Hospital., Washington D.C., buried: Ft. Lincoln Cemetery. Prince George's Co. MD.

Grew up in the family home in Blountville. Her future husband was a teacher at the Rhea's little red schoolhouse across the road from their house. As a young girl she as well as her siblings also attended this school. While James taught there, he lodged at theEarhart home and thus they met. He went back to college, finishing at Kings College and they married and moved to Washington D.C. where he was employed by the US Post Office as an attorney. There they raised their two boys. She died from leukemia.

Children:

423. i   James O'Delle BOUTON Jr. born 20-Apr-1921.

424. ii   Charles Earhart BOUTON born 16-Jun-1930.

355. William Herman EARHART born 1909, Sullivan Co.
TN, married Jamie Gladys KING, born about 1910, Sullivan Co.
TN. Twin of Martha Evalin Earhart.

Children:

i   Betty Ann EARHART born about 1932, Sullivan Co.
TN, married Alden Raymond MALONE, born about 1930.

ii   Peggy Sue EARHART born about 1934, Sullivan Co.
TN, married Barry SUSSMAN, born about 1935.

iii   Donnie Joe EARHART born about 1936, Sullivan Co.
TN, married Linda Ruth WITCHER, born about 1935.

iv   Barbara Kay EARHART born about 1938, Sullivan Co.
TN, married George Edmond WEAVER, born about 1935.

v   Billie Jean EARHART born about 1940, Sullivan Co.
TN, married Howard Lee TESTER, born about 1930.

vi   William Allen EARHART born about 1940, Sullivan
Co. TN, married Patricia 'Patty' Lee RUTTER,
born about 1940.

356. Ella EMERSON born 1895, TX?, married Robert Fitzhugh
NEWSOME, born about 1895, TX?

Children:

i   Robert Fitzhugh NEWSOME Jr. born about 1920, TX?

357. William Joseph RHEA Jr. born 17-Oct-1916, TX?, married
(1) Ida Mae LOWERY, born about 1916, married (2)
23-May-1940, Naomi G. LACY, born about 1916.

Children:

i   James L. RHEA born 1958.

ii   William Joseph RHEA III. born 19-Jun-1941,
married 18-Jun-1960, Nancy TRAVILLION, born about

1941.
iii   John Robert RHEA born 30-Sep-1951, married
      4-Aug-1972, Sonja Jean FLETCHER, born about 1951.
iv   Thomas Groves RHEA born 16-Aug-1953.

358. John Love RHEA born 19-Nov-1891, Tehuncana TX, married
Alma OWENS, born 25-Nov-1893, died 28-Jun-1914. John died
30-May-1946, Little Rock, Pulaski Co. AR, buried: Roselawn
Cemetery. Little Rock AR. Worked at Arkansas-Louisiana Gas
Co. Lived 300 High St. Little Rock Ark. Died of carcinoma of
lung. (Had pneumonectomy in 1955).

Children:
i   Florine RHEA born 3-Feb-1917, TX, married
    6-May-1939, James Maxwell RAILING, born
    2-Oct-1910.

359. Harriet Eleanor CARTRIGHT born 18-May-1900, Bluff City,
Sullivan Co. TN, married 24-Mar-1922, in Chattanooga TN,
Charles Vines WHITE, born 13-Nov-1900, Biltmore NC.

Children:
i   Charles Vines WHITE Jr. born about 1924, married
    28-Dec-1949, Mary Mcclaren COGHLON, born
    7-Dec-1924, Columbia MO.
425. ii   Rhea Jackson WHITE born 5-Feb-1926.
426. iii   Elizabeth Breaux WHITE born 15-Jul-1928.

360. Milburn Jonathan CARTRIGHT born 25-Aug-1914,
married Gertrude KELLY, born about 1914.

Children:
i   Jonathan CARTRIGHT born about 1940.

361. Dorothy Ruth CARTRIGHT born 27-May-1917, married
(1) 3-Sep-1939, Richard Crawford WILBUR, born about 1917,
married (2) 11-Sep-1948, William Wright ANDERSON, born
1917, Rockwood, Roane Co. TN.

Children:
427. i   Martha Lucille WILBUR born 9-Jan-1940.
428. ii   Dickie Ruth WILBUR born 27-Oct-1943.

362. Dorothy Lucille COLE born 20-Mar-1917, Sullivan Co. TN, married 12-Sep-1948, Estien Elkanah RICHARDSON, born 2-Feb-1917, Meadows of Dan, VA.

Children:
i   William Henry RICHARDSON born 13-May-1950, Galax VA, married 9-Aug-1969, Betty Jane NEWMAN, born about 1950.
ii   Ruth Ann RICHARDSON born 1-Feb-1952, Galax VA, married 16-Mar-1974, Gary Thomas GARDNER, born about 1952.

363. Seaton Tinsley PRESTON Jr. born 29-Aug-1921, FL?, married 26-Jul-1945, in Antwerp, Belgium, Aline DEBBAUT, born about 1921, Belgium?

Children:
429. i   Seaton Tinsley PRESTON III. born 19-Jun-1946.
430. ii   Christiane PRESTON born 4-Sep-1947.
431. iii   John PRESTON born 18-Mar-1949.
iv   Thomas PRESTON born 8-Sep-1950.
v   Philip PRESTON born 9-Aug-1956.

364. James Brainard PRESTON born 30-Mar-1923, FL?, married 14-Apr-1951, Cynthia Joan Houghton GLASSEN, born about 1923.

Children:
432. i   Cynthia Houghton PRESTON born 5-Mar-1952.
433. ii   James Brainard PRESTON Jr. born 8-Aug-1954.
iii   Martha Leigh PRESTON born 19-Mar-1960, married 21-Aug-1982, David Michael POWELL, born about 1960.

365. Frederick Leigh PRESTON born 27-Jan-1930, FL?, married 15-Jan-1955, Betty Louise AUMACK, born about 1930.

Children:
	i	Robert James PRESTON born 14-Aug-1916.
434.	ii	Frederick Leigh PRESTON Jr. born 10-Oct-1955.
435.	iii	Linda Louise PRESTON born 23-Oct-1956.
	iv	Rebecca Ann PRESTON born 11-Jun-1964.

Seventh Generation

366. William Rhea DAVIS born 1-Aug-1891, Moody, Howell Co. Missouri, married 18-Mar-1922, in Purdin, Linn Co. MO, Mattie Lou 'Lula' SMITH, born 17-Apr-1895, Browning, Linn Co. MO, (daughter of James Marion SMITH and Frances COTTER). William died 24-May-1964, Little Rock, Pulaski Co. ARK. Died of leukemia.

Rhea attended high school in Cabool Mo. and taught one term in a rural school in Texas Co. Met Lula while visiting his mother and stepfather in Purdin. Rhea and Lula's first home was in Cartney Mo. where he was postmaster and ran a general store. Moved to Little Rock where Rhea founded and ran the Davis Auto Wrecking Co.

Children:
436.	i	Atley Gene DAVIS born 16-Jan-1923.
437.	ii	Miriam Arlene DAVIS born 15-Nov-1925.
438.	iii	Margaret Lee DAVIS born 18-May-1931.

367. Henry Otis DAVIS born 5-Jun-1893, Bugg, Hickman Co. KY, married 1930, in MO?, Anna KING, born 1898, Texas Co. Missouri, (daughter of William KING and Lydia COVERT) died 17-Sep-1987, North Little Rock, ARK. Henry died 7-Nov-1955, North Little Rock, ARK.

Served in US Army during WWI. Joined without parents knowledge hoping to be sent overseas. Entire enlistment was in the US. Spent several years gold prospecting in the Rocky and Sierra Nevada Mountains after he was discharged. With brother Herschel founded Davis Rubber Co. in Little Rock. Traveled selling the products made from used auto tires. Retired in 1950 and went into construction until his death from a heart attack.

Children:
439. i   Jack DAVIS born 18-Feb-1931.
440. ii   James DAVIS born 1-Jun-1936.

368. Mary Carrigan 'Carrie' DAVIS born 2-Apr-1898, Tyrone, Texas Co. Missouri, married (1) 1926, in Cartney, Baxter Co. ARK, Joel Lee PRICE, born about 1898, MO?, died 1935, Little Rock, Pulaski Co. ARK, married (2) Herbert LOVETT, born about 1898, MO? She was struck by a car while crossing the street and never regained consciousness.

Children:
  i   Clyde Lee PRICE born 14-Aug-1924, Texas Co.
          Missouri, married in Tijuana, Baja California,
          Mexico, Glenna NOWLIN, born about 1924, CA?
          Attended Merchant Marine Academy. Sailed as
          first mate on fishing vessels out of San Pedro
          CA after the war. Later earned his Captain's
          license. Now port captain along gulf coast
          supervising the loading and unloading of ships
          in Texas ports. No children.
441. ii   Mary Alice PRICE born 25-Aug-1929.

369. Herschel S. DAVIS born 2-May-1900, Tyrone, Texas Co. Missouri, married 23-Aug-1950, in Little Rock, Pulaski Co. ARK, Barbara FRYER, born 25-Jan-1920, Morrilton, Conway Co. ARK, (daughter of Ray FRYER and Vickie GARRET). Herschel died 7-Nov-1993, North Little Rock, ARK. Married first Tressie who died in 1948.

He and brother started Davis Rubber in Little Rock, a recycling plant for automobile tires. After brother retired, he ran the business alone. Owned a large ranch a few miles north of Little Rock where he bred cattle and sold them to feed lots for finishing. He was also involved in other small businesses including a chain of car wash shops.

Children:

442.i   Steven Ray DAVIS born 9-May-1951.

  ii   Cole Thomas DAVIS born 6-Dec-1952, Little Rock, Pulaski Co. ARK, married 13-Aug-1983, DeAnna Lynn CULVER, born 1-Jul-1958, DesMoines, Iowa.

  iii   Phillip Earl DAVIS born 27-Feb-1956, Little Rock, Pulaski Co. ARK, married 18-Dec-1982, in North Little Rock, ARK, Melissa CINGOLARU, born 6-Nov-1959, Shreveport, Caddo Parish, LA.

  iv   Roger Herschel DAVIS born 25-Jul-1957, Little Rock, Pulaski Co. ARK, married 24-Nov-1984, in Midlothian, Cook Co. ILL, Donna NEIGHBOR, born about 1957.

443.v   Daniel Lee DAVIS born 6-Dec-1958.

370. Verna WOLFORD born 4-Oct-1911, Tyrone, Texas Co. Missouri, married in Houston, Texas Co. Missouri, Cecil BERLIN, born about 1911, MO? Married Cecil first. Divorced and married second Edward.

Graduated from Houston High School about 1929. 1994 lives in Ventura Co. CA.

Children:

444.i   Betty Jane BERLIN born 14-Jul-1933.

371. Joseph William WOLFORD born 15-May-1915, Houston, Texas Co. Missouri, married 21-Sep-1935, in Houston, Texas Co. Missouri, Hattie Jean BURRIS, born 15-Nov-1915, Morrison, Pawnee Co. OK, (daughter of Richard H. BURRIS and Hattie

Christine PENROSE).

Always lived near Houston where Joe worked with his father in the Wolford Monument Co. He ran the business after his father's death until his own son took over in 1980. Joe helps out (1994) in the shop when his son is in the field setting up stones.

Children:

i   Mary Christine WOLFORD born 29-Mar-1936, Houston, Texas Co. Missouri, married 28-May-1954, in Houston, Texas Co. Missouri, Carl Eugene WILLIAMS, born 20-Feb-1933, Plato, Texas Co. Missouri, died 17-Sep-1972, Fort Leonard Wood, Missouri. Graduated from Houston HS 1954. Both she and Carl worked at Fort Leonard Wood Mo. After Carl's death she attended Drury College, Springfield and earned her BS with a major in Business Administration and psychology. Graduated magna cum laude in 1981. Continued to work at the Corp. of Engineers at Ft Leonard Wood, in Memphis, at Vicksburg, Miss. and at St. Louis. Retired from federal service in 1992 after 31 years. Reared a nephew, Darren Wolford. Had no children.

ii   Carol Beatrice WOLFORD born 1-Feb-1940, Houston, Texas Co. Missouri, married 28-Dec-1963, in Houston, Texas Co. Missouri, Gilbert Dean MCPHERSON, born 14-Jul-1919, Ill, died 1-Dec-1987, Whitehall, ILL. Completed BS in elementary education at SW Missouri St. U. and MS in Education from Southern IL. U. Taught at Osage Mo. 2 years. After her marriage she moved to Whitehall, IL and there taught 5th grade ever since. Reared a niece, Stephanie Wolford but had no children of her own.

iii   Robert Bruce WOLFORD born 7-Dec-1943, Houston, Texas Co. Missouri, died 1944,

Springfield, Greene Co. Missouri.

iv   Howard Joseph WOLFORD born 20-Apr-1945,
Springfield, Greene Co. Missouri, married in
Licking, Texas Co. Missouri, Linda Kay HOLADAY,
born 14-Mar-1945, Los Angeles, CA. Spent one
year at Southwest Mo. State U. then 2 years in
the US Army. One year of service was in
Vietnam. He was an M.P. Now an Aircraft
Specialist in the National Guard with rank of
Master Sergeant. Proprietor of Wolford Monument
Co. in Houston. Received a BS from Tarkio
College in Bus. Administration Raised a nephew, Andrew
Wolford. Also adopted one son Jeffrey Dean
Wolford, born 9/3/1976.

445. v   Thomas Eugene WOLFORD born 3-Oct-1947.

446. vi   Steven William WOLFORD born 22-Jul-1956.

372. Lulu Faye URBACK born 28-Sep-1915, Purdin, Linn Co.
MO, married 9-Jan-1946, in Utica, Oneida Co. NY, Charles
Roderick BURTON, born about 1915.

Graduated Purdin HS 1932. BS from Southwest Mo. State U.
1941. MA from Washington U, St. Louis MO 1959. Taught 1 yr.
Gooch School near Purdin. After Pearl Harbor joined Fed. Govt. in
San Antonio TX where she met Charles who was stationed at Fort
Sam Houston. Taught AZ and NY returning to Lawrence KS when
Charles was discharged. After children were in school she taught
Nipher Jr. H. St. Louis Co. MO and Webster Grove HS. Moved
and taught Escondito HS north of San Diego. In 1961 was a
Fulbright Scholar to India, 1965 John Hay Fellow at the University
of Oregon. 1968 received grant to study at the East West Center at
the University of HI. Retired in 1981 and for 5 years enjoyed life of
leisure. At the time of Charles' death they had visited all 50 states
and 63 foreign countries.

She continues to live in San Diego and pursues her hobby of
genealogy. She is a volunteer librarian at two private libraries.

Children:

i   Charlene Rowena BURTON born 13-Nov-1946, Lawrence, Douglas Co. KS, married (1) David Bruce MILLER, born 13-Feb-1943, Naperville, ILL, married (2) William Joseph HAMLIN, born 25-Mar-1934, Deer Lodge, Montana. Graduated Kerney HS in San Diego, CA in 1964 with honors. Earned BS from Whittier College in 1971 and teaching certificate from Washington St. in 1972. Taught 1972-76 at Granite Falls HS. Left for the business world and from 1977 to 1994 was with Motor Trucks, Everett WA where she was systems manager for their computer system. 1994 lived in San Diego.

ii   Richard Roderick BURTON born 7-Oct-1948, Oakland, Alemeda Co. CA, married (1) 13-Jun-1970, in San Diego, CA, Katherine Jean KRASE, born 10-Aug-1951, Cincinnati, OH, married (2) 20-Sep-1992, in Palo Alto, CA, Laura DEYOUNG, born 5-Feb-1954, Manteno, ILL. Graduated from Kearney HS San Diego with honors in 1966. Earned BS at Cal Tech in 1970 and Ph.D. in computer science at U of CA in 1976. Worked 5 years in research dept. of Bolt, Beranel, and Newman, Boston. Joined Xerox, Palo Alto CA as a member of research team in 1978 and worked there 10 years. Began Windrose Consulting after that. Sailing is his favorite sport. Crewed a 40 ft yacht in the Pacific Cup Race in 1994.

373. Alice Marie URBACK born 9-Jul-1919, Purdin, Linn Co. MO, married (1) 2-Dec-1943, in Purdin, Linn Co. MO, Ralph Edward REBER, born 17-Oct-1917, Hiawatha KS, (son of Ralph REBER and Isabel ROBINSON) died 9-Feb-1968, married (2) 22-Oct-1983, in Topeka KS, John CRAGUN, born 12-Jul-1926, MI?, died 5-Mar-1993, Battle Creek, MI.

Attended Purdin HS until the last half of her senior year. Family moved to a farm near Batesville where she graduated in 1936. Taught elementary school in Purdin for 4 years. Worked as typist for Federal Government until her marriage. Lives 1994 in Blue Springs MO.

Children:

447. i   Diana L. REBER born 28-Nov-1946.
448. ii   Theodore 'Ted' REBER born 16-Mar-1951.
    iii   Timothy A. REBER born 12-Jun-1953, Manhattan, Riley Co. KS, married in Topeka, Shawnee Co. KS, Janet GRAVES, born about 1953, KS? 1994 worked for Consolidated Electrical Co. as journeyman electrician in San Antonio TX.

374. Inez Hazel WOLFORD born 25-Apr-1917, Houston, Texas Co. Missouri, married 1-Sep-1940, in Batesville, Independence Co AR, Robert Cotton BREWER, born about 1917, MO?, (son of Archer Lee BREWER and Katherine COTTON).

Graduated from Batesville HS in 1936. When her youngest child started to college she continued her education at Murry State U. in KY receiving a BS in Elementary Education in 1967 and later an MS. Taught 3 years in Paducah then started her own tutoring business.

Children:

    i   David BREWER born 10-Jun-1941, Batesville, Independence Co. AR, died 30-Dec-1983, Paducah, KY, buried: Batesville, Independence Co. AR. Died of brain cancer. Never married. Served in the US Navy for 2 years. His ship serviced planes which flew 'Agent Orange' into battle in Vietnam.
449. ii   Dana BREWER born 24-Apr-1943.
    iii   Robert Warren BREWER born 15-Aug-1944, New Orleans LA.
450. iv   Darlene BREWER born 27-Nov-1945.

375. Treva Mae WOLFORD born 25-Mar-1919, Houston, Texas
Co. Missouri, married (1) 21-Sep-1939, in Cave City, Sharp Co.
ARK, Carmen Cromorta JORDAN, born 11-Sep-1918, Concord,
Clebourne Co. ARK, (son of Grady JORDAN and Mary LONG)
married (2) Mack HUDDLESTON, born about 1819, MO? Twin.

Children:
451. i   Rene JORDAN born 24-Aug-1941.
452. ii   David Mack HUDDLESTON born 3-Mar-1952.

376. Reva WOLFORD born 25-Mar-1919, Houston, Texas Co.
Missouri, married Brockman WINFREY, born about 1919, MO?
Reva died 1-Feb-1980. Married 4 times. 4th husband was
Brockman. She worked for a fashion house in St. Louis and
studied fashion in Paris. Served in the Women's Marine Corps in
WWII and designed uniforms for the Corps.

Children:
453. i   Howard Brockman 'Brock' WINFREY born
         12-Nov-1953.
454. ii   Tamara WINFREY born 9-Dec-1958.

377. William Earnest WOLFORD born 23-Mar-1924, Cartney,
Baxter Co. ARK, married 25-Jun-1949, in Desota, Missouri,
Alice Ann MOTHERSHEAD, born 25-Jun-1930, Desota, Missouri.

Bill graduated from Batesville HS in 1946. Joined Army Transport.
After the war enrolled at Ark. College. Developed marble quarries.
Later manufactured block ice; did land developing and home
construction. Developed Wolfords Addition and Wolfords Quail
Valley in Batesville. Active in St. Paul's Episcopal Church. Lives
(1994) on a 300 acre farm 8 miles east of town.

Children:
455. i   Karen 'Kay' WOLFORD born 1-Nov-1951.
456. ii   Debra WOLFORD born 1-Nov-1951.
457. iii   Ann Alice WOLFORD born 17-Sep-1954.

iv   William Earnest WOLFORD Jr. born 11-Sep-1956,
      Batesville, Independence Co. AR, married (1)
      Kristy LAND, born 4-Mar-1956, Fayette, Chariton
      Co. MO, married (2) 13-Apr-1992, in Eureka
      Springs, ARK, Brenda Kay HAWKINS, born
      24-Apr-1953, Newport, ARK.

378. Charles Richard WOLFORD born 14-Feb-1929, Cartney,
Baxter Co. ARK, married 28-Oct-1957, in Dallas TX, June
Clyde HOLK, born about 1929, ARK?

Served in the Korean War. Graduated from the University of Tulsa
and for 17 years worked for the Ark. Industrial Commission as a
plant location consultant.

Children:
i   Shawna WOLFORD born 17-Feb-1959, Little Rock,
      Pulaski Co. ARK. Attended Batesville public
      schools while living with her uncle and aunt,
      Leonard and Venita Wolford. Finished High
      School in Little Rock. She was married briefly
      and presently (1994) is a single parent living in
      Florida with her daughter Roland June. Works
      as a bartender.

379. Bert HUGHES born 3-Mar-1888, Castle Rock, CO, married
4-Oct-1913, May WESTON, born about 1888, ILL?, died
1-Oct-1957, CA?, buried: National Cemetery. San Francisco CA.
Bert died 1973, Ill, buried: National Cemetery. San Francisco CA.

Served as supply officer in the quartermaster corps in WWI. Was
recalled to active duty in WWII with the rank of Lt. Col. Taught at
HS and Junior College level in Cicero IL for many years. Killed in
an automobile accident in Illinois about 1973.

Children:
458. i   Hallie Jean HUGHES born 7-Dec-1920.
459. ii   Helen HUGHES born 20-Jan-1922.

iii   George HUGHES born 9-May-1930, Western Springs, IL, married Silvia STOVALL, born about 1930.

380. Jane Preston BUCKLES born 11-Feb-1944, Sullivan Co. TN, married 13-Mar-1971, Robert C. HERSCH, born 17-Mar-1941, NC, died 18-Oct-1989, NC. Earned degrees from Univ. of Tennessee Knoxville, George Peabody College of Vanderbilt Univ. and West Ga. College. She, like her mother, is a librarian.

Children:

i   William Preston HERSCH born 14-Jul-1976, Maxton NC.

381. Jill RHEA born 1936, married (1) 1955, Thomas TEAGUE, born 1936, died 1956, married (2) Sherman F. DUDLEY, born about 1936.

Children:

i   Thomas TEAGUE Jr. born 19-Aug-1956.
ii   John Rhea DUDLEY born 29-Oct-1958.
iii   Jacqueline Shaw DUDLEY born 6-Apr-1961.

382. Jacqueline Ralston RHEA born 6-Apr-1938, married 1-Jun-1962, William MCCLEAN, born 1938.

Children:

i   Catherine Rhea MCCLEAN born 1963.
ii   Leigh Moore MCCLEAN born 1964.

383. Mayes Rhea WEBB born 13-Jun-1935, married Polly Ann GOGGIN, born 4-Jul-1934.

Children:

i   Kendrick Rhea WEBB born 1-Sep-1958.
ii   Jane Ann WEBB born 18-Jul-1961.

384. John Weber WEBB born 1937, married 28-Dec-1958, Virginia THOMPSON, born 5-Sep-1939.

Children:
i   John Weber WEBB Jr. born 18-Oct-1962.

385. James Robert THOMAS born 10-Nov-1856, married Matilda E. DICKSON, born 1-Jul-1858, Sullivan Co. TN, (daughter of George R. DICKSON and Sarah MILLER) died 3-Feb-1932.

Children:
460. i   William Mitchell THOMAS born 14-Oct-1883.
ii   Tollie G. THOMAS born 2-Feb-1887, Sullivan Co. TN
iii   Mary E. THOMAS born 1-Aug-1892, Sullivan Co. TN, married 17-May-1915, Sam J. HYDER, born about 1892. Mary died 29-Jan-1984.

386. Arthur Peter WINFREY III born 7-Oct-1934, married 3-Mar-1956, Eleanor Holton MARTIN, born 16-Apr-1934.

Children:
i   Arthur Peter WINFREY IV born 6-Aug-1957.
ii   William Addison WINFREY born 2-Nov-1958.
iii   Frances Holton WINFREY born 6-Feb-1961.
iv   Walter Rhea WINFREY born 27-Sep-1962.

387. John Crawford WINFREY born 2-Jul-1936, married Barbara STRICKLAND, born about 1936.

Children:
i   Mae Millicent WINFREY born 13-Apr-1962.

388. Constance Avalyn CRAWFORD born 1943, married Floyd Stuart BELLET, born 1929.
Children:
i   Ashley Megan BELLET born 1979.

389. James Taylor Rhea CRAWFORD Jr. born 1946, married Mary Pamela MARTIN, born 1948.

Children:
i   Leslie Kate CRAWFORD born 1980.

390. Cathryn Ann CRAWFORD born 1953, married Robert Stratton STAUFFER, born 1952.

Children:
i   Cathryn Elizabeth STAUFFER born 1985.

391. June CROSS born 14-Jun-1936, married 14-Mar-1953, Joseph David MORRELL, born 25-Oct-1929, Bluff City, Sullivan Co. TN, (son of David Edgar MORRELL and Rosa Belle CARRIER).

Children:
i   Jeffrey David MORRELL born 25-Jan-1955, Bluff City, Sullivan Co. TN, married Kathy Marie FRITTS, born about 1955.
ii   Kimberly Susan MORRELL born 12-Sep-1957, Bluff City, Sullivan Co. TN, married Thomas David CONERLY, born 28-May-1953.
iii   Michael Edgar MORRELL born 26-May-1967, Bluff City, Sullivan Co. TN.

392. Mary Pricilla WALKER born 4-Mar-1926, married 3-Sep-1948, Joseph Reeves LOCKE, born 3-Jul-1915.

Children:
i   Pricilla Walker LOCKE born 22-Jan-1952, married Michael L. DANIELS, born about 1952.
ii   Josiah Parker LOCKE born 19-Aug-1953.
iii   Joseph Reeves LOCKE born 31-Oct-1956.
iv   Mark Galloway LOCKE born 11-Jul-1958.

393. Arthur Winfrey WALKER born 24-Jan-1928, married 22-Jun-1950, Myrtle Jo BONE, born 31-Aug-1928.

Children:

i   Arthur Winfrey WALKER Jr. born 23-Sep-1954.
ii   Melanie Jo WALKER born 7-Mar-1957.
iii   Charles Allen WALKER born 9-Sep-1958.
iv   Mark Harmon WALKER born 1961.

394. Elizabeth Winfrey WALKER born 19-Jun-1931, married
5-Dec-1953, Thomas Lyle REID, born 17-Jun-1930.

Children:
i   Louise Elizabeth 'Betsy' REID born 29-Jun-1959.
ii   Martha Lyle REID born 29-Jul-1962.

395. Junius Galloway WALKER Jr. born 6-Aug-1934, married
19-May-1963, Virginia Ann BEARD, born 22-Dec-1940.

Children:
i   Junius Galloway WALKER III. born 11-Nov-1964.

396. Patsy Louise WALKER born 7-Nov-1935, married
18-Jul-1957, Allen Gooch KING, born 20-May-1933.

Children:
i   Allen Gooch King Jr. born 4-Sep-1958.
ii   Jane Winfrey KING born 17-Jun-1960.
iii   John Walker KING born 7-Jan-1964.

397. Carl Lee COOPER born 11-May-1908, Sullivan Co. TN,
married 8-Jul-1923, Lonna Pet FICKLE, born 10-Jan-1904
(daughter of Samuel Bruce FICKLE and Ellen Akard CROSS) died
22-Jun-1991. Carl died 1-Jun-1976, Sullivan Co. TN. Brother of
Perry and Sally.

Children:
i   Herschel Dove COOPER born 29-Nov-1925, Sullivan
        Co. TN, married 12-Oct-1949, in TN?, Eunice
        STEVENS, born about 1925.
461. ii Jacquie Lyn COOPER born 9-Dec-1932.
iii   Aradane Afton COOPER born about 1934, Sullivan

Co. TN, married Sallie BAKER, born about 1934,
TN? Aradane died 30-Dec-1972.

398. Wanda Blake COOPER born 1-Apr-1922, Sullivan Co. TN,
married 26-Sep-1942, in Sullivan Co. TN, Lake C. BARNES,
born 13-Mar-1919, Sullivan Co. TN, (son of Knaff J. BARNES
and Marjorie JOHNSTON).

Children:

462. i   Donna Jean BARNES born 4-Feb-1947.

399. Donald Weems COOPER born about 1925, married Mary
Elizabeth LOONEY, born about 1925, Sullivan Co. TN.

Children:

i   Charles COOPER born about 1950, Sullivan Co. TN.
ii   Paula COOPER born about 1952, Sullivan Co. TN?

400. Danny Rhea MASSEY born 6-Oct-1948, Sullivan Co. TN,
married 17-Mar-1972, in Bristol, Sullivan Co. TN, Vickie Lynn
WHITTAMORE, born about 1948, Sullivan Co. TN. 5th child.
1992 lived in Sanford subdivision which was developed from the
Dulaney farm.

Children:

i   Eric MASSEY born 10-Feb-1974, Sullivan Co. TN.
ii   Amy MASSEY born 5-Oct-1976, Sullivan Co. TN.

401. Charles Edwin CROUSE Jr. born 20-Sep-1946, married
6-Aug-1966, Lolita LARABEE, born about 1946.

Children:

i   Charles Edwin 'Ched' CROUSE III. born
      19-Jun-1970.
ii   Chanda Leigh CROUSE born 8-Dec-1971.
iii   Kevin Larabee CROUSE born 20-May-1973.

402. Karen Rhea CROUSE born 26-Jan-1950, married

21-Aug-1971, David S. HUNT, born about 1950.

Children:
i   Shannon Rhea HUNT born 24-Mar-1978.
ii   Joshua David HUNT born 19-Apr-1980.
iii   Kelly HUNT born 1 1983, died 1983.
iv   Laura Winfrey HUNT born 15-Dec-1983.

403. Linda Louise CROUSE born 15-Sep-1951, married 15-Jun-1974, Walter Louis COOK, born about 1951.

Children:
i   Jennifer Karen COOK born 27-May-1978.
ii   Walter Louis 'Luke' COOK Jr. born 5-Feb-1980.
iii   Hannah Louise COOK born 26-Jul-1981.
iv   Rhea Lynn COOK born 10-Jan-1983.

404. Helen Rhea LUCE born 7-Aug-1947, married 13-Sep-1969, Edwin Paul COPPEDGE, born 1947.

Children:
i   George Laurence COPPEDGE born 26-Oct-1975.

405. Lynn HARRISON born 16-Sep-1941, Tampa Fl, married 20-Jun-1962, in Charlottesville, VA, Donald Wayne GARDNER, born 20-Apr-1935, VA?

Worked at State Farm Insurance as a loss prevention specialist in 1995. Had gone to nursing school in Charlottesville VA and there met her husband.

Children:
463.i   Stephen Allen GARDNER born 7-Oct-1964.
ii   David Todd GARDNER born 19-Jun-1967, VA?, married 27-Jul-1991, Christine Marie STURM, born 10-Apr-1966. Majored in anthropology at Mary Washington College in Fredricksburg VA.

406. Richard Hanslow HARRISON Jr. born 23-Jun-1944, Louisiana, married 30-Jun-1972, Ellen Doris Katharina STEGLICH, born 17-Oct-1947, Germany.

Had fellowship at Purdue. Had received engineering degree at Virginia Tech. Works as a systems production manager for Baltimore Aircoil.

Children:
i   Mark Gotthard HARRISON born 6-Apr-1976.

407. Thomas Edward RHEA Jr. born 2 1945, married (1) 1-May-1966, Donna Fern THOMAS, born 12-Jul-1947, married (2) 28-Nov-1981, Karen Patricia EVANS, born 1948. Retired from the US Navy on 30 September 1993 at Norfolk VA. Served for 20 years. Works at Micromax, a computer manufacturing company. Active in Church of the Ascension (Episcopal).

Children:
i   Thomas Edward RHEA III. born 29-Jan-1972.
ii   Lynnette Frances RHEA born 28-Jan-1977.

408. Allene Adele RHEA born 23-Sep-1946, married 1-Jun-1967, Johnnie Dale GRIMES, born 17-Oct-1947.

Children:
464. i   Rachel Lenette GRIMES born 28-Oct-1969.
ii   Katherine Allene GRIMES born 19-Jul-1972.
    Married on June 24, 1995
iii   Rebecca Jane GRIMES born 16-Apr-1972.
iv   Victoria Rhea GRIMES born 12-Oct-1983.

409. George Matthew RHEA born 6-Oct-1950, married 14-Aug-1971, Gail Anita RUSSELL, born 24-Nov-1949.

Children:
i   April Anita RHEA born 12-Oct-1977.

ii   Stephen Matthew RHEA born 13-Jun-1983.

410. Sarah Elizabeth RHEA born 27-Dec-1951, married 19-May-1973, Robert James WHITE, born 22-Apr-1951, Smithville, Dekalb Co. TN? 1995 works at Dekalb Co. Hospital.

Children:
i   Elizabeth Adele WHITE born 23-Aug-1976, Smithville, Dekalb Co. TN.
ii   James Harrison WHITE born 2-Apr-1980, Smithville, Dekalb Co. TN.
iii   John Rhea WHITE born 8-Sep-1983, Smithville, Dekalb Co. TN.

411. Richard Card RHEA born 20-Feb-1956, OK?, married 30-Oct-1981, Lanney Louise COOPER, born 20-Feb-1957.

Children:
i   Amy Elizabeth RHEA born 30-Jan-1983.
ii   Bradley Adam RHEA born 26-Sep-1985.
iii   Amanda LeeAnn RHEA born 14-Jul-1987.
iv   Melissa Annette RHEA born 9-Jan-1990.

412. Herbert Card RHEA born 20-Feb-1956, VA?, married 4-Dec-1976, Nellie LaVonne FRY, born 9-Oct-1955, VA? Twin.

1994 moved to Jenks OK, a suburb of Tulsa. Working as athletic trainer for Jenks Public Schools.

Children:
i   Joshua Glen RHEA born 1-Dec-1980. Confirmed in the Episcopal Church at Hollins College, Roanoke VA in 1994.
ii   Ashley Marie RHEA born 8-Mar-1984.

413. Robert Eugene RHEA born 6-Nov-1958, married 1-Aug-1981, Lisa Jane MARTIN, born 19-Aug-1960.

Children:

i   Alexander Samuel RHEA born 29-Jul-1992, Nashville, Davidson Co. TN.

414. Stephen Herbert RHEA Jr. born 3-Jul-1949, married 6-Mar-1982, Leigh SCHOPFER, born 20-Mar-1952.

Children:

i   Emily Keith RHEA born 7-Nov-1983.

ii   Elizabeth Leigh RHEA born 29-May-1986.

415. James Samuel RHEA Jr. born 6-Sep-1943, married 7-Apr-1966, Rebecca Lee OZIER, born 22-Jun-1944.

Children:

i   Lee Ann RHEA born 24-Dec-1968.

ii   Jamie Rebecca RHEA born 17-Nov-1972.

iii   Samantha Courtney RHEA born 2-Sep-1983.

416. David Charles RHEA born 18-May-1951, married 16-Aug-1974, Mary Patricia RILES, born about 1951.

Children:

i   David Charles RHEA Jr. born 16-Aug-1980.

ii   Chad Alan RHEA born 4-Feb-1986.

417. James Wilson SNOWDEN born 27-Jun-1941, married 15-Feb-1963, Betty Lou WHITE, born about 1941.

Children:

i   Any Denise SNOWDEN born 9-Dec-1963.

ii   James Wilson SNOWDEN Jr. born 25-Dec-1972.

418. Sarah Ann SPENGLER born 2-Sep-1957, married Allen Lee JANKE, born about 1957.

Children:

i   Zachary Arthur JANKE born 29-Sep-1984.

419. Thomas Watkins RHEA Jr. born 28-Nov-1934, married
13-Jun-1958, Suzanne MARSHALL, born 17-Jan-1940.

Children:
i   Susan Blanche RHEA born 12-Sep-1962, married
       14-May-1983, William Selby KENNEDY V, born
       13-Jul-1960.
ii   Martha Boyd RHEA born 17-Sep-1964.

420. Lawrence S. EARHART born 29-Aug-1918, Bristol, Sullivan
Co. TN, married Lynda, born about 1918. Lawrence died
19-Apr-1974, Sullivan Co. TN.

Children:
465. i   Robert Joseph EARHART born 1956.
ii   Charles Phillip EARHART born 1956,
       Bristol, Sullivan Co. TN. Twin.

421. Margaret Kathleen EARHART born 24-Nov-1915,
Blountville, Sullivan Co. TN, married June 1939, Theodore Dale
'Col.' PERRY, born circa 1920.

Children:
466. i   James Samuel 'Dr.' PERRY born circa 1950.
ii   Margaret Louise 'Meg' PERRY born about 1950,
       Sullivan Co. TN, died Arlington VA. Died at
       age 8.

422. Etta Elizabeth EARHART born 1-Mar-1917, Bristol,
Sullivan Co. TN, married 12-Apr-1936, in Elizabethton TN,
Ford Monroe CALDWELL, born 1914, Giles Co. VA, (son of
Archibald CALDWELL and Neva FRANCUM).

In 1935 as a senior at Bristol TN HS she fell in love with a football
hero from King College, 'Race Horse' Caldwell. He came to King
College from Crosspore NC in 1933. He worked at Moore-Earhart

for 38 years. At Rhea family reunion in 1932, modeled Elizabeth McIlwain's wedding dress (now in Rocky Mount NC Museum). A picture from that day is in 'Families and History of Sullivan Co., 1992.

Children:
467. i   Harriet Ann CALDWELL born 29-Jul-1937.
468. ii   Joyce Eveleen CALDWELL born 5-Sep-1940.
469. iii   Ford 'Buddy' CALDWELL Jr. born 31-Mar-1947.

423. James O'Delle BOUTON Jr. born 20-Apr-1921, Washington D.C., married 30-Jun-1949, in Washington D.C., Erin CONNOR, born 11-Jul-1923, Greenwood SC, (daughter of Hix CONNOR and Erin Cleora HIPP). James died 7-Mar-1995, North Myrtle Beach, Horry Co. SC, buried: Ft. Lincoln Cemetery. Prince George's Co. MD.

Family lived in Langdon section of Washington DC off Mills Av. where he was born. When he was 4 they left their upstairs rented portion of that house and moved to their own home on Monroe St. in Wash. DC. Grew up in Washington D.C.

Each summer the family would travel back to the Holston Valley area of East Tennessee to visit with Jim's mother's family. Many family photographs show Jim as a young boy in East Tennessee during these visits including one where at the age of 2 he is feeding the chickens with grandma Emma Powell Earhart.

Graduated from McKinley High School in Washington DC January 31, 1941. Attended American University in Washington DC February 1941 to June 1942. Completing a year before he was drafted in the Army.

Entered Army June 23, 1942 as a private and was discharged from AAA School Company, Davis NC as a Corporal December 12, 1942. Serial Number 33191739. He immediately entered service on December 23, 1942 for Officers Training School.

Commissioned 2nd Lt. in Anti-Aircraft Artillery OCS, 1942.
Instructor AAA School at Camp David NC April 1943 through
May 1944. Platoon Officer in AAA and Infantry May 1944
through June 1945. Commanded approximately 200. Special
Service Officer June 1945 through 1946. During his service,
made 5 trips on ship to European ports aboard troop
transport. He was finally discharged from active service as
a Captain on August 1, 1946 at the Fort Meade Separation
Center in Maryland. His serial number then O-1048687.

August 1946 to 20 November 1950 worked as Postal Clerk at
the main US Post Office in Washington D.C.

From February 1947 through June 1950 attended Benjamin
Franklin University in Washington DC at night. Completed
the required courses including Commercial Law, Accounting
and Economics to earn a BS in 1950 while working at the post
office during the day.

Met his wife Erin on blind date arranged by friends. Married June
30, 1949 in a simple ceremony due to the illness of his mother who
died the following month. Using veterans benefits, bought their first
home at 2106 Woodberry St. Hyattsville MD.

November 21, 1950 to August 19, 1951 worked in Washington
DC, US Army Department, Ordinance Requirements Branch as a
Supply Requirements Clerk.

August 19, 1951 through August 30, 1952 was a Supply
Requirements Analyst. Assembled audits, prices and
availability of major ordinance items.

August 31, 1952 through April 10, 1953 was a Supply
Assistant, GS-8 for the Army. Responsible for reviewing and
analyzing supply data and making recommendations pertaining
to Army programs concerning ordinance in foreign nations.
Office in Washington DC.

April 1953 promoted to General Supply Assistant.
Assisted in control of the guided missile section stock of
ordinance.

April 1959 became a civilian General Supply Officer
and later for US Army. Worked under the Chief of NICP
Management providing staff supervision and direction in the
supply management activities of field installations.
Primarily involved in the Guided Missile and Special Weapons
section.

February 1963 a Major Item Program Manager for U.S. Army HQ.
Responsible for he coordination and administration of
various phases of material readiness- procurement schedules,
program authorizations, financial management for military
electronics, mobility equipment, weapon systems, ammunition
and missiles used by the US Army.

On April 15, 1978 after 32 years of Civil Service he retired
from his position at the HQ US Army Material Development and
Readiness Command, 5001 Eisenhower Av., Alexandria VA. His
last position, Supply Management Representative.

In 1978 moved to North Myrtle Beach SC to a home they designed
on the second fairway of Robbers Roost Golf Course where they
enjoyed many years of travel, golf, friends and relaxation earned
from these years of work.

February 1994 he suffered a heart attack. Although he had
reduced heart function, through good diet and exercise, he
achieved a higher level of health and energy in 1994 than he
had for many years previously. However, on March 7, 1995
after awaking that morning, he collapsed stricken by a heart
attack which took his life.

Services were held at the Trinity Methodist Church in North
Myrtle Beach. He now rests with his mother and youngest
daughter at Fort Lincoln Cemetery, Maryland.

Children:
470. i   Janet Erin BOUTON born 3-Jun-1953.
    ii   Sandra Louise BOUTON born 16-Aug-1955,
         Washington D.C., died 20-Oct-1958, Prince
         George's Co. MD, buried: Ft. Lincoln Cemetery. Prince
         George's Co. MD. Died of liver disease.

424. Charles Earhart BOUTON born 16-Jun-1930, Washington
D.C., married in Washington D.C., Carol WHITCRAFT, born
5-Aug-1930.

Went to McKinley High School with Carol. Charlie went to U. of
Maryland and Carol to American U. Through ROTC, he became
attached to the Airforce and was stationed in NM where Mark was
born. Returning to Wash DC after service they lived on N.H. Av.
and he worked at Naval Ordinance Lab. Attended George
Washington U at night for Law Degree. Went to work for Swift
Foods Co. and after obtaining degree was transferred to IL where
he worked for Swift and its sucessor company unitl he retired.
They now live in Florida.

Children:
471. i   Mark Earhart BOUTON born 10-Sep-1953.
472. ii   Leslie Ann BOUTON born 5-Mar-1956.
473. iii   Clare Lynn BOUTON born 9-Oct-1961.

425. Rhea Jackson WHITE born 5-Feb-1926, Chattanooga TN,
married 18-Sep-1954, Joe Ketchin MCALPHINE, born about
1926, Union SC.

Children:
    i   Tirzah Laurens WHITE born about 1955.
    ii   James Jackson WHITE born about 1957.
    iii   John Kelly WHITE born about 1959.

426. Elizabeth Breaux WHITE born 15-Jul-1928, Chattanooga
TN, married Milton Randolph BUNDSCHU, born about 1922.

Children:
i   Milton Randolph BUNDSCHU Jr. born about 1850.
ii   Patricia Breaux BUNDSCHU born about 1952.
iii   Katherine Marie BUNDSCHU born about 1958.

427. Martha Lucille WILBUR born 9-Jan-1940, Rockwood, Roane CO TN, married 19-Dec-1959, in Rockwood, Roane CO TN, Donald H. RENEGAR, born about 1940.

Children:
i   Amy Lucille RENEGAR born 10-Jan-1960, Anaheim CA.
ii   William Lawson RENEGAR born 1-Apr-1970, Santa Fe, CA.

428. Dickie Ruth WILBUR born 27-Oct-1943, married (1) 1960, Rolland Eugene MCCULLOUGH, born about 1943, married (2) 1967, Paul Douglas THOMAS, born about 1943, married (3) 1962, Thomas Lynn MARTIN, born about 1943.

Children:
i   Paul Anthony THOMAS born 5-Nov-1961. First named David Eugene McCullogh. Later adopted by Paul Thomas and name legally changed.
ii   William Mark THOMAS born 20-Jan-1968.
iii   Virginia Ruth THOMAS born 29-Dec-1963. Originally named Virginia Ruth Martin, later adopted by Paul Thomas and name legally changed.

429. Seaton Tinsley PRESTON III born 19-Jun-1946, married 6-Sep-1975, Anita HULEFELD, born about 1946.

Children:
i   Anne Katherine PRESTON born 29-Apr-1979.
ii   Robert Tinsley PRESTON born 20-Apr-1982.
iii   Susanna Debbaut PRESTON born 2-Dec-1983.

430. Christiane PRESTON born 4-Sep-1947, married about 1980,

William WALKER, born about 1947.

Children:
i   Colin WALKER born 15-Jul-1981.

431. John PRESTON born 18-Mar-1949, married 28-Oct-1972, Sean OTIS, born about 1949.

Children:
i   Patrick PRESTON born 17-Sep-1977.
ii   Tommy PRESTON born 23-Apr-1981.

432. Cynthia Houghton PRESTON born 5-Mar-1952, married 2-Feb-1974, Erwin Jay PINKHAM, born about 1952.

Children:
i   Matthew Owen PINKHAM born 30-Aug-1975.
ii   Jessica Heather PINKHAM born 30-Jun-1980.

433. James Brainard PRESTON Jr. born 8-Aug-1954, married 24-Aug-1974, Peggy Anne SMOYER, born about 1954.

Children:
i   Andrew James PRESTON born 19-Dec-1979.
ii   Scott Roy PRESTON born 23-Feb-1984.

434. Frederick Leigh PRESTON Jr. born 10-Oct-1955, married 11-Oct-1980, Corrima SMITH, born about 1955.

Children:
i   Melissa PRESTON born 27-Feb-1982.

435. Linda Louise PRESTON born 23-Oct-1956, married 23-Oct-1956, Charles SNYDER, born about 1956.

Children:
i   JoAnn SNYDER born 16-Jun-1980.
ii   Cynthia SNYDER born 9-Jan-1982.

Eighth Generation

436. Atley Gene DAVIS born 16-Jan-1923, Cotter, Baxter Co.
ARK, married 11-Mar-1945, in Little Rock, Pulaski Co. ARK,
Sarah Elizabeth 'Betty' CLEAVER, born 27-May-1925, Little
Rock, Pulaski Co. ARK.

Graduated from Little Rock Central HS and Little Rock Jr. College
before enlisting in the Army Air Corps. After his discharge he
worked with his father in Davis Wrecking Co. In 1950's he
transformed it into a manufacturing and truck equipment
distribution business (Davis Trailer and Equip. Co.) Later began
collecting antique cars.

Children:
i   Diane Elizabeth DAVIS born 10-Feb-1946, Little
       Rock, Pulaski Co. ARK, married (1) Gary
       WALQUIST, born 10-Dec-1943, ARK?, died
       14-Feb-1976, Little Rock, Pulaski Co. ARK,
       married (2) 7-Jan-1977, in Little Rock, Pulaski
       Co. ARK, George Edward PETERS, born about 1946,
       ARK? Teaches government at Little Rock
       Central High (1994).
474. ii   Debra Lee DAVIS born 24-Aug-1948.
iii   Rhea Edward DAVIS born 23-Jun-1951, Little
       Rock, Pulaski Co. ARK. Graduated from Little
       Rock HS. Received BS from U. of Ark. in computer
       science. Worked for Arkansas Power and Light
       and Dillards Department Store. Moved to Dallas and
       worked as computer analyst for Neiman-Marcus,
       then to Conway Ark for Axiom Corp. 1994 lived
       in Little Rock.

437. Miriam Arlene DAVIS born 15-Nov-1925, Cartney, Baxter
Co. ARK, married 1-Aug-1945, in Little Rock, Pulaski Co.

ARK, Eldon Eugene DENT, born 3-Jul-1918, Crane, Missouri, (son of Thomas DENT and Bessie MYERS) died 12-Jun-1990, Dallas TX. Miriam died 16-Sep-1970, St. Louis, Missouri, buried: Roselawn Cemetery, Little Rock AR.

She graduated from Little Rock Central HS, and attended Little Rock Jr. College for 1 year then graduated from U. of Chicago. Died of Leukemia.

Children:
i   Rebecca Ann 'Becky' DENT born 14-Dec-1946, Little Rock, Pulaski Co. ARK. Works for Burlington Northern Railroad.
475. ii   Laura Sue 'Susie' DENT born 13-Sep-1948.
476. iii Donna Jean DENT born 22-Aug-1951.
iv   Thomas Oliver DENT born 17-Oct-1953, Little Rock, Pulaski Co. ARK.

438. Margaret Lee DAVIS born 18-May-1931, Little Rock, Pulaski Co. ARK, married 23-Dec-1957, in Little Rock, Pulaski Co. ARK, Richard Menifee MOOSE, born 2-Feb-1932, Jacksonville ARK.

Graduated from Little Rock Central HS and Barnard College NYC. She studied drama and went on to the NYC Playhouse, a school of drama. She is the author of the novel 'Happy Days'.

Children:
477. i   Jeffrey Menifee MOOSE born 29-Nov-1958.
ii   Amanda Davis MOOSE born 10-Jul-1963, Alexandria VA. Graduated Wesleyan College, CT. Now creative director for a film production company in Los Angeles CA. Once worked as an assistant to Robert Redford in Sun Valley Idaho.

439. Jack DAVIS born 18-Feb-1931, Little Rock, Pulaski Co. ARK, married (1) 25-Jun-1952, Marley Jo HOLMES, born 1932, ARK?, married (2) 1976, Linda HUMBLE, born about 1931,

ARK?, married (3) 1978, Patricia Ann BURNEY, born about 1931, ARK?

Attended Little Rock HS and U. of Ark. Received a degree in mechanical engineering. In 1955 he organized his own construction company.

Children:
478. i   Lucinda Kay DAVIS born 17-Sep-1953.
479. ii   Granger William DAVIS born 7-Sep-1956.

440. James DAVIS born 1-Jun-1936, Little Rock, Pulaski Co. ARK, married 25-Aug-1957, June Ellen WHITE, born about 1936.

Earned degree from Hendrix College and MD degree from U. of Ark. First practiced in Salem Ark. Later built and operated with June, a clinic in Mt. Ida Ark. In Feb. 1993 they sold the clinic to St. Joseph's Hospital in Hot Springs.

Children:
480. i   Mark Stuart DAVIS born 27-Oct-1959.
     ii   Clark Steven DAVIS born 19-Dec-1960, Little Rock, Pulaski Co. ARK, married 21-Jul-1984, in Conway, ARK, Karen BALLARD, born about 1960, ARK? Works for Ciba-Geigy as a research and production chemist. Ph.D. from Texas A&M in 1989.
481. iii James Nathan DAVIS born 12-Jun-1963.

441. Mary Alice PRICE born 25-Aug-1929, Pickeran Hill, Pulaski Co. ARK, married Carl Edwin HEIZMAN, born about 1940, ARK?, died 1982, Little Rock, Pulaski Co. ARK.

Earned BA at U of Ark. in French and social studies. Taught US History and French for several years. She was State Information and Crusade Director for the American Cancer Society and later Executive Directory of the Central Ark chapter of the March of Dimes. 1994 Marketing Director of Woodland Heights Retirement Center in Little Rock.

Children:
482.i   Angela HEIZMAN born 16-Jun-1953.
483.ii   Eric HEIZMAN born 5-Jul-1955.

442. Steven Ray DAVIS born 9-May-1951, Little Rock, Pulaski
Co. ARK, married 21-Jul-1979, in Kermit, Dunklin Co.
Missouri, Sharon Diane DEAN, born 8-Aug-1956, St. Louis,
Missouri.

Did undergraduate work at Vanderbilt U. and earned law degree at
Texas U., Austin.

Children:
i   Rachel Amber DAVIS born 15-Jun-1980, MO?
ii   Elizabeth Marie DAVIS born 27-Sep-1985, MO?

443. Daniel Lee DAVIS born 6-Dec-1958, Little Rock, Pulaski
Co. ARK, married 26-Aug-1978, in Conway, ARK, Judith
TAYLOR, born 19-Jul-1958, Conway, ARK.

Children:
i   Alexander Herschel DAVIS born 8-Mar-1979,
      Conway, ARK.
ii   Christopher Lee DAVIS born 26-Apr-1984, Conway,
      ARK.

444. Betty Jane BERLIN born 14-Jul-1933, Houston, Texas Co.
Missouri, married 13-Dec-1949, in Las Vegas, NV, Robert F.
YOUNG, born about 1932, MO? 1994 working with the Food
Bank in Ventura Co. California. Planned to retire in 1994.

Children:
i   Jeannine YOUNG born 29-Oct-1951, Bakersfield,
      CA, married Glenn Patrick YOUNG, born about 1951,
      CA?
484.ii   Robert C. YOUNG born 12-Dec-1952.
485.iii   Jeanette YOUNG born 11-Apr-1961.

486. iv   John YOUNG born 13-Feb-1961.
487. v   Donald Edward YOUNG born 11-Jul-1964.
488. vi   Terri YOUNG born 1966.

445. Thomas Eugene WOLFORD born 3-Oct-1947, Waynesville, Missouri, married 13-Apr-1969, in Billings, Montana, Thelma Diana UTKE, born about 1947, Montana?

Graduated from Southwest Missouri St. U. in 1969 and was commissioned a 2nd Lt. in the US Army. Served 2 years in Vietnam. Taught mathematics at Seymur Mo. Lived in St. Charles MO 2 years and now is in the US Army Reserves with the rank of Captain. Lives in 1993 in Olive Branch, Miss. and is in the paper products business.

Children:
i   Bryan Thomas WOLFORD born 23-Jan-1972, Charles, Missouri. Graduated from Air Force Academy June 1993.
ii   Laurie Ann WOLFORD born 29-Aug-1973, Charles, Missouri.
iii   Mark Kilpatrick WOLFORD born 17-Jul-1975, Charles, Missouri?
iv   Melanie Gail WOLFORD born 17-Jun-1977, Olive Branch, DeSoto Co., Miss.
v   James Christopher WOLFORD born 25-May-1982, Olive Branch, DeSoto Co., Miss.

446. Steven William WOLFORD born 22-Jul-1956, Cabool, Texas Co. Missouri, married 10-Oct-1976, in Almagardo, Mexico, Rochelle Bettina REIS, born about 1956, Mexico?

Graduated from Houston HS in 1974. Worked in grocery store then joined the US Air Force. Attended college while in the Air Force. 1994 a pharmaceutical specialist working for the Veterans Administration in San Antonio TX.

Children:

i   Stephanie WOLFORD born 8-Feb-1979, George Air Force Base, San Bernadino CA.

ii   Darren WOLFORD born 22-Aug-1982, Wiesbaden, Germany.

iii   Andrew WOLFORD born 15-Nov-1983, San Antonio, TX.

447. Diana L. REBER born 28-Nov-1946, Manhattan, Riley Co KS, married in Topeka, Shawnee Co. KS, James FERGUSON, born 12-Aug-1947, Topeka, Shawnee Co. KS.

Graduated Topeka HS in 1965. Received BS from Central Mich. U, MBA from Texas U. Taught Junior HS in Saginaw Mich. and HS in San Antonio. Took job at San Antonio Savings and Loan working up to VP of Personnel Training before retiring to become a full time mother in 1986.

Children:

i   Kenneth Edward FERGUSON born 28-Jan-1984, San Antonio, TX.

ii   Clare Marie FERGUSON born 2-Feb-1986, San Antonio, TX.

448. Theodore 'Ted' REBER born 16-Mar-1951, Manhattan, Riley Co. KS, married (1) Cynthia Sue NEILL, born 27-Nov-1951, Topeka, Shawnee Co. KS, married (2) 7-Dec-1991, in Kansas City KS, Linda Althea 'Lin' ELZEY, born 15-Feb-1949, Hutchinson, KS. Employed by Dit-MCO in Kansas City for 10 years (1994).

Children:

i   Christopher Andrew REBER born 20-Apr-1977, KS.

ii   Shonda Rene REBER born 11-Sep-1979, KS.

iii   Rebecca Ann REBER born 27-Nov-1982, KS.

449. Dana BREWER born 24-Apr-1943, Memphis TN, married in Clarksburg, Lewis Co. WV, David Richard JACKSON, born about 1943, WV?

Graduated from Reidland HS, Paducah KY in 1961, 3rd in her class. BS in home economics in 1965 from Murray State U, Murray KY. Taught Home Economics at Emmerson HS, Gary IND. 1967 resigned to become a Pioneer, full-time volunteer Bible Education as one of Jehovah's witnesses. Sent to Russel KS. There pioneered and supported herself teaching chemistry and biology half day. Assigned to Weston WV where she met David in 1973 an elder in the congregation.

Children:
i   Derek JACKSON born 6-Oct-1976, Kingwood, WV.
ii   Darren JACKSON born 22-Jan-1979, Kingwood, WV.
iii   Douglas JACKSON born 13-Nov-1980, Kingwood, WV.

450. Darlene BREWER born 27-Nov-1945, New Orleans LA, married 1971, in Bowling Green, Warren Co. KY, Kenneth Wayne LAMB, born 3-Feb-1942, Bowling Green, Warren Co. KY.

Graduated from Redland HS, Paducah KY. Received limited scholarship to Murray State where she received BS in music. MS in Exceptional Education from Western KY U in 1989. Taught music at Cocoa Elementary School. 1970 moved to Bowling Green where she continued Pioneering as a Jehovah's Witness until the birth of her first child in 1975. 1987 returned to College and began teaching special education at Russelville HS.

Children:
i   Eric Wayne LAMB born 20-Oct-1975, Bowling Green, Warren Co. KY.
ii   Evan Todd LAMB born 28-May-1979, Bowling Green, Warren Co. KY.
iii   Zachary David LAMB born 7-May-1985, Nashville, Davidson Co. TN.

451. Rene JORDAN born 24-Aug-1941, Batesville, Independence Co. AR, married Donna Joyce HARRISON, born 21-Aug-1941,

Neb.?

Earned BS in mathematics from U. of Ark 1963. Teaching
certificate from U. of Utah 1964. Taught for 4 years and earned
MS in Library Science from Emporia State U. Taught library
science at Kansas State before becoming Director of the
Clinch-Powell Regional Library of Clinton TN in 1973. 3 years later
became head of Branch Services at Knoxville TN public library and
since 1982 has been head of Technical Services. Edits 'Tennessee
Ancestors' the genealogical Journal of East TN Historical Society.

Children:
i   Carol Jean JORDAN born 4-Aug-1964, KS.
     Adopted.
ii   Seth Michael JORDAN born 16-Mar-1965, KS.
iii   Jill Sharon JORDAN born 4-Jan-1967, KS.
iv   Matthew Rhea JORDAN born 25-Oct-1971, KS.
v   Chad Austin JORDAN born 25-Oct-1971, KS.
vi   Benjamin Rene JORDAN born 24-May-1973, KS.

452. David Mack HUDDLESTON born 3-Mar-1952, Batesville,
Independence Co. AR, married Pam BROWN, born 7-Jul-1956,
Pine Bluff, ARK.

Earned BS in business administration from Ark State U. 1974.
Insurance underwriter with USF&G Insurance Co. in Little Rock
for 5 years. Since 1979 worked for Cashion Co., an insurance
company, as Vice President. Lives in Sherwood Ark. (1992).

Children:
i   Justin Hugh HUDDLESTON born 10-Jan-1981, ARK.
ii   David Grant HUDDLESTON born 2-Feb-1984, ARK.

453. Howard Brockman 'Brock' WINFREY born 12-Nov-1953,
Martinsburg, WV, married 21-Feb-1972, in Winchester, Frederick
Co. VA, Lynn Ruth MASTERS, born 12-Aug-1949, Los Angeles,
CA.

Children:
i   Kia Breanna WINFREY born 6-Mar-1973, Fairfield, Solano Co. CA.
ii   Brockman Yancey WINFREY born 27-Nov-1974, San Diego, CA.
iii   Travis Brant WINFREY born 10-Sep-1976, Manassas, Prince William Co. VA.
iv   Cambray Nicole WINFREY born about 1979, Fredericksburg, Spotsylvania Co. VA.
v   Clinton Masters WINFREY born 11-Apr-1981, Fredericksburg, Spotsylvania Co. VA.
vi   Lark Afton WINFREY born 2-Nov-1982, Fredericksburg, Spotsylvania Co. VA.

454. Tamara WINFREY born 9-Dec-1958, Martinsburg, Berkeley Co. WV, married William B. ARMEL, born about 1958, VA?

Children:
i   Jennifer ARMEL born 1980, WV?

455. Karen 'Kay' WOLFORD born 1-Nov-1951, Batesville, Independence Co. AR, married 8-Aug-1970, in Batesville, Independence Co. AR, Allen Rutherford CROUCH, born 1951, Batesville, Independence Co. AR.

BA from Arkansas College majoring in English. A full time homemaker until her divorce, when she began working at Approved Home Medical as a data entry clerk. Does organic gardening, quilts and is a wildlife enthusiast.

Children:
489. i   Amy Elizabeth CROUCH born 9-Jul-1973.
ii   Nathan Allen CROUCH born 4-Apr-1977, Batesville, Independence Co. AR.

456. Debra WOLFORD born 1-Nov-1951, Batesville, Independence Co. AR, married 8-Feb-1975, in Batesville,

Independence Co. AR, William DABOLL, born 15-Dec-1949, Chicago, Cook Co, IL. BA in biology from Hendrix College.

Children:
i   Sarah Elizabeth DABOLL born 5-Oct-1977.
ii   William Wolford DABOLL born 19-Oct-1979.
iii   Matthew Briggs DABOLL born 3-Mar-1982.

457. Ann Alice WOLFORD born 17-Sep-1954, Batesville, Independence Co. AR, married 28-Jun-1975, in Batesville, Independence Co. AR, Kenneth Grady VICKERS, born 11-Oct-1954, Stillwater, OK.

Children:
i   Alice Ann VICKERS born 3-Oct-1979, Sherman, Grayson Co. TX.
ii   John Grady VICKERS born 21-Mar-1984, Sherman, Grayson Co. TX.

458. Hallie Jean HUGHES born 7-Dec-1920, Marion, Williamson Co. ILL, married Robert RANK, born about 1920, WI?, died about 1992.

Children:
490. i   Steven George RANK born 20-Apr-1948.
491. ii Mark Robert RANK born 18-May-1955.

459. Helen HUGHES born 20-Jan-1922, Marion, Williamson Co. ILL, married 17-Jun-1948, in Western Springs, ILL, Lowell Charles GIBSON, born about 1922, ILL?

Graduated from Ill.Wesleyan U. with major in speech and English. Taught until her marriage. After rearing her children for 12 years, taught for 17 years until she retired in 1981.

Children:
492. i   Carma Mae GIBSON born 24-Feb-1951.
493. ii Beth Marie GIBSON born 8-Jul-1952.
iii   John Lowell GIBSON born 5-Dec-1954, Hazel

Crest, ILL. Valedictorian of his class in
1973. Graduated from Wheaton College in 1977.
Did graduate work at Columbia Bible College,
SC.. Went to Ireland as a college summer intern
in 1975. Does volunteer work at nursing homes
as a minister and presently works at Sears as a
Salesman. Single and lives at home (1994).
494. iv   Michelle Jeanne GIBSON born 10-Dec-1960.

460. William Mitchell THOMAS born 14-Oct-1883, Sullivan Co.
TN, married 25-Dec-1904, in Sullivan Co. TN, Mary Elizabeth
DICKSON, born 12-Dec-1871, Sullivan Co. TN, (daughter of
Charles L. DICKSON and Sarah Melissa MOODY) died
5-Feb-1955, Sullivan Co. TN. William died 7-Apr-1959, Johnson
City, Washington Co. buried: East Lawn Memorial. Park, Sullivan
Co. TN.

Children:
i   Grace THOMAS born 12-Aug-1912, Sullivan Co. TN,
married 24-Dec-1934, Luther Floyd BROYLES, born
about 1912.

461. Jacquie Lyn COOPER born 9-Dec-1932, Sullivan Co. TN,
married 11-Mar-1958, in TN?, Calvin DISHNER, born about 1932.

Children:
i   Davane Lee DISHNER born about 1955.
ii   Lari Beth DISHNER born about 1957.

462. Donna Jean BARNES born 4-Feb-1947, Sullivan Co. TN,
married 1965, in Sullivan Co. TN, Eddie HOBBS, born
10-Jul-1945, Sullivan Co. TN.

Children:
i   Lisa Ellen HOBBS born 1966, Memphis TN.
ii   Elizabeth Ann HOBBS born 9-Nov-1972, Bristol,
Sullivan Co. TN.

463. Stephen Allen GARDNER born 7-Oct-1964, VA?, married

6-Jul-1991, Robin Elizabeth LOGERWELL, born 30-Dec-1963, TN? 1995 broadcast editor for USA TODAY in Arlington VA.

Children:
i   Joshua Thomas Logerwell GARDNER born 19-Feb-1989.
ii   Kelsey Erin GARDNER born 7-Nov-1991.

464. Rachel Lenette GRIMES born 28-Oct-1969, married 11-Aug-1989, Douglas O'Neal ALLEN, born 3-Nov-1969.

Children:
i   Brittney Annette ALLEN born 14-Nov-1991.
ii   Whittney Allene ALLEN born 1991.

465. Robert Joseph EARHART born 1956, Bristol, Sullivan Co. TN, married Shelia, born about 1956. Twin. Lives on the old Rhea homeplace on Rt. 11 E across from the Bristol Speedway.

Children:
i   Philip EARHART born about 1981, Bristol, Sullivan Co. TN.
ii   Allen EARHART born about 1985, Bristol, Sullivan Co. TN.

466. James Samuel 'Dr.' PERRY born circa 1950, married.

Children:
i   Theodore 'Thad' Leland PERRY born about 1967, Bristol, Sullivan Co. TN. Working on Doctorate of Psychology at Vanderbilt University (1993).
ii   Margaret 'Meg' Alice PERRY born about 1974, married Claude W. MILLICAN III, born about 1975. Graduated from Vanderbilt University.
iii Alexa D. PERRY born about 1977, Blountville, Sullivan Co. TN.

467. Harriet Ann CALDWELL born 29-Jul-1937, Bristol,

Sullivan Co. TN, married Otto Maurice SPANGLER, born circa 1937.

Children:

i Otto 'Chuck' Maurice SPANGLER Jr. born about 1960, married Mary, born about 1960. In 1995 the family was living in Suffolk, England where Mary was stationed with the US Air Force.

495. ii Victor SPANGLER born about 1962.

496. iii Elizabeth SPANGLER born about 1964.

468. Joyce Eveleen CALDWELL born 5-Sep-1940, Bristol, Sullivan Co. TN, married 1958, William FLANNAGAN, born circa 1940.

Children:

i William 'Chip' FLANNAGAN Jr. born about 1961, St. Louis, Missouri.

ii Cindy Marie FLANNAGAN born about 1965, St.Louis, Missouri, married Michael STEEN, born about 1965, MO?

469. Ford 'Buddy' CALDWELL Jr. born 31-Mar-1947, Bristol, Sullivan Co. TN, married (1) Sheila wife of Ford CALDWELL, born about 1947, married (2) Kim BOONE, born 1955. 1995 lives in Plano TX. Works for a chemical company.

Children:

i Brett CALDWELL born about 1975. 1995 was student at Texas Tech.

470. Janet Erin BOUTON born 3-Jun-1953, Washington D.C., married 23-Oct-1976, in U of Maryland Chapel, Edward Francis FOLEY III, born 13-Oct-1954, Asheville, Buncombe Co. NC, (son of Edward Francis FOLEY II and Marguerite Evelyn GUILKA).

Born Doctors Hospital. Lived early years in Washington suburb Lewisdale MD. Moved to Largo MD and graduated from Frederick Sasscer High School in 1971. 1971-73 attended Prince George Community College and later graduated from U. of Maryland B.A. in 1975. Married. Worked at Friendship Savings and Loan as Assistant Manager. Left her job to raise her family in NY and in Columbia MD. In 1996 moved to Singapore where her husband is Director and Treasurer of Caterpillar in Asia.

Children:
i   Michael James FOLEY born 26-Oct-1979, Holy Cross Hospital, Silver Spring, Montgomery Co. MD.
ii   David Edward FOLEY born 28-Sep-1982, Southside Hospital, Bayshore, Nassau Co. NY.
iii   Ryan Connor FOLEY born 18-Apr-1988, Howard Co. Hospital. Columbia, Howard Co. MD.

471. Mark Earhart BOUTON born 10-Sep-1953, Albuquerque, Bernillo Co. NM, married 1-Sep, in IL?, Suzie LEGAULT, born about 1953. Graduate of Williams College. Later received Ph.D.

Children:
i   Lindsey LeGault BOUTON born 28-May-1987, Burlington VT.
ii   Grace Dorothy BOUTON born 28-Dec-1992, Burlington VT.

472. Leslie Ann BOUTON born 5-Mar-1956, Washington D.C., married James PETERSON, born 1954. Degree in Russian Language.

Children:
i   Brooke Bouton PETERSON born 8-Oct-1989, Manchester MO.
ii   Christa Whitcraft PETERSON born 1-Sep-1990, Manchester MO.

473. Clare Lynn BOUTON born 9-Oct-1961, Aurora, Kane Co, IL,

married 22-Jul-1979, Myles HANSEN.

Children:
i   Reuben Henry HANSEN born 1-Sep-1992, Alexandria VA.
ii   Madeleine June HANSEN born 17-Mar-1995, Washington D.C.

Ninth Generation

474. Debra Lee DAVIS born 24-Aug-1948, Little Rock, Pulaski Co. ARK, married 6-Apr-1974, in Little Rock, Pulaski Co. ARK, Michael Reece MCQUEEN, born 6-Apr-1974.

Graduated from Louisiana State U with degree in marketing. Worked as a buyer for Dillards Department Store and MM Cohen Co. in Little Rock. Now works for C.R. Gibson Co. covering the State of Maryland (1994). 1995 lives in Columbia MD.

Children:
i   Laura Elizabeth MCQUEEN born 23-Apr-1977.
ii   Katherine Davis MCQUEEN born 25-Jul-1980.

475. Laura Sue 'Susie' DENT born 13-Sep-1948, Little Rock, Pulaski Co. ARK, married 8-Jun-1968, William A. LEWIS, born 3-Sep-1948, Kansas City MO. Received degree in music from U. of Kansas.

Children:
i   William A. LEWIS Jr. born 25-Dec-1972, Tripoli, Libya.
ii   Thomas E. LEWIS born 2-Aug-1978, Rio de Janerio, Brazil.
iii   Laura K. LEWIS born 12-May-1980, Rio de Janerio, Brazil.

476. Donna Jean DENT born 22-Aug-1951, Little Rock, Pulaski

Co. ARK, married 4-Aug-1973, in St. Louis, Missouri, Robert
E. 'Rory' MCCARTHY Jr., born 16-Jul-1947, White Plains NY.

Children:
i   Jeremy MCCARTHY born 3-Feb-1976, St. Louis,
Missouri.
ii   Christopher MCCARTHY born 23-Mar-1978,
St. Louis, Missouri.

477. Jeffrey Menifee MOOSE born 29-Nov-1958, Mexico City,
Mexico, married 1988, Mary SHUTAK, born about 1958,
Wash? Graduated from the Institute of Art. Self employed
graphic artist. Lives in Seattle, Washington.

Children:
i   Elias Menifee MOOSE born 3-Aug-1989, Bainbridge
Island, Wash.

478. Lucinda Kay DAVIS born 17-Sep-1953, ARK, married
17-Dec-1971, Alan HALL, born about 1953, ARK?.

Children:
i   Teri Lyn HALL born 17-Mar-1976, ARK?
ii   Scott Alan HALL born 21-May-1980, ARK?

479. Granger William DAVIS born 7-Sep-1956, ARK, married
25-Oct-1985, in Little Rock, Pulaski Co. ARK, Vikki Elaine
HAIGHT, born 14-May-1960, ARK?

Children:
i   Aaron William DAVIS born 28-Nov-1986.
ii   Brian Allen DAVIS born 11-Aug-1990.
iii   Christopher James DAVIS born 5-Jul-1993.

480. Mark Stuart DAVIS born 27-Oct-1959, Little Rock, Pulaski
Co. ARK, married 21-Jul-1978, Tamela Gale CHADWICK, born
about 1959, ARK.

Children:
i   Kirk DAVIS born 1984, Hot Springs, ARK.

481. James Nathan DAVIS born 12-Jun-1963, Little Rock, Pulaski Co. ARK, married Shari MYERS, born about 1963, TX? Ph.D. in microbiology in 1990 from U. of Texas. Researching leukemia.

Children:
i   Daughter DAVIS born 1-Sep-1994.

482. Angela HEIZMAN born 16-Jun-1953, Little Rock, Pulaski Co. ARK, married George Lawrence JEGLEY, born 1-Nov-1952, Cincinnati, OH.

BA in political science from Hendrix College, and Law degree from U. of Ark Law School. Served one and a half years as a Master in the Arkansas Juvenile Court System. 1990 was appointed judge over Involuntary Commitments. Assistant Attorney General with specialty in family law in Ark.

Children:
i   Amanda Jane JEGLEY born 25-Dec-1981, Little Rock, Pulaski Co. ARK.
ii   Patrick Adam JEGLEY born about 1985, Little Rock, Pulaski Co. ARK.

483. Eric HEIZMAN born 5-Jul-1955, Little Rock, Pulaski Co. ARK, married Leslie DOUBLEDAY, born 5-Feb-1957, Tulsa, OK.

BS in microbiology from U of Ark. Acquired real estate brokers license and became commercial property manager, consultant and appraiser. Worked for several 'failed' Saving and Loan institutions disposing and managing their properties.

Children:
i   Katherine HEIZMAN born 8-May-1987, Little Rock,

Pulaski Co. ARK.

484. Robert C. YOUNG born 12-Dec-1952, Bakersfield, CA, married 4-Oct-1977, in Ventura, CA, Susan B. DOWNING, born about 1952, CA?

Children:
i   Neill YOUNG born 1977, CA?
ii   Scott YOUNG born 1979, CA?
iii   Lindsay YOUNG born 1982, CA?

485. Jeanette YOUNG born 11-Apr-1961, Ventura, CA, married (1) 31-Oct-1985, Jamie MALAND, born about 1958, CA?, married (2) Jeffrey M. HAMMOND, born about 1958, CA?

Children:
i   Sarah Jane MALAND born 31-Oct-1986, CA?
ii   Courtney HAMMOND born 1980, CA?

486. John YOUNG born 13-Feb-1961, Ventura, CA, married 1992, Christy.

Children:
i   Daughter YOUNG born 5-Aug-1993.

487. Donald Edward YOUNG born 11-Jul-1964, Ventura, CA, married (1) Dena DAVENPORT, born about 1964, married (2) 14-Feb-1987, Susan McMAHON, born about 1964, married (3) 1-Sep-1992, Tracy SMITH, born about 1964.

Children:
i   Charity Denise YOUNG born 23-Sep-1984.
ii   Chelsie Nadine YOUNG born Mar-1989.
iii   Donald Edward YOUNG Jr. born 7-Jan-1993.

488. Terri YOUNG born 1966, Ojai, CA, married 1990, in Ventura, CA, Thomas BARNUM, born about 1966.

Children:
i   Michael Thomas BARNUM born 1-Nov-1990, CA?
ii   Jessica Lynn BARNUM born 1-Jun-1993, CA?

489. Amy Elizabeth CROUCH born 9-Jul-1973, Batesville, Independence Co. AR, married James Pawnee BRADLEY, born 3-Jun-1971, Batesville, Independence Co. AR. Graduated from Sulphur Rock HS with honors.

Children:
i   Andrew James BRADLEY born 11-Jul-1993, Batesville, Independence Co. AR.

490. Steven George RANK born 20-Apr-1948, Milwaukee, WI, married Mary Beth BALISTERAS, born about 1948, WI?

Attended Wisconsin State College and earned MA from U of Wisconsin. Teaches in Sturgeon Bay Wisconsin public schools (1994).

Children:
i   Gina RANK born about 1973, WI? Married but no children (1994).
ii   Laura RANK born about 1975, WI?

491. Mark Robert RANK born 18-May-1955, Milwaukee, WI, married Ann DEUTCH, born about 1955, WI?

Ph.D. from U of Wisconsin . Teaches sociology at Washington U, St. Louis MO. Published book "Living on Welfare".

Children:
i   Elizabeth RANK born 1991, MO?
ii   Kathy RANK born 1993, MO?

492. Carma Mae GIBSON born 24-Feb-1951, Madison, WI, married 21-Sep-1975, in Hammond, Indiana, Larry Wayne MORELY, born about 1955, WI?

Graduated from Indiana U. Gary, Ind. as pre-med student in 1973. Graduated from University Medical School in 1977 with double honors. Completed residency in psychiatry in 1981. Became chief of VA Medical Center Psychiatric Dept. in Indianapolis and remained there for 10 years. Later went into private practice at St. Vincent Hospital as a psychiatrist.

Children:
i   Rockie MORELY born 9-Feb-1983, Indiana.
ii   Heather MORELY born 19-Feb-1987, Indiana.
iii David MORELY born 19-Feb-1987, Indiana. Twin.

493. Beth Marie GIBSON born 8-Jul-1952, Madison, WI, married 2-Aug-1975, Jon Russell OHARA, born 15-Aug-1954, Stromburg, Nebraska. Graduated Wheaton College in 1974. Attended Moody Bible Institute as a grad student in 1975. Taught 3 years in McColl Junction Nebraska and 3 years in Boone Gravie Ind. (1978-1981). Home schooled her 3 older boys for several years and is now home schooling the younger girls (1994).

Children:
i   Patrick Jon OHARA born 18-Nov-1981, Indiana.
ii   Kevin Lowell OHARA born 14-Jun-1983, Indiana. Twin.
iii Evan Russell OHARA born 14-Jun-1983, Indiana.
iv   Heidi Beth OHARA born 1988, Indiana.
v   Mary Helen OHARA born 13-Jan-1991, Indiana.

494. Michelle Jeanne GIBSON born 10-Dec-1960, Hazel Crest, ILL, married 21-Dec-1985, in South Holland, IL, Joseph Michael BENSON, born about 1960, IL?

Graduated from Illiana Christian HS in 1979. Graduated from Columbia Bible College, SC in 1983. Taught kindergarten in a Christian School 1984-85 and 1st and 2nd grades in Gary Indiana public schools 1985-88. Now home schools her two children (1994).

Children:
i   Nathaniel Joseph BENSON born 1-Jul-1988, IND?
ii   Andrew Wesley BENSON born 22-Aug-1991, GA?

495. Victor SPANGLER born about 1962, married Ronica. 1995 lived on a boat with family in Daytona Fl.

Children:
i   Elise SPANGLER born about 1990.

496. Elizabeth SPANGLER born about 1964, married Mr. BERGE, born about 1964.

Children:
i   Christopher BERGE born about 1990.

Anderson, Rhea, <u>Sullivan Co.
Blountville, Citizens, Homes,
and Reminisences</u>, Address
delivered before the Histolical
Society of Washington Col. VA,
Washington Co. Historical
Society, Abington VA 1944

Armstrong, Zella, <u>Notable
Southern Famalies</u>, Lookout
Publishing, Chatanooga TN
1922

Bradshaw, Bessie and Carter,
Helen, Sullivan County -
Blountville Cemetery,
unpublished transcript
Blountville Library vertical
files, 1936

Bristol Herald Courier, Bristol
TN-VA August 17, 1934,
*Rhea-Breden Celebration;
Virginia's Interest Therein*, L. P.
Summers

DAR Vertical Files, Washignton
D.C. *Joesph Rhea*

Holston Territory Genealogical
Society, <u>Familes and History of
Sullivan Co. Tennessee Volume
1 1779-1992.</u>, Walsworth
Printing 1992

Knoxville News-Sentinal, Sept.
9, 1993, "The Rheas: First they
were Campbells" , Fred Brown.

Knoxville Sentinal, Knoxville
TN, Nov. 28, 1908, *"Lives and
Character of Rhea
Descendants"*, Nelson,
Summers.

Knoxville Sentinal, Knoxville
TN, Sept. 19, 1908, *"Joseph
Rhea Family; School
Benefactors"*, Nelson, Summers.

Massengill, Samuel E., <u>The
Massengills, Massengales and
Variants 1472-1931</u>, King
Printing Co. Bristol TN, 1931

McBride, Robert, <u>Biographical
Directory of the Tennessee
General Assembly</u>, Vol.1,
Tennessee State Library and
Archives, 1975

Rhea Family Papers, Tennessee
Historical Society, Nashville,
TN, Assession Number THS 10,
Date of Procession Completion
3/18/1966 , Property of
Tennessee Historical Society,

Rhea, John, *Memoir of the Rhea Famliy,* unpublished papers written about 1830, Vertical Files Bristol TN Public Library.,

Rhea, Rev. Joseph, unpublished personal journal of 1769, boxed with *The Rhea Papers*, State Library and Archives, Nashville TN, property of Tennessee

Historical Society, Nashville TN
Rhea, Robert, <u>Rhea Chronicle</u>, Vol.1 Issue 1, May 1994

Rhea, Robert, <u>Rhea Chronicle</u>, Vol.1 Issue 2, Feb. 1995

Rhea, William L., Unpublished manusript, *Genealogy of the of Rhea Family,* 1895

Sherman,Karen , <u>Sullivan County Cemeteries</u>

Spoden, Muriel C., <u>Historic Sites of Sullivan County</u>, Kingsport Press, 1976

Sullivan Co. News, Aug., 8, 1985, *"Historic Book to Be Published"*, Editor

U. S. 1850 Census , Sullivan Co. TN, National Archives.

U. S. 1860 Census , Sullivan Co. TN, National Archives.

U. S. 1870 Census , Sullivan Co. TN, National Archives.

U. S. 1880 Census , Sullivan Co. TN, National Archives.

U. S. 1910 Census , Sullivan Co. TN, National Archives.

Descendants of Rev. Joseph Rhea

Descendants of Rev. Joseph Rhea